ABAP Development for SAP® NetWeaver BI:
User Exits and BAdIs

SAP® Essentials

Expert SAP knowledge for your day-to-day work

Whether you wish to expand your SAP knowledge, deepen it, or master a use case, SAP Essentials provide you with targeted expert knowledge that helps support you in your day-to-day work. To the point, detailed, and ready to use.

SAP PRESS is a joint initiative of SAP and Galileo Press. The know-how offered by SAP specialists combined with the expertise of the Galileo Press publishing house offers the reader expert books in the field. SAP PRESS features first-hand information and expert advice, and provides useful skills for professional decision-making.

SAP PRESS offers a variety of books on technical and business related topics for the SAP user. For further information, please visit our website: *www.sap-press.com.*

Daniel Knapp
SAP NetWeaver BI 7.0 Migration Guide
2008, 181 pp.
978-1-59229-228-8

Thorsten Franz, Tobias Trapp
ABAP Objects: Application Development from Scratch
2008, 505 pp.
978-1-59229-211-0

JayaKumar M. Pedapudi
Test-Driven Development with ABAP Objects
2009, app. 330 pp.
978-1-59229-248-6

J. Andrew Ross
SAP NetWeaver BI Accelerator
2008, 260 pp.
978-1-59229-192-2

Dirk Herzog

ABAP Development for SAP® NetWeaver BI: User Exits and BAdIs

Galileo Press

Bonn • Boston

ISBN 978-1-59229-255-4

© 2009 by Galileo Press Inc., Boston (MA)
2nd Edition, updated and revised

2nd German Edition published 2008 by Galileo Press, Bonn, Germany.

Galileo Press is named after the Italian physicist, mathematician and philosopher Galileo Galilei (1564–1642). He is known as one of the founders of modern science and an advocate of our contemporary, heliocentric worldview. His words *Eppur si muove* (And yet it moves) have become legendary. The Galileo Press logo depicts Jupiter orbited by the four Galilean moons, which were discovered by Galileo in 1610.

Editor   Stefan Proksch
English Edition Editor   Justin Lowry
Translation   Lemoine International, Inc., Salt Lake City, UT
Copyeditor   Julie McNamee
Cover Design   Jill Winitzer
Photo Credit   Getty Images/Yann Layma
Layout Design   Vera Brauner
Production Editor   Kelly O'Callaghan
Typesetting   Publishers' Design and Production Services, Inc.
Printed and bound in Canada

Contents

Preface to the 2nd Edition

Don't we all sometimes need a gentle shove in the right direction? Since I moved in 2000 from controlling (CO) software development in Walldorf to business intelligence (BI) consulting in Berlin, I've continuously increased my ABAP programming knowledge of Business Add-Ins (BAdIs) and user exits in SAP® NetWeaver Business Intelligence 7.0 (SAP NetWeaver BI). I now can safely claim to be an expert in this field. As a result, I constantly receive requests for ideas and solution proposals from many different industries. I had the idea of writing a book on this topic, but as a father and husband, I often avoided this extra work until the editorial department at SAP PRESS asked if I was interested in writing a publication on my specific field of expertise. My publications from the SAP Developer Network (SDN), which frequently deal with these subjects, obviously had raised some interest.

It's hard to believe that two years have passed already since the first edition was published. During that time, I've received a lot of positive feedback from readers. And even in the classes I taught, I often saw my book on the desks of the trainees. Consequently, it didn't surprise me when I was asked by the editorial department to update the book and have it published in the new format of the "SAP Essentials" series.

In particular, this gives me the opportunity to write about a subject that I have been dealing with extensively in the past two years — planning. Since the publication of the first edition, I've been part of a team involved with a relatively large planning project. This project comprised the entire sales and distribution planning process of a large German industrial concern. The functional requirements were pretty high because the solution was supposed to be rolled out to several hundreds of employees in a short time frame.

I had already written dozens of exit functions previously; however, those functions represented transactions on regular BI cubes. That specific project, however, gave me the pleasure of getting to know the entire bandwidth of the exits. Consequently, I received the message that it isn't possible to create more than 99 function modules in 1 function group for the first time. So, those of you who still feel bored despite the exits described in this book will definitely have more than enough work when it comes to planning. Both in the new Chapter 6, User Exits in Planning, and in all other chapters, it's very important to not only describe the syntax but also the purpose for which the user exits are applied.

In addition, the new format allows me to describe several topics in greater detail, specifically the expert routine in transformation. In fact, the — admittedly brief — example I described in the first edition is the only known and publicly available sample expert routine. To close this gap, I extended the comprehensive sample transformation by an additional example that demonstrates how you can implement the same task using the expert routine.

However, despite all that this book includes, it can't solve all problems that occur in your daily work with SAP NetWeaver BI. My usual answer to the question as to which reports can be mapped by a BI system is: "Any report that you can describe using an algorithm. It's rather a question of how much work is needed to implement the report." However, we must not forget the other side of the coin in this context: data modeling. And if the condition in the query once again doesn't show the correct totals and values, then you should check whether it's easier to obtain the result by using an additional field that's filled via a user exit and contains a corresponding filter.

I would like to thank all those people who supported this project, particularly my colleagues, Regine Stechow and Jeff Prochnow; my boss, Joachim Repsch; Stefan Lindner, who introduced me to the secrets of business intelligence; my colleagues at BI-RIG, especially Rudolf Hennecke; the guys at BI development who provided me with valuable information; my former boss, Harald Stuckert, who had made it possible for me to join SAP; my former mentor, Frank Freitag, who showed me all of the tricks in ABAP; and all those who supported me in my career at SAP.

Many thanks also to all those SDN members, and above all to Mark Finnern, Craig Cmehil, and Robert Negro. Thanks to you, developing is even more fun than it used to be.

However, my biggest thank you goes to my wonderful wife and my beloved children who never complained about all that free time I had to sacrifice for the work on this book. I thank you very much and look forward to our common future.

Dirk Herzog
Senior Consultant Business Intelligence
SAP Deutschland AG & Co. KG

1   Introduction

Many consultants have established a kind of love-hate relationship with the topic of ABAP programming within SAP NetWeaver Business Intelligence. Because not everyone can get their programming knowledge from the SAP development division, I advised all BI consultants who contacted me to attend courses in ABAP programming. The big advantage for experienced BI consultants of the numerous user exits and BAdIs is that, instead of a simple standard reporting based on the business content, they allow for implementation of reporting that is tailored to specific user requirements and reduces the costs for the user by automating many tasks. This creates a significant added value. The amount of implementation work to be done in this context is actually much smaller than implementing the Oracle or Microsoft SQL Server databases that are often brought into play by the old "IT stagers." SAP NetWeaver BI is most appealing because it allows you to concentrate on implementing your business requirements while it implements performant data acquisition and storage functions. In doing so, it's often more efficient than your own implementations.

You also should take into account that SAP NetWeaver BI 7.0 is a reporting tool that enables formatted reporting, a clean print output through the integration of Adobe, and the output in Microsoft Excel, as well as in a Web browser and even mobile reporting. These capabilities make very obvious the advantages of a standard product such as SAP NetWeaver BI over customer-specific island solutions.

But success means work, and SAP has provided us with a lot of work in the form of user exits. In many cases, the problem isn't implementing the specific requirements, but finding the right user exit for the relevant requirements. The goal of this book is to describe the standard exits that are used in every BI project and to explain when and how these exits are used. Taking a quick glance into this book might answer some of your questions in the future.

Target Group

The book is intended for BI consultants who only have basic knowledge of ABAP, and for ABAP programmers who have no experience with SAP NetWeaver BI but who are involved in discussions with many BI users about their specific requirements. Because different target groups are involved, I use as few specific terms as possible and provide simpler descriptions wherever I can.

But even the more experienced BI consultants will find new ideas and suggestions in the examples used in this book. For example, the extraction of exchange rates for reporting purposes and the option to load a sorted hierarchy from Microsoft Excel and to automatically sort the parent-child relationships correctly are requirements that go beyond the usual BI project standards.

These examples are used to demonstrate that even very complex requirements of which many consultants would say, "BI can't do that" can be implemented with a limited amount of work if you choose the right exits.

Structure of This Book

Chapter 2, Performance, of this book starts us off with a discussion of the performance of ABAP developments because this aspect often represents a critical issue in BI programming.

The actual user exits and BAdIs are then described in the sequence in which the data runs through the exits:

- ▶ **Chapter 3**, User Exits and BAdIs in the Extraction Process, introduces you to the extraction of data from the source system.

- ▶ **Chapter 4**, User Exits in Data Import Processes, describes the data-staging process, that is, the flow of data that takes place between the time of its entry into SAP NetWeaver BI and the time it's stored in the data target.

- ▶ **Chapter 5**, User Exits and BAdIs in Reporting, describes the options available to you to manipulate the reporting process via ABAP programming.

- ▶ **Chapter 6**, User Exits in Planning, describes the user exits both in the old planning process of SAP Business Planning and Simulation (SAP BW-BPS) and in the new SAP NetWeaver BI Integrated Planning.

- ▶ **Chapter 7**, Summary, contains a brief summary of the results found in this book.

The **Appendix**, Additional Extension Options, provides you with the naming conventions of DDIC (Data Dictionary) objects for typical BI objects.

Requirements

The examples used in this book are mainly based on SAP NetWeaver 7.0 Business Intelligence. However, with a few exceptions that are specifically mentioned during the course of the descriptions, you can also implement the examples in SAP Business Information Warehouse (SAP BW) 3.x. The descriptions of the user exits with regard to extraction apply to all versions of the service API supported by SAP, that is, from Version 2004_1 onward.

To keep the examples simple, the use of ABAP Objects is avoided as much as possible. Even though everyone who deals with ABAP should also include ABAP Objects, I know from my own experience that many of my colleagues only have a limited knowledge of ABAP Objects. And because the advantages of ABAP Objects with regard to exit programming in SAP NetWeaver BI are only minor, I prefer to use function modules instead to ensure that you'll understand the examples. Those of you who have a good knowledge of ABAP Objects won't have any problems with modifying the examples accordingly.

However, for the BI Integrated Planning discussed in Chapter 6, User Exits in Planning, it isn't possible to omit ABAP Objects. For this reason, this chapter includes a step-by-step guide to introduce beginners to the subject. In the past two years, the development toward ABAP Objects has proceeded so rapidly that I recommend everyone who is involved in this subject to at least deal with the basics.

2   Performance

Performance is always important for ABAP programming in SAP NetWeaver BI. And, because even medium-sized SAP ERP installations involve data-loading processes with several million records, particularly in initial loading processes or monthly loadings, it's critical that literally every single routine is programmed to be as high performing as possible.

SAP NetWeaver BI includes many loading processes consisting of several hundred and up to a few thousand data records. But even in those cases, you should design the routines to be as efficient as possible, even if it's just for practice purposes. Besides, a change of the business processes or the data model can suddenly multiply the data volume of a loading process.

> **Example: Loading Annual Report Data**
>
> This can happen when a bank replaces its legacy system with a new one, which means that not only the internal accounts must be processed for the annual report but also all current accounts and deposits from private customers. In a real project, this would cause the data volume to increase from 3 million data records to approximately 15 million data records for the quarterly statement. A fivefold increase and more is far from uncommon.

If, in this example, you can reduce the performance per data record from 2ms to 1ms, the runtime decreases from 8 hours to 4 hours. So even negligent programming can at least double the performance.

Apart from the obligatory avoidance of database accesses, the most important factors in high-performance programming in the SAP NetWeaver BI environment are the consistent use of table types and the use of field symbols.

2.1   Table Types in ABAP

For each type of access, there's a table type available in ABAP that provides the ideal performance; you just have to find the right table type. However, this is often not very difficult because we don't write entire programs but instead use the user exits to specifically enrich certain details. For this reason, the tables are accessed only at a few points.

In general, ABAP provides three different table types:

▶ **Standard tables**

Standard tables (STANDARD TABLE) are neither restricted with regard to sorting aspects nor with regard to their access. You can sort them in any way, access them with any key, insert new records at any point, and use them in any situation.

This flexibility, however, reduces the system performance. In particular, the read accesses to standard tables are significantly slower because often the entire table must be searched to find the relevant data record.

▶ **Sorted tables**

Sorted tables (SORTED TABLE) are sorted by a specific key. This key doesn't need to be unique. All accesses that go through this key or a leading part of the key are significantly faster than accesses to standard tables. Accesses that don't use this key are no faster than accesses to standard tables. In addition, the buildup of sorted tables is slower because the sorting always must be adhered to.

There are two main advantages to sorted tables: Records with duplicate keys can be automatically avoided, and sorted tables are significantly faster for loops with partly qualified keys. Important to the performance of sorted tables is the sequence of the key fields. The sequence you choose should guarantee that all accesses can provide the leading key fields.

Programming Examples for Table Types

The sorted table L_TO_DEMO has the key fields K1, K2, K3, and K4 in this order. With similar hit quantities, the command

```
LOOP AT l_to_demo WHERE K1 = 'XYZ'.
ENDLOOP.
```

would be significantly faster than the similar command

```
LOOP AT l_to_demo
  WHERE K2 = 'ABC'
  AND K3 = '123'
  AND K4 = '0'.
ENDLOOP.
```

In the first variant, a binary search determines the exact point at which the value of K1 is XYZ. Then the table is processed row by row until the value of K1 is no longer XYZ. Due to the table sorting, all relevant rows can be found in this way.

The second variant does not contain any information on K1. The existing sorting of the table is therefore useless, so the entire internal table must be read to find the relevant lines.

▶ **Hashed tables**

Hashed tables (HASHED TABLE) are essential for programming exits in SAP NetWeaver BI, so you should become familiar with them. Because we can only provide a brief overview at this point, you should refer to the documentation available in the SAP Help Portal (*http://help.sap.com*) or in the SAP Developer Network (*http://sdn.sap.com*). Both sources provide a lot of information for beginners and experts.

Hashed tables are tables that can be primarily accessed via a key that's stored in the table definition, as opposed to standard and sorted tables where an index is used for the access. The access via a key can be carried out within a constant amount of time and is nearly independent of the table size. This property is particularly useful if the table is accessed only at one or at just a few points. This is often the case in SAP NetWeaver BI because we don't develop a complete application, but just carry out specific data enrichment and cleansing processes at individual points.

Example: Deriving Master Data Attributes

During an upload of transaction data, a profit center is to be derived from the master data attributes of the cost center, provided the interface does *not* deliver a profit center. The corresponding code could look like the one shown in Listing 2.1.

```
IF comm_structure-profit_ctr = SPACE.
* No profit center delivered.
  IF l_th_costcenter[] IS INITIAL.
*   No cos  center attributes have been,
*   loaded up to this point. All
*   currently valid cost center attributes
*   will therefore be loaded into table
*   L_TH_COSTCENTER now.
    SELECT * FROM /bi0/qcostcenter
      INTO TABLE l_th_costcenter
```

```
      WHERE objvers = 'A'
      AND   datefrom <= sy-date
      AND   dateto   >= sy-date.
  ENDIF.
  READ TABLE l_th_costcenter
    INTO  l_s_costcenter
    WITH TABLE KEY
      co_area    = comm_structure-co_area
      costcenter = comm_structure-costcenter.
  IF SY-SUBRC = 0.
    RESULT = l_s_costcenter-profit_ctr.
  ELSE.
    RESULT = 'DUMMY'.
  ENDIF.
ELSE.
  RESULT = comm_structure-profit_ctr.
ENDIF.
```

Listing 2.1 Example of a Data Enrichment Process

It's very likely that the L_TH_COSTCENTER table is only read at one point in the exit and that it contains several thousand entries. If now several tens of thousands of data records are added from a DataSource, it's obvious that the READ TABLE statement must be executed very quickly. For this reason, the best table type to use here is a hashed table because it's accessed through one key only. The table definition, for instance, reads as follows:

```
DATA: l_th_costcenter
  TYPE HASHED TABLE OF /bi0/qcostcenter
  WITH UNIQUE KEY co_area costcenter
  INITIAL SIZE 0.
```

2.2 Loops and Read Accesses to Tables

To help you find the optimal read access to tables at any time, Table 2.1 contains a list of the possible table accesses, including their effects on the runtime. Just pick out the type of access most frequently used in your implementation, and then derive the table type you should use to obtain optimal system performance. You also can check whether performance problems with a specific table access type can be resolved by using an alternative command with a different table type.

Access Type	Standard Table	Sorted Table	Hashed Table
READ TABLE WITH KEY	The table is scanned row by row (full table scan) until a relevant data record is found: O(n).	A full table scan is carried out: O(n).	A full table scan is carried out: O(n).
READ TABLE WITH TABLE KEY	A full table scan is carried out: O(n).	A binary scan is used to find the data record: O(log n).	A hashed process is used to find the record in an almost constant time period: O(1).
READ TABLE ... INDEX ...	The access occurs in almost constant time: O(1).	The access occurs in almost constant time: O(1).	Not possible.
LOOP AT TABLE WHERE ...	The entire table is scanned: O(n).	If the WHERE clause contains the first part of the key with a query on =, a binary search is performed up to the entry point. After that, only those entries are run through that have the relevant values: O(log n + m). Otherwise, a loop across the entire table is created: O(n).	The entire table is scanned: O(n).

Table 2.1 Effects of Table Accesses

The so-called *O notation* that is specified after the explanations refers to the factor by which the access time increases along with the table size (see Table 2.2).

Factor in O Notation	Description
O(1)	The access time is constant.
O(n)	The access time is proportional to the number of table entries n.
O(log n)	The access is proportional to the logarithm of the number n of entries.
O(m + log n)	The access is proportional to m + log n, where m represents the number of hits, and n the number of table entries.

Table 2.2 Meaning of the O Notation

It also depends on various factors such as the number and sorting of the records in a table to determine which table is faster in specific cases. However, surveys have shown that even with a few table entries, hashed tables have a significant advantage over sorted tables, and sorted tables in turn are faster than standard tables (*https://weblogs.sdn.sap.com/pub/wlg/2615*).

2.3   Field Symbols

Another option for optimizing the system performance is to use field symbols. The use of field symbols predominantly aims at reducing the time needed for moving content from one variable into another, especially when moving the content of a table row into the associated work area. Field symbols are particularly useful when you have to deal with very wide tables that contain many entries. Such tables occur often in SAP NetWeaver BI.

Also, because field symbols are referenced indirectly, they enable you to keep the code as dynamic as possible. This is useful in SAP NetWeaver BI because, in practice, changes to the data model occur much more often than many users allow for during the project phase.

The overall performance increase caused by the use of field symbols is rather limited. But that shouldn't prevent you from using field symbols, even in noncritical cases, to get familiar with the method so that you know what to do when the extractor must be adjusted to handling a daily volume of, say, 2 million data records.

Table 2.3 contains an overview of the most important commands for using field symbols.

Command	Description	Remark
`FIELD-SYMBOLS: <fs> TYPE type.`	The field symbol `<fs>` is defined.	You should always use typed field symbols. If necessary, you can type field symbols using the types `ANY` and `ANY TABLE`.
`ASSIGN var TO <fs>.`	The field symbol `<fs>` is assigned the variable `var`.	Instead of the `var` variable, you can also use the field symbol `<fs>` in this command until `<fs>` is assigned to a different variable.
`<fs> = 123.`	The field symbol `<fs>` is assigned the value 123.	The variable `var` is assigned the value 123 if `var` has been assigned to the field symbol `<fs>`.
`LOOP AT tab ASSIGNING <fs>.`	During the loop, the field symbol `<fs>` is assigned the current row of table `TAB`.	Because this command doesn't copy any data into the header, the biggest performance increase can be obtained when using wide tables and tables that contain other tables. In general, this variant provides an increase in performance from five loop passes onward.
`READ TABLE tab ASSIGNING <fs>.`	The field symbol `<fs>` is assigned the result of the `READ` command.	The command provides performance increases for tables of 1,000 bytes or more. If you want to change the table contents using `MODIFY`, you can even obtain performance increases for tables of 100 bytes.[1]

Table 2.3 Using Field Symbols[1]

---

1 When using a field symbol, the `MODIFY` command can be omitted so that you can directly modify the contents of the field symbol. In hashed tables and sorted tables, modifying the key fields is not permitted.

2.4   Database Accesses and Cache

Despite the use of multiprocessor machines today, the database still represents the bottleneck in the extraction process because SAP NetWeaver BI must move large quantities of data to the database. If, in addition, the database is strained with frequent read accesses, the load times can become significantly longer.

Example of Selecting a Table Type

Listing 2.2 shows a characteristic derivation in an update rule. All it does is perform a conditional attribute derivation. If no profit center is transferred, the time-dependent master data table of the cost centers is read. The profit center currently assigned to the cost center is determined from that table and then returned.

```
IF comm_structure-profit_ctr IS INITIAL.
  SELECT SINGLE * FROM /bi0/qcostcenter
    INTO l_s_costcenter
    WHERE costcenter = comm_structure-costcenter
    AND   co_area = comm_structure-co_area
    AND   datefrom <= sy-date
    AND   dateto   >= sy-date
    AND   objvers  = 'A'.
  IF sy-subrc = 0.
    RESULT = l_s_costcenter-profit_ctr.
  ELSE.
    RESULT = comm_structure-profit_ctr.
  ENDIF.
ENDIF.
```

Listing 2.2   Example of a Bad Implementation

This or a similar example can be found in many BI systems where employees with little or outdated ABAP knowledge implement the characteristic derivation.

If a profit center is transferred only rarely, the database is strained by many single-record accesses that don't even have unique keys and that are very time-consuming because the `<= sy-date` and `>= sy-date` queries are used.

A much better solution is the example shown previously in Listing 2.1, which only requires one access to the database and provides an optimal performance through the use of hashed tables.

In general, the cache method used in Listing 2.1 is very well suited for SAP NetWeaver BI. Because of the separation into several data packages that are distributed across different processes, you can never be sure that a global cache variable has been correctly filled in a previous data package. For this reason, you should use the following query to ensure that no new select process is carried out in the database when the cache is full: `IF l_th_costcenter[] IS INITIAL`.

This happens, for instance, if you select the options ONLY PSA and UPDATE IN DATA TARGETS in the InfoPackage. If you do that, all data packages are processed in the same work process after they have been loaded into the *persistent staging area* (PSA), that is, into the storage area where the source system data is stored without any prior conversion. This way, you can preserve the cache across different data packages. However, parallelization isn't possible in this case, which means that generally you won't be able to obtain any performance increase.

3 User Exits and BAdIs in the Extraction Process

This chapter describes the options available for modifying the data records during an extraction process in the source system by using ABAP. SAP distinguishes between two basic techniques:

- *User exits* are function modules provided by SAP that contain in the customer namespace an include that can be modified by the developer.
- *Business Add-Ins* (BAdIs), on the other hand, are interfaces provided by SAP development that can be implemented. This technique originates from ABAP Objects.

3.1 Usage Options

User exits are used in an extraction if the standard extractors made available by SAP don't provide the expected data or the required functionality, for instance, in authorization or time checks.

A distinction must be made here. Is the issue that the available standard extractors don't provide the required data in its entirety so that individual records or fields must be provided separately? Or, are there no standard extractors available that can access the required tables? In the latter case, you must create generic extractors that access the tables. For complex selections, you may even have to write your own function modules.

The following usage types are often seen.

- **Enhancement of a standard extractor by individual fields**
  Sometimes, a standard extractor provided by SAP won't contain all of the fields you need. Suppose, for example, that you want the extractor for goods movements, which by default contains only the delivering warehouse, to also provide the destination warehouse when carrying out a stock transfer.

▶ **Enhancement of a standard extractor by additional records**
This is particularly necessary if the complementary records are based on information that is no longer available in SAP NetWeaver Business Intelligence (SAP
NetWeaver BI). The standard extractors used in overhead cost controlling usually provide the sender and recipient of a clearing. However, in multilevel clear-
ings in SAP R/3 (now SAP ERP), the first sender in the clearing chain is still
stored in the ORIGINAL OBJECT field.

The extraction process merges several data records into one if the records differ
in their original objects. If, however, this information on the original object is
needed, each data record must be divided across the different original objects.

▶ **Masking specific fields**
A company can have a complex cost-center structure. During the extraction
process in the SAP NetWeaver BI system of the parent company, for instance,
certain details are supposed to be hidden by replacing the last two (numerical)
characters with 00.

▶ **Authorization checks**
As an example, the extraction of accounting data in SAP NetWeaver BI should
only be possible when the accounting period has been closed. This way, you
can make sure that all assessments in financial accounting are completed at the
time of the extraction.

3.2   Generic Extractors

Generic extractors or DataSources enable you to extract data from the source system that isn't provided via standard extractors, for example, data that is stored in
customer-specific tables. The generic extractors even allow you to program simple
extractors by yourself.

To create a generic extractor, you can use Transaction RSO2, which allows for the
creation, modification, and display of generic DataSources. The transaction enables
the modification of DataSources for transaction data, master data attributes, and
texts. However, you can't use transactions to create DataSources for hierarchies.
With regard to hierarchies, there's no other way than to use the DataSources provided by SAP or to load the hierarchies from flat files.

In the following sections, we'll create a generic DataSource that extracts exchange
rates from table TCURR. This can be necessary if — for instance — you want to

provide the users with a report that contains necessary information on current exchange rates.

1. When you call Transaction RSO2 (see Figure 3.1), you can specify a name for the DataSource. Create a TRANSACTION DATA DataSource, and assign the name `DS_GENERIC_DEMO_TCURR` to it.

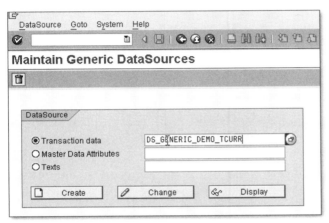

Figure 3.1 Maintaining a Generic DataSource

In general, you must adhere to the same naming conventions for DataSources as for InfoObjects in SAP NetWeaver BI; that is, the DataSource must not begin with a number. You should make it a habit to begin the name of a DataSource with "DS_," although this isn't a must. If your company maintains specific conventions in this respect, you should comply with them. If necessary, you can also adopt and adjust naming conventions for programs.

When extracting data from tables or views, you should include the name of the table or view in the DataSource name so that you can easily recognize the contents of the DataSource without having to look at the details. You can use a prefix to indicate the application or project that is responsible for the DataSource, but note that such pieces of information should also be transferred by choosing the appropriate application component.

2. After you've entered the name, click on the CREATE button. The system displays a dialog box in which you can select the application component and decide whether the data is extracted from a table or database view, from an ABAP query, or from a function module (see Figure 3.2).

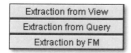

Figure 3.2 Selecting the Type of Extraction

The following sections focus on the extraction from a table or view. The extraction from an ABAP query is useful if you already use ABAP queries. The extraction via a function module occurs only rarely and is beyond the scope of this book.[1]

3. First, you must choose an application component; in this case, that's DEMO_BW. When creating your own DataSources, you should make sure that you also create your own application components in the standard application component hierarchy. You can do that in the standard Implementation Guide (IMG) for SAP NetWeaver BI using Transaction SBIW via BUSINESS INFORMATION WAREHOUSE • POST-PROCESS DATASOURCES • EDIT DATASOURCES AND APPLICATION COMPONENT HIERARCHY. In this process, all DataSources are included in the application component hierarchy, and you can insert new application components via the INSERT command and also post-edit the existing DataSources (see Figure 3.3).

You can structure the application components according to your requirements. For example, you can insert an application component at the appropriate location in the component structure provided by SAP for each project. It's also possible to insert a DS_OWN component containing the text, "Proprietary DataSources," which can then be further structured for each project or responsibility.

Figure 3.3 Post-Editing DataSources

---

1 If you're interested, take a look at the well-documented function module, RSAX_BIW_GET_DATA_SIMPLE, which demonstrates the most important techniques involved in extracting data via a function module. Listing 3.5 later in this chapter introduces another technique that enables you to completely avoid using your own function modules.

4. After you select the application component, you must enter the table. In this case, that's TCURR (see Figure 3.4). Then select SAVE.

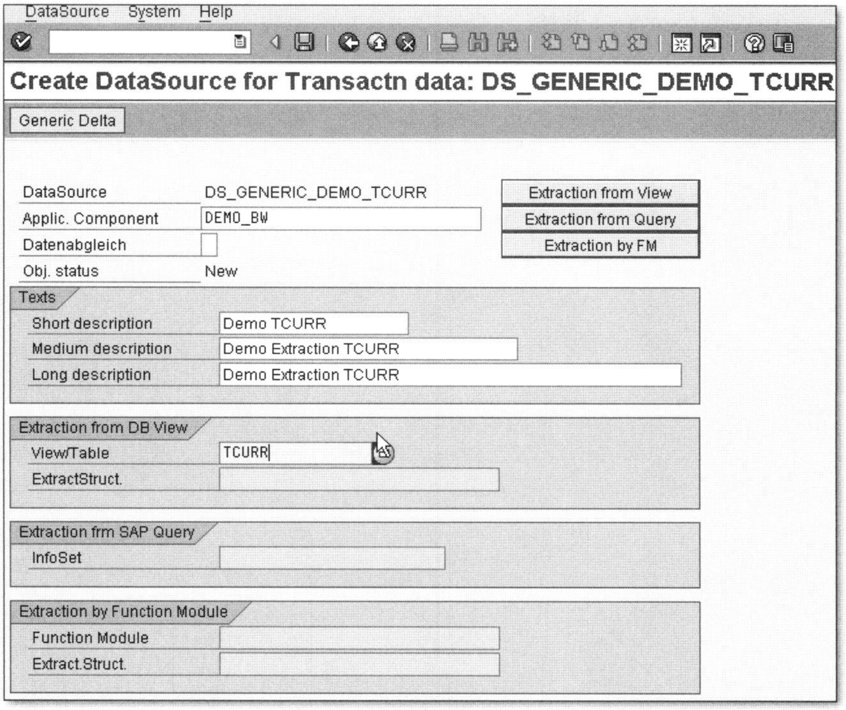

Figure 3.4 Creating the Generic DataSource

Practical Tip: Generic Delta

We won't use the GENERIC DELTA button here (see Figure 3.4, top-left corner). However, this button can sometimes be important.

Not only does a generic delta enable the generic extractor to provide a full upload but also a delta upload, which includes only the changes since the last upload. For this purpose, the service API that enables the generic extraction must be able to determine which data records have changed since the last extraction. This can be ensured by specifying a field that must always be filled in ascending order, such as LAST CHANGED BY, TIME STAMP, or RUNNING NUMBER. Document numbers are generally inappropriate because documents can be cancelled retroactively and the previous document numbers are then usually changed. Also, different number ranges often exist for different types of documents.

5. In the dialog box that displays next, you can select the fields you want to include as selection fields in the data package. Here, you should select the exchange rate type (KURST) and the date as of which the exchange rate is valid (GDATU) in the SELECTION column shown in Figure 3.5.

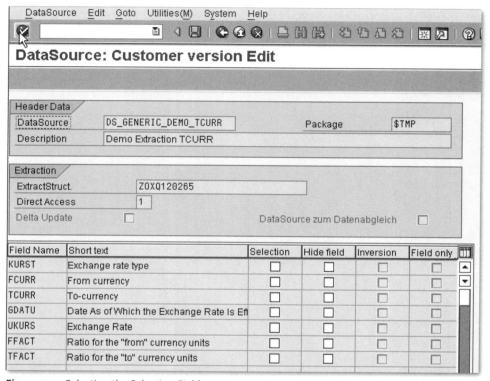

Figure 3.5 Selecting the Selection Fields

6. Basically, the extractor for table TCURR is completed, and you can check it using the extractor checker (Transaction RSA3). However, you'll see that the results don't meet the expectations. The format of the Valid-from date looks rather weird, for example, 79939898, and the FACTOR FROM and FACTOR TO fields never contain any values. For this reason, we'll employ a user exit in the following sections to adjust those fields.

3.3   User Exit RSAP0001

Both the standard extractors provided by SAP and the generic extractors can be extended via user exit `RSAP0001`. When doing so, the individual data packages provided by the service API are transferred to the user exit so you can manipulate the entire data package. This means you can change the contents of individual fields and delete or add complete rows. Usually, the same options are also available in the start routine of the transfer rules.

The BI user who doesn't have much time to study the theoretical details of designing data warehouses is often forced to ask which of the many user exits should be used to customize the data. Particularly with regard to the extraction of data, it's often not clear which changes should be made in SAP NetWeaver BI and which ones in the source system. The following examples provide you with ideas and hints concerning some aspects you should take into account when making your decision.

▶ **Extending fields and data records**
The question of where exactly the derivation should occur can be answered rather easily because often data are extended that are already contained in existing source-system tables. In that case, it doesn't make much sense to transfer the tables into SAP NetWeaver BI to enrich the extracted data there. The data-extension process should instead occur in the source system.

▶ **Masking Specific Fields**
The masking of specific fields can occur without difficulty both in SAP NetWeaver BI and in the source system. The implementation process itself is similar in both systems. Here, you should base your decision on the actual requirements. If the BI team considers it advisable to cleanse the data to obtain a uniform set of data, and if it's the BI team that sets the rules, the cleansing process should actually take place in SAP NetWeaver BI. This way, you can also change the rules in SAP NetWeaver BI at a later stage, if needed. You can carry out a potential restructuring process from the persistent staging area (PSA) without difficulty.

If, on the other hand, the data owner in the source system says that he only wants to provide a certain detailing, he should also be responsible for the implementation. In the sample cost center name-masking mentioned earlier, for instance, he would have to adjust all transaction data as well as all attribute, text, and hierarchy extractors.

▶ **Authorization checks**

In general, you should carry out authorization checks in the source system to prevent certain power users in SAP NetWeaver BI from accessing data they shouldn't have access to (or at least not at present). Because SAP NetWeaver BI isn't to be used to bypass any corresponding limitations in the source system, the source system must be protected against such accesses from SAP NetWeaver BI.

▶ **Conversions**

SAP NetWeaver BI often requires a specific conversion, for instance, that a specific field content must be alpha-converted. If possible, you should carry out those kinds of adjustments directly in SAP NetWeaver BI because at a later stage, several BI systems often access the same source systems, and those BI systems don't necessarily have to have the same requirements regarding conversion. To not lose any flexibility in this context and to preserve the original status of the data in all BI systems as much as possible, you should try to avoid a conversion in the source system.

Now we need to apply two changes to the generic extractor DS_GENERIC_DEMO_TCURR we created: correctly convert the Valid-from date, and correctly fill the FACTOR FROM and FACTOR TO fields.

3.3.1 How to Use the Exit

First you must tell the system that you want to use user exit RSAP0001 from now on. As is the case with all user exits, you can do that via Transaction CMOD.

1. For this example, create a new project called "BW_EXT" (see Figure 3.6).

2. In the dialog box that appears next, enter a text for the project, for instance, "Extractor extensions for BW." Then click on the COMPONENTS button. A list displays that contains the components you want to use. In this case, you only need user exit RSAP0001.

3. The system then displays an overview of the function modules that are available for this user exit. The user exit RSAP0001 contains four function modules, one each for transaction data DataSources, attribute DataSources, text Data-Sources, and hierarchy DataSources (see Table 3.1).

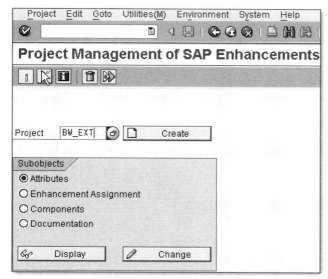

Figure 3.6 Maintaining SAP Extension Projects

Type of DataSource	Function Module
Transaction data	EXIT_SAPLRSAP_001
Master data attributes	EXIT_SAPLRSAP_002
Master data text	EXIT_SAPLRSAP_003
Hierarchies	EXIT_SAPLRSAP_004

Table 3.1 Function Modules in User Exit RSAP0001

Because you created a transaction data DataSource, you need function module EXIT_SAPLRSAP_001 for transaction data. This module contains the interface described in Listing 3.1.

```
IMPORTING
  VALUE(I_DATASOURCE)
      TYPE RSAOT_OLTPSOURCE
  VALUE(I_ISOURCE)
      TYPE SBIWA_S_INTERFACE-ISOURCE
  VALUE(I_UPDMODE)
      TYPE SBIWA_S_INTERFACE-UPDMODE
TABLES
  I_T_SELECT TYPE SBIWA_T_SELECT
```

```
   I_T_FIELDS TYPE SBIWA_T_FIELDS
   C_T_DATA
   C_T_MESSAGES STRUCTURE BALMI OPTIONAL
EXCEPTIONS
   RSAP_CUSTOMER_EXIT_ERROR
```

Listing 3.1 Interface of User Exit EXIT_SAPLRSAP_001

4. However, the extensions you want to implement are not directly included in the function module because the module is located in the SAP namespace, so the implementation would represent a modification. Instead, the following statement is added to the function module: `INCLUDE ZXRSAU01`. This include statement is located in the customer namespace and can be created by double-clicking. Whenever this function module is called, the include statement is processed. In an activated project in Transaction CMOD, this occurs once per data package, which is sent along with a transaction data DataSource to SAP NetWeaver BI.

3.3.2 Structured Composition of the ZXRSAU01 Include

Before discussing the details of what you can do with this include, you should know what you can't do with it. For example, you should *never* implement the actual logic in the standard include. Because the include is used by *every* extractor, it gradually develops into a monster containing several thousands of rows. And, because it's used by many projects, the include is transported regularly and regularly brings semi-completed corrections into the live system, which — in a best-case scenario — only produces some data spaghetti. In the worst case, this problem can cause all extractors to fail because of syntax errors.

You therefore should choose the following procedure. A central distribution mechanism is implemented in the include statement; depending on the DataSource, this mechanism calls a subroutine, a function module, or a method. For example, the include statement could be implemented as shown in Listing 3.2.

```
DATA: l_d_fmname(30) TYPE c.
CONCATENATE 'Z_DS_' i_datasource(25)
            INTO l_d_fmname.
TRY.
  CALL FUNCTION l_d_fmname
    EXPORTING
      I_DATASOURCE  = I_DATASOURCE
```

```
      I_ISOURCE     = I_ISOURCE
      I_UPDMODE     = I_UPDMODE
    TABLES
      I_T_SELECT    = I_T_SELECT
      I_T_FIELDS    = I_T_FIELDS
      C_T_DATA      = C_T_DATA
      C_T_MESSAGES  = C_T_MESSAGES
    EXCEPTIONS
      RSAP_CUSTOMER_EXIT_ERROR = 1
      OTHERS                   = 2
      .
    IF SY-SUBRC <> 0.
      RAISE RSAP_CUSTOMER_EXIT_ERROR.
    ENDIF.
CATCH CX_SY_DYN_CALL_ILLEGAL_FUNC.
* No exit implemented, no need to do
* anything here.
ENDTRY.
```

Listing 3.2 Sample Implementation of ZXRSAU01

Then you can modify every DataSource by creating a function module called Z_DS_<DataSource> that contains the interface of function module EXIT_SAPLR-SAP_001. If this function module doesn't exist, the data package isn't changed as required.

This way you can also avoid transport problems. The extension becomes active when the function module is transported, irrespective of other changes that may be implemented in the include statement or in other extensions. The example shown in Listing 3.2 also makes redundant the frequently used CASE statement that often specifies several dozens of DataSources.

The actual contents of the extension are often very much the same. Because you can connect more than one BI system to the source system, you should avoid an aggregation of data and the deletion of entire data records. This means that basically there are only two alternatives available to extend DataSources. You can either fill or modify entire field contents or add entire rows. For both options, typical patterns are available for how the extension is structured.

Case 1: Filling or Modifying Fields of the Extract Structure

Listing 3.3 contains the typical code lines for filling additional fields. A loop across table C_T_DATA into a typed field resolves the problem that table C_T_DATA is of the ANY TABLE type and can therefore be structured differently depending on the Data-Source from which it's called. The error is captured by a corresponding message in table C_T_MESSAGES. In this context, certain mapping tables frequently don't contain any entries for the values.

```
FIELD-SYMBOLS: <fs_data> TYPE EXT_STRUCT.
* The field contains the extract structure of the
* DataSource as type. The extract structure can be
* found in Table ROOSOURCE in the EXSTRUCT field.
LOOP AT c_t_data ASSIGNING <fs_data>.
   CALL FUNCTION 'Z_FILL_MY_DATASOURCE'
* Specifically written function that performs the filling of
* data. In this context, errors can occur if certain
* values are not contained in customizing tables.
        CHANGING
           c_s_data    = <fs_data>
        EXCEPTIONS
           mapping_error  = 1
           OTHERS         = 2.
   IF SY-SUBRC <> 0.
     PERFORM append_sy_message
* Here messages from the function module are
* transferred to the error table.
        USING sy-msgty
              sy-msgid
              sy-msgno
              sy-msgv1
              sy-msgv2
              sy-msgv3
              sy-msgv4
        CHANGING
              c_t_messages.
   ENDIF.
ENDLOOP.
```

Listing 3.3 Typical Implementation for Filling Data Records

If you need mapping tables in SAP NetWeaver BI, you can create them as DataStore objects or InfoObjects and then access the tables directly via the code. For the Data-Store object, that's table /BIC/A<DSName>00; for the InfoObject, it's table /BIC/P<IObjName>.

Both the DataStore and the InfoObject can be easily loaded from Excel tables using standard BI tools, which significantly simplifies updating the tables. In addition, SAP NetWeaver BI provides a simple maintenance process for InfoObjects.

Case 2: Adding Data Records to the Data Package

A typical example of adding data records is the splitting up of each record of the data package into one or more records. The code could then appear as shown in Listing 3.4:

```
FIELD-SYMBOLS: <fs_data> TYPE EXT_STRUCT.
* The field contains the extract structure of
* the DataSource as type EXT_STRUCT. The extract
* structure can be found in Table ROOSOURCE
* in the EXSTRUCT field.
DATA: l_t_data type standard table of EXT_STRUCT
* Intermediate table containing the new data.
                WITH NON-UNIQUE DEFAULT KEY
                INITIAL SIZE 0.


LOOP AT c_t_data ASSIGNING <fs_data>.
   CALL FUNCTION 'Z_FILL_MY_DS_TABLE'
* Specifically written function that performs the filling of
* data. In this context, errors can occur if certain
* values are not contained in customizing tables.
      EXPORTING
         i_s_data      = <fs_data>
      CHANGING
         c_t_data      = l_t_data
* The code presupposes that table C_T_DATA can contain
* data records that are not deleted.
      EXCEPTIONS
         mapping_error  = 1
         OTHERS         = 2.
```

```
   IF SY-SUBRC <> 0.
       PERFORM append_sy_message
* Here, messages from the function module are transferred
* to the error table.
         USING sy-msgty
               sy-msgid
               sy-msgno
               sy-msgv1
               sy-msgv2
               sy-msgv3
               sy-msgv4
         CHANGING
               c_t_messages.
   ENDIF.
ENDLOOP.
c_t_data[] = l_t_data[].
* The determined rows are returned.
```

Listing 3.4 Typical Implementation for Adding Data Records

If the tables can't be derived per data record but from the entire data package, you could modify the code in Case 1 in such a way that the loop is removed and the entire code is transferred to the function module. Note, however, that this type of implementation doesn't provide access to the complete dataset but only to the contents of the data package. Particularly when extracting data from SAP ERP systems, you shouldn't rely on a specific type of sorting, nor should you assume that you can access all records in a data package for specific keys. For example, the posting lines for a document number could be distributed to two different data packages.

However, you can define a generic extractor on a custom table using the selected extract structure and then insert exactly 1 data record in that table. In a data-extraction process from SAP NetWeaver BI, exactly 1 data record is then transferred in a data package, and you can implement a completely customized logic in the exit described in this chapter. The drawback of this method is that the entire set of data is transferred in one data package. If more than 100,000 data records exist, the internal tables become very large and can affect system performance and stability. In that case, you should revert to the described generic extractor with function module.

3.3.3 Implementing the User Exit EXIT_SAPLRSAP_001 for Currency Extraction

Let's now get back to our DataSource, DS_GENERIC_TCURR_DEMO. You want to invert the date field and fill the exchange rate factors row by row. This can be implemented as shown in Listing 3.5.

```
FIELD-SYMBOLS: <fs_tcurr> TYPE TCURR.
* The generic extractor refers to table TCURR and thus
* it has Extract Structure TCURR.
DATA: l_s_message TYPE balmi.
* l_s_message is used to fill error messages.
LOOP AT c_t_data ASSIGNING <fs_tcurr>.
*    Change date

*    Fill exchange rate factors
  STATICS: s_t_tcurf TYPE SORTED TABLE OF TCURF
*    Table TCURF contains the required exchange rate factors.
          WITH UNIQUE KEY KURST FCURR TCURR GDATU
          INITIAL SIZE 0.
  FIELD-SYMBOLS: <fs_tcurf> TYPE TCURF.
  IF s_t_tcurf IS INITIAL.
    SELECT * FROM TCURF INTO TABLE s_t_tcurf.
  ENDIF.
  LOOP AT s_t_tcurf ASSIGNING <fs_tcurf>
       WHERE
           KURST = <fs_tcurr>-kurst AND
           FCURR = <fs_tcurr>-fcurr AND
           TCURR = <fs_tcurr>-tcurr AND
           GDATU >= <fs_tcurr>-gdatu.
    EXIT. " Use first record found.
  ENDLOOP.
  IF SY-SUBRC <> 0.
* Read factors with inverted currency
    LOOP AT s_t_tcurf ASSIGNING <fs_tcurf>
         WHERE
           KURST = <fs_tcurr>-kurst AND
           FCURR = <fs_tcurr>-tcurr AND
           TCURR = <fs_tcurr>-fcurr AND
           GDATU >= <fs_tcurr>-gdatu.
      EXIT. " Use first record found.
    ENDLOOP.
    IF SY-SUBRC <> 0.
```

```
*       No factors found, then set factors to 1
*       and output error message.
        <fs_tcurf>-ffakt = 1.
        <fs_tcurf>-tfakt = 1.
        l_s_message-msgty = 'E'. " error message
        l_s_message-msgid = 'ZCURR'. " Message class
        l_s_message-msgno = '001'. " Error number
        l_s_message-msgv1 = <fs_tcurr>-kurst.
        l_s_message-msgv2 = <fs_tcurr>-tcurr.
        l_s_message-msgv3 = <fs_tcurr>-fcurr.
        l_s_message-msgv4 = <fs_tcurr>-gdatu.
        COLLECT l_s_message INTO c_t_messages.
      ELSE.
*       Here, the factors are swapped to avoid making
*       a distinction later. <fs_tcurr>-ffakt
*       is only used as a clipboard here.
        <fs_tcurr>-ffakt = <fs_tcurf>-ffakt.
        <fs_tcurr>-ffakt = <fs_tcurf>-tfakt.
        <fs_tcurr>-tfakt = <fs_tcurr>-ffakt.
      ENDIF.
    ENDIF.
    <fs_tcurr>-ffakt = <fs_tcurf>-ffakt.
    <fs_tcurr>-tfakt = <fs_tcurf>-tfakt.

ENDLOOP.
```

Listing 3.5 Deriving the Fields in Table TCURR

The biggest problems in Listing 3.5 are the logic used for the loop across table S_T_ TCURF and the query of the date. The logic is as follows: The VDATE field contains an inverted date, namely 99999999. However, you need the record with the date that is smaller than or equal to the key date. The inversion causes the plus/minus sign to change, which means you must use "greater than" for the query instead of "less than." The sorted table makes sure that you'll find the smallest data record that fulfills the condition.

If you compare all of this with a customized program in SAP ERP or SAP NetWeaver BI that enables you to view current exchange rates, you'll see that the only programming code you need is the logic. That consists of the inversion of the date and the additional reading of the exchange rate factors. Due to the logic of inverted factors, this can't be attained via a view. All of the programming code needed for the selection and output, and which you would probably have to implement in the ALV grid, can be avoided and replaced by the data-modeling technique in SAP NetWeaver BI, which is much easier and structured more clearly. Considering the number of exchange rates to be expected, it's unlikely that we'll have to cope with any performance problems.

3.3.4   Using the Hierarchy Exit

Because the user exit interface for hierarchies differs significantly from that of other exits, it's described here by using an example. The example contains the following scenario.

You want to use the standard extractor OCOSTCENTER_HIER to load a cost-center hierarchy. This cost-center hierarchy contains many levels so that you can't differentiate parent nodes from child nodes when navigating through the hierarchy. For this reason, you'll have each hierarchy node preceded by the corresponding level. The code needed for this hierarchy adjustment is shown in Listing 3.6.

```
DATA: LD_HIENODE TYPE RSAP_S_HIENODE,
      LD_FOLDERT TYPE RSAP_S_FOLDERT,
      LD_OLDNAME     LIKE C_T_HIENODE-NODENAME,
      LD_LASTNODE02  LIKE C_T_HIENODE-NODENAME.

CASE I_S_HIEBAS-HCLASS.
* Hierarchy for 0COSTCENTER
  WHEN '0101'.

* Change existing node names
    LOOP AT C_T_HIENODE INTO LD_HIENODE.
      CHECK LD_HIENODE-IOBJNM = '0HIER_NODE'.
*      Save old node name first
      LD_OLDNAME = LD_HIENODE-NODENAME.
*      Build new node name as <LVL>_<KNOTENNAME>
      LD_HIENODE-NODENAME(2)    = LD_HIENODE-TLEVEL.
      LD_HIENODE-NODENAME+2(1)  = '_'.
      LD_HIENODE-NODENAME+3     = LD_OLDNAME(16).
      MODIFY C_T_HIENODE FROM LD_HIENODE.
*      Then implement node text

*      Read old node name
      READ TABLE C_T_FOLDERT INTO LD_FOLDERT
              WITH KEY
              LANGU = SY-LANGU
```

```
                        IOBJNM = 'OHIER_NODE'
                        NODENAME = LD_OLDNAME.
         CHECK SY-SUBRC = 0.
*        Record found? Then change node name.
         LD_FOLDERT-NODENAME = LD_HIENODE-NODENAME.
         MODIFY C_T_FOLDERT FROM LD_FOLDERT INDEX SY-TABIX.
      ENDLOOP.
* End of OCOSTCENTER hierarchies
   WHEN OTHERS.
ENDCASE.
```

Listing 3.6 Example of Using the Hierarchy Exit

In this example, you want the nodes of the cost-center hierarchy to also contain the level number instead of the descriptions used in the SAP ERP system. So, if a node of the cost center hierarchy is called K4711 and is located at level 5, its name in SAP NetWeaver BI is 05_K4711.

This must be done in two places: in table C_T_HIENODE, which contains the position of the nodes within the hierarchy, and in table C_T_FOLDERT, which contains the node texts. In the preceding example, a loop is made across table C_T_HIENODE. If the entry is a hierarchy node and not a cost center, the level is added as a prefix, and then the corresponding entry in C_T_FOLDERT is read and adjusted.

The interface of the hierarchy exit is described in Listing 3.7. What is essential in this interface is the information provided by I_DATASOURCE and I_S_HIER_SEL to determine the hierarchy. Depending on the destination of the exit, the most frequently used tables are C_T_HIENODE, which contains the hierarchy structure, and the text tables, C_T_HIETEXT and C_T_FOLDERT. Otherwise, you probably won't use this user exit very often.

```
IMPORTING
  VALUE(I_DATASOURCE) TYPE
                      RSAOT_OLTPSOURCE
*      Name of DataSource
  VALUE(I_S_HIEBAS) TYPE  RSAP_S_HIEBAS
*      Basic attribute (=InfoObject) of the hierarchy
  VALUE(I_S_HIEFLAG) TYPE  RSAP_S_HIEFLAG
*      Hierarchy flags for time-dependence, versions,
*      intervals, etc.
  VALUE(I_S_HIER_SEL) TYPE
                      RSAP_S_HIER_LIST
```

```
*       Selected hierarchy
   VALUE(I_S_HEADER3) OPTIONAL
*       Hierarchy header in SAP NetWeaver BI
TABLES
   I_T_LANGU TYPE   SBIWA_T_LANGU
* Languages installed in SAP BW/BI (for texts)
   C_T_HIETEXT TYPE   RSAP_T_HIETEXT
* Texts of the hierarchy
   C_T_HIENODE TYPE   RSAP_T_HIENODE
* Hierarchy node information
   C_T_FOLDERT TYPE   RSAP_T_FOLDERT
* Texts of the nodes for the hierarchy
   C_T_HIEINTV TYPE   RSAP_T_HIEINTV
* Intervals in hierarchy
   C_T_HIENODE3 OPTIONAL
* All nodes of the hierarchy (flexible structure)
   C_T_HIEINTV3 OPTIONAL
* All intervals of the hierarchy (flexible structure)
   C_T_MESSAGES STRUCTURE   BALMI OPTIONAL
* Messages
EXCEPTIONS
   RSAP_CUSTOMER_EXIT_ERROR
```

Listing 3.7 Interface of Function Module EXIT_SAPLRSAP_004

3.3.5   Surrogate for the Generic Hierarchy Extractor

One of the biggest problems of the generic extractor is that it doesn't enable you to create hierarchy extractors. To resolve this problem, you can also use hierarchy exits.

For example, if you want to use an exit to load a hierarchy into an InfoObject called HIEROBJ, you must perform the following steps:

1. Create an InfoObject, HIEREXP, as a copy of InfoObject HIEROBJ.

2. Generate the export DataSource of the object.

3. Bind the DataSource HIEREXP_HIER to InfoObject HIEROBJ.

4. Implement your logic for DataSource HIEREXP_HIER in the hierarchy exit.

5. Create a dummy hierarchy with a node at InfoObject HIEREXP.

6. Create an InfoPackage to load the hierarchy.

7. Load the hierarchy.

At this point, you should not underestimate the complexity of the BI hierarchy. To implement the parent-child-next relationships, you must implement some more complex algorithms. Section 4.1, Transformation, in Chapter 4 contains an example of this.

3.3.6 Transferring Parameters to the User Exit

In very rare cases, you may want to transfer parameters from SAP NetWeaver BI to the user exit, for example, when you use time-consuming exits that are not always necessary, but in which you don't want to program hard case distinctions. In this situation, you should proceed as follows.

1. Include a ZZ_USE_EXIT field in the extract structure via an append structure.
2. Mark this field as a SELECTION FIELD. After the corresponding replication and activation, the field can be selected in the InfoPackage.
3. In table I_T_SELECT, all selections are transferred to the user exit where they can be used. So you should use the key FIELDNM = 'ZZ_USE_EXIT' to read the table and use the value transferred there to control the user exit. The corresponding code could be implemented as shown in Listing 3.8.

```
DATA: L_S_SELECT LIKE LINE OF I_T_SELECT.
L_S_SELECT-LOW = 'N'.
* Default: do not process exit
READ TABLE I_T_SELECT INTO L_S_SELECT
  WITH KEY FIELDNM = 'ZZ_USE_EXIT'.
IF ( L_S_SELECT-LOW = 'Y' ) OR
   ( L_S_SELECT-LOW = 'J' ).
* Run user exit
  CALL FUNCTION 'EXIT_LOGIC'
     ...
ENDIF.
```

Listing 3.8 Controlling the Exit via an InfoPackage

This way, you could carry out a currency conversion and transfer the exchange rate type in the InfoPackage. Don't forget to transfer the value from the selection in the InfoPackage to the ZZ_USE_EXIT field at the end. Otherwise, you'll be surprised that no records have been transferred to SAP NetWeaver BI.

3.4   BAdI RSU5_SAPI_BADI

The BAdI `RSU5_SAPI_BADI`[2] exists in parallel to user exit `RSAP0001`. It's one of various BAdIs provided by SAP to enable customers to gradually replace the old user exits with BAdIs. The BAdI is also available in SAP ERP with the new plug-ins.[3]

3.4.1   Methods

It contains two methods: a `DATA_TRANSFORM` method for all transaction data, attributes, and text DataSources; and a `HIER_TRANSFORM` method for all hierarchy DataSources. Compared to the RSAP0001 exit, the interface has almost not changed at all. If you create a BAdI[4] and copy the old code from the exit into it, you probably won't have to make any adjustments to continue using the old code.

The `DATA_TRANSFORM` method that you use to adjust transaction data, attribute, and text DataSources contains the interface listed in Table 3.2.

Parameter/Field	Description
I_DATASOURCE	Name of the DataSource for transaction and master data
I_UPDMODE	Update mode (full, delta)
I_T_SELECT	Requested selection criteria
I_T_FIELDS	Requested fields
C_T_DATA	Table containing extracted data
C_T_MESSAGES	Error log

Table 3.2 Interface of Method DATA_TRANSFORM

Compared to the old interface, only two parameters have been removed: `I_ISOURCE` and `I_CHABASNM`. Both parameters are obsolete and can be queried via `I_DATASOURCE`.

---

2 SAP Note 691154 always contains an up-to-date description of the BAdI.

3 The BAdI is provided along with the software components SAP_BASIS and PI_BASIS and is available as of SAP_BASIS 6.20 or PI_BASIS 2004_1, respectively.

4 Section 5.2, "Virtual Key Figures and Characteristics," contains further information on creating a BAdI.

Some major changes have been implemented in the interface of the hierarchy extension (see Table 3.3).

Parameter/Field	Description
I_DATASOURCE	Name of the DataSource for hierarchies
I_S_HIEFLAG	Hierarchy control flag for basic characteristics (time-dependent, and so on)
I_S_HIER_SEL	Selected hierarchy
I_T_LANGU	Table of required languages
C_T_HIETEXT	Name of the hierarchy (language-dependent)
C_T_HIENODE	Directory of hierarchy nodes
C_T_FOLDERT	Texts of nodes that can't be posted to
C_T_HIEINTV	Table of hierarchy intervals
C_T_MESSAGES	Error log

Table 3.3 Interface of Method HIER_TRANSFORM

What's missing here is the parameter I_S_HIEBAS that used to indicate the basic InfoObject of the hierarchy and could be derived from the DataSource name. Moreover, the interface no longer contains the parameters that were used for flexible hierarchies: I_S_HEADER3, C_T_HIENODE3, and C_T_HIEINTV3. The reason is that the BAdI doesn't support flexible hierarchies. This doesn't entail any significant limitations in your daily work.

3.4.2 Advantages and Disadvantages

We deliberately described the extension of the extraction via the exit before going into the details of extending the extraction via the BAdI. In existing systems, it will probably be the exit that is implemented, and most of the time, you'll want to avoid replacing the exit with the BAdI. For this reason, the extension via the exit is probably used more widely than the extension via the BAdI. Nevertheless, you shouldn't carry out new extensions by using an exit but rather create a BAdI to do that.

A BAdI has the advantage that you can create separate implementations per DataSource or project. This allows you to separate the implementations, which is very important with regard to transports. In that case, the central distribution mechanism described is no longer needed.

Unfortunately, this method isn't adequately supported. It would be advantageous if the BAdI could be restricted to one or more DataSources. Instead you must include a CASE request in each BAdI to query the DataSource.

There's one more disadvantage, which actually should be regarded as an advantage. Because BAdIs are object implementations, you must use the limited ABAP Objects syntax.

Generally speaking, this BAdI with its simple interface and logic is certainly one of the easiest ways to begin with the technique of implementing BAdIs. Moreover, it's a future-proof implementation method because SAP is more likely to discontinue its support of user exits than discontinue the BAdI.[5]

---

5 So far, SAP has not stated that it would stop supporting the user exit. Therefore, you shouldn't assume that this statement implies the opposite.

4 User Exits in Data Import Processes

Whereas the adjustment of extractor results predominantly occurs only with selected DataSources, most data import processes in SAP NetWeaver Business Intelligence involve a user exit that is run through between the DataSource and the InfoProvider. This may be done for conversion purposes, for the derivation of new characteristics, or for data cleansing. Because the entire logic of SAP NetWeaver BI has been changed significantly in SAP NetWeaver 7.0, Section 4.1, Transformation, provides a detailed description of the transformation options that have been newly implemented. Compared to the options available in the transfer and update rules, the transformation options have been extended substantially and provide new features.

The only "disadvantage" is that methods are generated instead of form routines, which is why the code of the exit itself is checked for the more rigid syntax of ABAP Objects. However, those of you who want to become more engaged in this subject matter will probably consider this an advantage because it enables you to employ a clean and consistent way of programming. And those of you who don't want to be involved still have the chance to call a function module and return to the good old ABAP syntax.

4.1 Transformation

The method of transformation newly introduced for SAP NetWeaver 7.0 standardizes the transfer and update rules taken from SAP BW 3.x. Although the transfer rules were only applied between DataSources and InfoSources and the update rules only between InfoSources and InfoProviders,[1] the transformation can be used to link any DataSource to the data targets.

In addition, you have the option to display the rules graphically. Figure 4.1 shows the graphical display of the transformation in SAP NetWeaver 7.0. The DataSource

---

[1] Technically speaking, an InfoSource is also included during a data update from a DataStore object into an InfoProvider. You can see that by displaying the generated objects in the Administrator Workbench.

and target are specified in the header next to the name of the transformation. Below the header, the graphic displays a section of the DataSource structure, and the right-hand part of the graphic displays a section of a rule group. The rule group is a structure that corresponds to the structure of the data target. It's supposed to enable you to derive several data records in the data target from one source record, as is possible in SAP BW 3.x. The arrows displayed in the graphic indicate which fields of the DataSource are transformed into the corresponding fields of the data target.

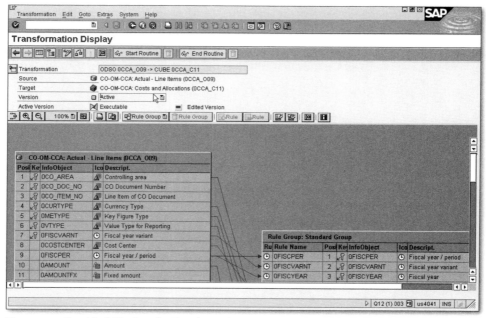

Figure 4.1 Graphical Display of a Transformation

Along with the improved exit implementation options, you should use the transformation option for newly created objects in SAP NetWeaver 7.0. It depends on each individual case whether it's worthwhile to convert the old data flows. In any event, you should consider when only InfoObject assignments are used in the update or transfer rules and when you can delete the InfoSource being used. In all other cases, it's only worth the effort if you want to revise the rule completely anyway, you'll benefit from the advantages provided by the new routines, or if you have to standardize the routines to keep a clear overview of SAP NetWeaver BI. The last issue is especially necessary in enterprise data warehouses; in fact, anyone who has carried out at least three different projects with three different project teams will likely agree that it's absolutely necessary to implement a certain structure.

The transformation contains a total of five exits:

- Exit for determining the key figures and data fields[2]
- Exit for determining the characteristics and key fields[3]
- Start routine
- End routine
- Expert routine

The expert routine completely replaces the graphical modeling process and enables you to convert each data package from the source into the target structure in a single routine. In SAP NetWeaver 7.0, the end routine and the expert routine have been newly implemented in the transformation, whereas the transfer and update rules in SAP BW 3.x only contained the first three exits. In the following sections, you'll see how much the end routine and the expert routine can improve your life as a programmer.

4.1.1   Deriving Characteristics

The derivation of characteristics and key fields is certainly the simplest type of derivation in the context of BI exits because it contains the fewest variants. The characteristic derivation is required in many different scenarios, for instance, if fields from the source system aren't delivered, if the fields in the source system have a different structure from those in SAP NetWeaver BI, if a conversion needs to be performed, or if time characteristics must be converted for which no standard conversion has been implemented.

To create a routine for deriving characteristics:

1. Double-click on the characteristic for which you want to create the routine. This takes you to the RULE DETAILS dialog box.

---

2 If you update into an InfoCube, only the key figures are calculated, whereas if you update into a DataStore object (in a SAP BW 3.x: ODS object) all data fields are calculated. In an InfoObject, it's the attributes and texts that are calculated.

3 Similarly, in this exit, the characteristics are determined in an InfoCube, and the key fields in a DataStore, while the value of an InfoObject and of compounded characteristics, if available, are determined in an InfoObject.

2. Here you must select the ROUTINE item in the RULE TYPE field. Then you can create the routine by clicking on the CREATE button next to the field (see Figure 4.2).

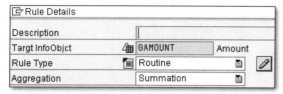

Figure 4.2 Creating a Routine

SAP NetWeaver BI then generates a main class that will contain only the implementation. Listing 4.1 shows the generated code. The data input consists of the record number, the number of data records, the source structure of the current data record, and some information on the status of the data import process. The required output should contain the characteristic value and some status information.

```
PROGRAM trans_routine.
*---------------------------------------*
*        CLASS routine DEFINITION
*---------------------------------------*
*
*
*---------------------------------------*
CLASS routine DEFINITION.
  PUBLIC SECTION.

    TYPES:
      BEGIN OF _ty_s_SC_1,
*   InfoObject: 0METYPE Key Figure Type.
        METYPE        TYPE /BI0/OIMETYPE,
      END   OF _ty_s_SC_1.
    TYPES:
      BEGIN OF _ty_s_TG_1,
*     InfoObject: 0METYPE Key Figure Type.
        METYPE    TYPE /BI0/OIMETYPE,
      END   OF _ty_s_TG_1.
  PRIVATE SECTION.
    TYPE-POOLS: rsd, rstr.
*$*$ begin of global -
* insert your declaration only below this line *-*
... "insert your code here
*$*$ end of global -
```

```
* insert your declaration only before this line *-*

    METHODS
      compute_0METYPE
        IMPORTING
          request        TYPE rsrequest
          datapackid     TYPE rsdatapid
          SOURCE_FIELDS TYPE _ty_s_SC_1
        EXPORTING
          RESULT    TYPE _ty_s_TG_1-METYPE
          monitor   TYPE rstr_ty_t_monitor
        RAISING
          cx_rsrout_abort
          cx_rsrout_skip_record.
ENDCLASS.  "routine DEFINITION


*---------------------------------------*
*       CLASS routine IMPLEMENTATION
*---------------------------------------*
*
*---------------------------------------*
CLASS routine IMPLEMENTATION.

  METHOD compute_0METYPE.
    DATA:
      MONITOR_REC    TYPE rsmonitor.
*$*$ begin of routine -
* insert your code only below this line *-*
... "insert your code here
*-- fill table "MONITOR" with values of structure
*-   "MONITOR_REC" to make monitor entries
... "to cancel the update process
*    raise exception type CX_RSROUT_ABORT.
... "to skip a record
*    raise exception type CX_RSROUT_SKIP_RECORD.

*    result value of the routine
     RESULT = .
*$*$ end of routine -
* insert your code only before this line *-*
  ENDMETHOD.    "compute_0METYPE
ENDCLASS.         "routine IMPLEMENTATION
```

Listing 4.1 Generated Characteristic Derivation Method

If you're not yet familiar with object-oriented programming, don't panic. Because the main class is predefined, you can focus entirely on implementing the logic and don't need to bother about inheritance, interfaces, attributes, and so on. At this point, that's much easier even than implementing a BAdI.

But let's take a detailed look at Listing 4.1. At the beginning, two types are defined: _ty_s_SC_1 and _ty_s_TG_1. The contents of both types depend on the fields you want to link to each other in the graphical modeling process. In the simplest case, it's only the field OMETYPE of the DataSource that is linked to the field OMETYPE of the data target. Therefore, both types obtain exactly this field.

In the subsequent section, you can define global data objects. All data definitions that you make here occur in all routines created in this transformation so that you can transfer data from one routine into another.

The next section of the listing contains the definition of the method. ABAP Objects distinguish between the definition and the implementation of the method, which is why the interface is first defined at this stage. In addition to the request and data package numbers, the interface contains the structure SOURCE_FIELDS as import parameter. The type of this structure is defined as _ty_s_SC_1 and contains the selected fields of the source structure. The only available export parameters are the RESULT field for the result and the MONITOR table for the error messages. The RETURNCODE and ABORT flags that are available in SAP BW 3.x are now replaced by corresponding exceptions. To skip the data record, you should insert the statement RAISE cx_rsrout_skip_record, whereas RAISE cx_rsrout_abort enables you to abort the entire processing of the data package. The new development can be regarded as a significant step forward, given that the handling of the RETURNCODE parameter wasn't very intuitive in SAP BW 3.x. It used to behave differently in the transfer rules, where it didn't cause any error message, and in the update rules, where it actually did produce errors.

Apart from that, the implementation is almost identical to that of the transfer and update rules in SAP BW 3.x, despite the fact that some parameter names have been slightly changed. This means that you don't need to learn anything new and can simply copy the existing code in almost all cases.

The only restriction is that the more rigid ABAP Objects syntax is checked here. But those of you who simply can't do without the tables and headers and all those other precious gadgets in ABAP just need to call a function module at this point to have the entire range of ABAP relics at your disposal again.

Example: Removing Special Characters

A typical problem that regularly occurs when importing data from external systems is that input fields such as family names and addresses can contain special characters, for instance, in foreign addresses or incorrect entries. The best way to catch them is to use a routine. In Listing 4.2, all special characters are replaced by blank space characters in an InfoObject called NAME that has the type CHAR(60).

Simple routines such as this one significantly increase the stability of the import processes and reduce the maintenance requirements.

```
METHOD compute_NAME.
    DATA:
        MONITOR_REC    TYPE rsmonitor.
*$*$ begin of routine -
* insert your code only below this line *-*
    DATA: l_d_offset LIKE sy-index.
    CONSTANTS: c_allowed(100) TYPE c
        value 'ABCDEFGHIJKLMNOPQRSTUVWXYZ1234567890_'.
    RESULT = SOURCE_FIELDS-/BIC/NAME.
* Only capitals are permitted, hence convert to capitals.
    TRANSLATE RESULT TO UPPER CASE.
    DO 60 TIMES.
        l_d_offset = sy-index - 1.
        IF RESULT+l_d_offset(1) CO c_allowed.
*        Character allowed, don't do anything
        ELSE.
*        Character not allowed, replace with blank space character
            RESULT+l_d_offset(1) = ' '.
        ENDIF.
    ENDDO.
*$*$ end of routine -
* insert your code only before this line *-*
    ENDMETHOD.     "compute_NAME
```

Listing 4.2 Method for Removing Special Characters

4.1.2 Deriving Key Figures

The derivation of key figures and data fields occurs almost as often as the derivation of characteristics and key fields. For example, it's used for simple calculations (invoice amount = catalog price + extras – discount). However, characteristics derivations also occur here if the characteristics are contained in the data component of DataStore objects.

The derivation of key figures and data fields in the transformation can be as simple as the derivation of characteristics; it even uses exactly the same routine. There is one little difference, and that's the calculation of units in the routine.

Here is how that now works:

1. You must select a key figure in your data target and double-click on it to open the RULE DETAILS dialog box that you're already familiar with (see Figure 4.3).

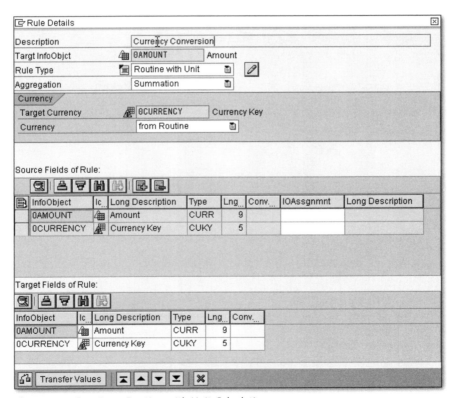

Figure 4.3 Creating a Routine with Unit Calculation

2. Then you can select the ROUTINE WITH UNIT entry under the RULE TYPE item.

3. Click on the CHANGE button next to the rule type to open the ABAP Editor. The system then automatically generates the code shown in Listing 4.3.

```
PROGRAM trans_routine.

*-----------------------------------------*
*       CLASS routine DEFINITION
*-----------------------------------------*
*
*-----------------------------------------*
CLASS routine DEFINITION.
  PUBLIC SECTION.
    TYPES:
      BEGIN OF _ty_s_SC_1,
*       InfoObject: 0AMOUNT Amount.
        AMOUNT      TYPE /BIO/OIAMOUNT,
*       InfoObject: 0CURRENCY Curr. Key.
        CURRENCY    TYPE /BIO/OICURRENCY,
      END   OF _ty_s_SC_1.
    TYPES:
      BEGIN OF _ty_s_TG_1,
*       InfoObject: 0AMOUNT Amount.
        AMOUNT      TYPE /BIO/OIAMOUNT,
*       InfoObject: 0CURRENCY Curr. Key.
        CURRENCY    TYPE /BIO/OICURRENCY,
      END   OF _ty_s_TG_1.
  PRIVATE SECTION.

    TYPE-POOLS: rsd, rstr.

*$*$ begin of global -
* insert your declaration only below this line *-*
... "insert your code here
*$*$ end of global -
* insert your declaration only before this line *-*
    METHODS
      compute_0AMOUNT
        IMPORTING
          request      TYPE rsrequest
          datapackid   TYPE rsdatapid
          SOURCE_FIELDS  TYPE _ty_s_SC_1
        EXPORTING
```

```
         RESULT    TYPE _ty_s_TG_1-AMOUNT
      CURRENCY TYPE _ty_s_TG_1-CURRENCY
       monitor  TYPE rstr_ty_t_monitor
      RAISING
       cx_rsrout_abort
       cx_rsrout_skip_record.
ENDCLASS.    "routine DEFINITION


*---------------------------------------*
*       CLASS routine IMPLEMENTATION
*---------------------------------------*
*
*---------------------------------------*
CLASS routine IMPLEMENTATION.

  METHOD compute_0AMOUNT.

    DATA:
      MONITOR_REC     TYPE rsmonitor.

*$*$ begin of routine -
* insert your code only below this line *-*
... "insert your code here
*-- fill table "MONITOR" with values of structure
* "MONITOR_REC" to make monitor entries
... "to cancel the update process
*    raise exception type CX_RSROUT_ABORT.
... "to skip a record
*    raise exception type CX_RSROUT_SKIP_RECORD.

*    result values of the routine
    RESULT = .
    CURRENCY = .

*$*$ end of routine -
* insert your code only before this line    *-*
  ENDMETHOD. "compute_0AMOUNT
ENDCLASS.    "routine IMPLEMENTATION
```

Listing 4.3 Key Figure Calculation with Unit Output

You can use the key figure calculation with unit output for two different types of units: quantity units and currencies. Although you should calculate currencies using a corresponding currency conversion key, the preceding routine is the only way to perform a quantity unit conversion.

You might need to convert currencies; otherwise, the process terminates because data records are imported that don't contain any information on the amount or source currency. In that case, you should perform the currency conversion by yourself. Listing 4.4 shows you how to do that.

```
CLASS routine IMPLEMENTATION.

  METHOD compute_0AMOUNT.
*   Here the provided currency is converted
*   into Euro.If no currency is delivered,
*   0 Euro is returned.
.
    DATA:
      MONITOR_REC    TYPE rsmonitor.

*$*$ begin of routine -
* insert your code only below this line *-*
... "insert your code here
*-- fill table "MONITOR" with values of structure
*-  "MONITOR_REC" to make monitor entries
... "to cancel the update process
*    raise exception type
*         CX_RSROUT_ABORT.
... "to skip a record
*    raise exception type
*         CX_RSROUT_SKIP_RECORD.
*    result values of the routine
  IF SOURCE_FIELDS-CURRENCY IS INITIAL.
    RESULT = 0.
    CURRENCY = 'EUR'.
  ELSE.
    CALL FUNCTION
        'CONVERT_TO_LOCAL_CURRENCY'
      EXPORTING
        DATE            = sy-datum
        FOREIGN_AMOUNT  =
          SOURCE_FIELDS-amount
        FOREIGN_CURRENCY =
          SOURCE_FIELDS-currency
        LOCAL_CURRENCY   = 'EUR'
```

```
        TYPE_OF_RATE    = 'M'
     IMPORTING
        LOCAL_AMOUNT    = RESULT
     EXCEPTIONS
        OTHERS          = 1.
  IF sy-subrc = 0.
    CURRENCY   = 'EUR'.
  ELSE.
    RESULT    = SOURCE_FIELDS-amount.
    CURRENCY = SOURCE_FIELDS-currency.
  ENDIF.
*$*$ end of routine -
* insert your code only before this line *-*
  ENDMETHOD. "compute_0AMOUNT
ENDCLASS.    "routine IMPLEMENTATION
```

Listing 4.4 Currency Conversion in the Transformation

A somewhat easier alternative is to set the currency 0CURRENCY to EUR in the start routine. However, if the currency is updated into an additional field, it can make an important difference if you update Euro or no-currency data.

The only routine that's missing in the transformation compared to the old update rules is the routine containing the return table. In most cases, this routine can be replaced with the end routine described in Listing 4.5 in the next subsection, although in some rare cases, you have to revert to the expert routine. Even though this may require some additional work, the SAP decision to avoid the routine was certainly right. Regarding the return table, it was always unclear in which sequence the individual exits would be called, and this could be very confusing.

4.1.3 Start Routine in the Transformation

The start routine is primarily used to format the source data. You should use the start routine whenever the source system delivers the data in a different form than is expected by SAP NetWeaver BI. For example, you should carry out conversions if cost types are delivered without alpha conversion or if the date format is 01.05.06. At this point, you can also already delete data records from the source system that aren't needed in SAP NetWeaver BI. In general, it's more efficient to carry out several data operations in the start routine instead of splitting them up into single routines, especially if those routines require the same intermediate results for their calculations.

You can also efficiently scale down the data package in the start routine. Because the entire data package is contained in an internal table, you can reduce the data quantity efficiently by using the `DELETE SOURCE_PACKAGE WHERE ...` statement. Implementing an exception in the characteristic routine for the same purpose is much less efficient because the data records first have to be specifically formatted for the characteristic calculation—a time-consuming task.

You can create the start routine either through the transformation menu by selecting INSERT • CREATE START ROUTINE or by clicking on the relevant button (see Figure 4.4).

Figure 4.4 Button for Creating a Start Routine

The importing parameters of the start routine are the request as well as the data package ID; its exporting parameter is the table containing the error records. The most important parameter, however, is the actual `SOURCE_PACKAGE` table that contains the data records and is defined as a changing parameter.

The annoying thing about the start routine in Release 3.x was that the fields that were contained in the InfoCube often were actually missing in the start routine. This effect can almost be neglected because of the existence of the end routine. For this reason, you should mainly use the start routine for initializations, data cleansing, and deleting redundant data records.

In the example in Listing 4.5, we'll first delete invalid characters from the data package and then initialize a master data table.

```
PROGRAM trans_routine.


*------------------------------------------*
*        CLASS routine DEFINITION
*------------------------------------------*
*
*------------------------------------------*
CLASS routine DEFINITION.
  PUBLIC SECTION.
```

```
    TYPES:
      BEGIN OF _ty_s_SC_1,
*        InfoObject: 0CO_AREA Contr. area.
         CO_AREA TYPE /BI0/OICO_AREA,
*        InfoObject: 0CO_DOC_NO CO Doc.No.
         CO_DOC_NO TYPE /BI0/OICO_DOC_NO,
* ...
      END   OF _ty_s_SC_1.
    TYPES:
      _ty_t_SC_1
        TYPE STANDARD TABLE OF _ty_s_SC_1
        WITH NON-UNIQUE DEFAULT KEY.
  PRIVATE SECTION.

    TYPE-POOLS: rsd, rstr.

*$*$ begin of global -
* insert your declaration only below this line *-*
  DATA: g_t_costcenter
          TYPE /bi0/qcostcenter
          WITH UNIQUE KEY
              co_area
              costcenter
              objvers
              dateto.
*$*$ end of global -
* insert your declaration only before this line *-*
    METHODS
      start_routine
        IMPORTING
          request     TYPE rsrequest
          datapackid TYPE rsdatapid
        EXPORTING
          monitor TYPE rstr_ty_t_monitors
        CHANGING
          SOURCE_PACKAGE TYPE _ty_t_SC_1
        RAISING
          cx_rsrout_abort.
ENDCLASS.           "routine DEFINITION


*---------------------------------------*
*       CLASS routine IMPLEMENTATION
```

```
*----------------------------------------*
*
*----------------------------------------*
CLASS routine IMPLEMENTATION.

*----------------------------------------*
*        Method start_routine
*----------------------------------------*
*        Calculation of source package via
*        start routine
*----------------------------------------*
*    <-> source package
*----------------------------------------*
  METHOD start_routine.
*=== Segments ===

    FIELD-SYMBOLS:
      <SOURCE_FIELDS>    TYPE _ty_s_SC_1.

    DATA:
      MONITOR_REC       TYPE rstmonitor.

*$*$ begin of routine -
* insert your code only below this line *-*
... "insert your code here
*--  fill table "MONITOR" with values of structure
* "MONITOR_REC" to make monitor entries
* First delete those lines that have an order
* as partner projects.
  DELETE SOURCE_PACKAGE WHERE
     PIOBJSV = '0COR'.
* Then initialize the cost center table.
DATA: r_cctr TYPE RANGE OF
        /bi0/oicostcenter, "Ranges table for
                            "cost centers
      w_cctr LIKE LINE OF r_cctr. "Header for r_cctr
  CLEAR w_cctr.
  w_cctr-sign   = 'I'.  "Including selection
  w_cctr-option = 'EQ'. "Query similarity
* A ranges table containing all cost centers is built
* up in the following loop.
  LOOP AT source_package
    ASSIGNING <SOURCE_FIELDS>.
```

```
   w_cctr-low = <SOURCE_FIELDS>-costcenter.
   COLLECT w_cctr into r_cctr.
 ENDLOOP.
* Then those cost centers are imported into the
* global table that are also available in the
* data package.
 SELECT * FROM /bi0/qcostcenter
   INTO TABLE g_t_costcenter
   WHERE costcenter IN r_cctr
   AND   objvers = 'A'.

... "to cancel the update process
*    raise exception type
*          CX_RSROUT_ABORT.

*$*$ end of routine –
* insert your code only before this line *-*
 ENDMETHOD.       "start_routine
ENDCLASS.         "routine IMPLEMENTATION
```

Listing 4.5 Example of a Start Routine, Including Generated Method

Both techniques described here are typical of start routines. When the start routine in SAP BW Release 3.x was the only routine in which the complete data package was calculated, it was often used for many different calculations. Logically speaking, however, this should be part of the end routine.

4.1.4 End Routine in the Transformation

The end routine in the transformation is predominantly used to post-edit the data. Here you should calculate new fields that aren't delivered directly, determine additional check sums that are to be updated in the data target, and adjust the data to the data target.

You also can use the end routines for validation purposes. For instance, you can first calculate the sales figures per customer and then delete all data records in the end routine in which the sales figures per customer are below $10,000. However, whether the calculation takes place in the start routine or end routine usually depends on other considerations, particularly whether the fields required for calculating the algorithms are actually updated into the data target.

Example: Selecting the Position of the Calculation

We want to update a cost center category CCTRCAT into a data target. The cost center category can be derived from the cost center and the load-unload identifier. Each cost center category consists of approximately 100 cost centers. The DataSource only contains the cost center. The following 4 different locations are available for carrying out the calculation:

▶ Choosing the end routine here is the cleanest way because the data enrichment isn't used for data-staging purposes. However, the derivation is only possible here if the cost center is updated anyway. Otherwise, it doesn't make sense to increase the data by factor 100.

▶ The start routine can always be used for calculation purposes, but note that it may be necessary to add the CSTCAT field to the DataSource even if the field remains empty where the data originated. This extension of the DataSource can usually be done without any problem, but you should document it well because follow-up projects might rely on the fact that the field is delivered from the data's origin.

▶ You also can perform the calculation in the characteristic derivation method. It actually makes sense to do that here, although the process affects system performance more than using the start and end routines. On the other hand, you don't need to adjust the source or data target structures.

▶ You can also replace the entire transformation with an *expert routine*. This is particularly useful if the source and target fields contain many differences. However, in that case, you must program every single field derivation, and you can't use any standard currency conversion.

There is no silver bullet regarding the best routine to be used. You have to decide case by case which solution is best.

Take a look at the generated method of an end routine (see Listing 4.6). The end routine clearly mirrors the start routine. The only difference in the code is that the name of the SOURCE_PACKAGE from the start routine is RESULT_PACKAGE in the end routine.

```
PROGRAM trans_routine.

*----------------------------------------*
*        CLASS routine DEFINITION
*----------------------------------------*
*
*----------------------------------------*
CLASS routine DEFINITION.
  PUBLIC SECTION.
```

```
      TYPES:
        BEGIN OF _ty_s_TG_1,
* InfoObject: 0FISCPER Fiscal year / per.
          FISCPER TYPE /BIO/OIFISCPER,
* InfoObject: 0FISCVARNT Fiscal year var.
          FISCVARNT TYPE /BIO/OIFISCVARNT,
*  ...
        END   OF _ty_s_TG_1.
      TYPES:
        _ty_t_TG_1
          TYPE STANDARD TABLE OF _ty_s_TG_1
          WITH NON-UNIQUE DEFAULT KEY.
    PRIVATE SECTION.
      TYPE-POOLS: rsd, rstr.

*$*$ begin of global -
* insert your declaration only below this line *-*
... "insert your code here
*$*$ end of global -
* insert your declaration only before this line *-*
      METHODS
        end_routine
          IMPORTING
            request     TYPE rsrequest
            datapackid TYPE rsdatapid
          EXPORTING
            monitor TYPE rstr_ty_t_monitors
          CHANGING
            RESULT_PACKAGE TYPE _ty_t_TG_1
          RAISING
            cx_rsrout_abort.
ENDCLASS.          "routine DEFINITION


*----------------------------------------*
*        CLASS routine IMPLEMENTATION
*----------------------------------------*
*
*----------------------------------------*
CLASS routine IMPLEMENTATION.

*----------------------------------------*
*        Method end_routine
```

```
*-------------------------------------------*
*       Calculation of result package via
*       end routine
*-------------------------------------------*
*    <-> result package
*-------------------------------------------*
  METHOD end_routine.
*=== Segments ===

    FIELD-SYMBOLS:
      <RESULT_FIELDS>     TYPE _ty_s_TG_1.

    DATA:
      MONITOR_REC      TYPE rstmonitor.

*$*$ begin of routine -
* insert your code only below this line *-*
... "insert your code here
*--  fill table "MONITOR" with values of structure
*-  "MONITOR_REC" to make monitor entries
... "to cancel the update process
*     raise exception type CX_RSROUT_ABORT.

*$*$ end of routine -
* insert your code only before this line *-*
  ENDMETHOD.        "end_routine
ENDCLASS.           "routine IMPLEMENTATION
```

Listing 4.6 Generated Method of an End Routine

4.1.5 Expert Routine in the Transformation

Both the start and end routines can't be programmed efficiently unless the source and target data of the derivation formulas are available in the InfoProvider and in the InfoSource. In real life, however, this isn't always the case.

SAP NetWeaver 7.0 provides a new solution to this problem. The expert routine allows you to implement the transformation of source data into target data completely by yourself. However, if you implement this routine, you also must fill the entire target structure, including the units and, if necessary, a currency conversion. Note that if an attribute derivation is necessary as well, you must do that manually.

The most complex part, however, is probably error handling because the expert routine doesn't provide you with a simple monitor table but rather a `LOG` object of the `CL_RSBM_LOG_CURSOR_STEP` class. Not only does this object receive the messages, but it also provides the complete message tree. It probably represents the biggest obstacle for inexperienced programmers because it presupposes comprehensive object-oriented programming knowledge.

Compared to the standard transformation, the expert routine also has advantages regarding system performance. In the standard transformation process, a routine is called for each field of the data target to fill the field. If you implement a simple field assignment, it only contains a simple assignment instruction. In that case, the entire overhead that's involved in structuring the data record is naturally much slower than the simple `MOVE-CORRESPONDING` command that would be used in the expert routine at this point.

Another important reason you should use the expert routine is that by doing so you can obtain a history of the transformation. If transformations change frequently, it can be important to track which transformation rules were used for the import of certain data. In the standard version, this is only possible if you documented the rules clearly in Microsoft Word, for example. However, if you store the expert routine in a method, you can use the ABAP change history at any time to track when a transport was imported into the live system and the status of a specific data package at a certain point in time. This option requires that the Info-Cube be uncompressed so that the request ID used to identify the point in time is still stored in the InfoCube.

Deciding what to do in the expert routine is relatively simple: If you don't use the expert routine for performance reasons, you should at least use it whenever you need both the start and end routines for the derivations and when you need several complex routines for characteristic and key figure derivations

You can only create the expert routine via the following menu: EDIT • CREATE EXPERT ROUTINE. When you create an expert routine, the appearance of the transformation changes, as shown in Figure 4.5. As you can see in the figure, the many different links have been replaced by an arrow that's called EXPERT ROUTINE.

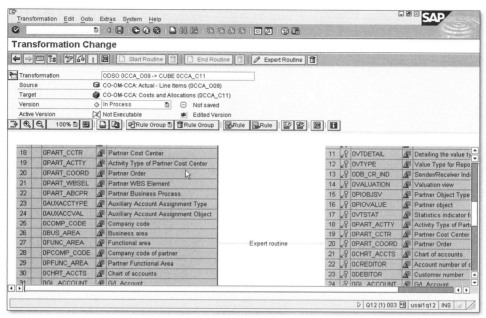

Figure 4.5 Transformation with Expert Routine

After the routine has been created, the system automatically generates the program code shown in Listing 4.7.

```
PROGRAM trans_routine.


*----------------------------------------*
*        CLASS routine DEFINITION
*----------------------------------------*
*
*----------------------------------------*
CLASS routine DEFINITION.
  PUBLIC SECTION.

    TYPES:
      BEGIN OF _ty_s_SC_1,
*       InfoObject: 0CO_AREA Cont. area.
        CO_AREA          TYPE /BI0/OICO_AREA,
* InfoObject: 0CO_DOC_NO CO Doc. Number.
*       ...
*       Field: RECORD.
        RECORD           TYPE  RSARECORD,
```

```
      END   OF _ty_s_SC_1.
    TYPES:
      _ty_t_SC_1
        TYPE STANDARD TABLE OF _ty_s_SC_1
        WITH NON-UNIQUE DEFAULT KEY.
    TYPES:
      BEGIN OF _ty_s_TG_1,
*   InfoObject: 0FISCPER Fiscal year/per.
    FISCPER         TYPE /BIO/OIFISCPER,
*   InfoObject: 0FISCVARNT Fisc. year var.
    FISCVARNT       TYPE /BIO/OIFISCVARNT,
*   ...
*      Field: RECORD.
        RECORD          TYPE RSARECORD,
      END   OF _ty_s_TG_1.
    TYPES:
      _ty_t_TG_1
        TYPE STANDARD TABLE OF _ty_s_TG_1
        WITH NON-UNIQUE DEFAULT KEY.
  PRIVATE SECTION.
    TYPE-POOLS: rsd, rstr.

*$*$ begin of global -
* insert your declaration only below this line *-*
... "insert your code here
*$*$ end of global -
* insert your declaration only before this line *-*
    METHODS
      expert_routine
        IMPORTING
          request      TYPE rsrequest
          datapackid   TYPE rsdatapid
          SOURCE_PACKAGE TYPE _ty_t_SC_1
          log TYPE REF TO cl_rsbm_log_cursor_step
        EXPORTING
          RESULT_PACKAGE TYPE _ty_t_TG_1.
    METHODS
      inverse_expert_routine
        IMPORTING
          i_r_selset_outbound   TYPE REF TO
                                cl_rsmds_set
          i_th_fields_outbound  TYPE
                                rstran_t_field_inv
```

```
              i_r_universe_inbound   TYPE REF TO
                                     cl_rsmds_universe
         CHANGING
            c_r_selset_inbound    TYPE REF TO
                                     cl_rsmds_set
            c_th_fields_inbound   TYPE
                                     rstran_t_field_inv
            c_exact               TYPE
                                     rs_bool.
ENDCLASS.               "routine DEFINITION


*---------------------------------------*
*       CLASS routine IMPLEMENTATION
*---------------------------------------*
*
*---------------------------------------*
CLASS routine IMPLEMENTATION.


*---------------------------------------*
*       Method expert_routine
*---------------------------------------*
*       Calculation of result package via
*       expert routine
*---------------------------------------*
*    -> package of source segments
*    <- result package
*---------------------------------------*
  METHOD expert_routine.
*=== Segments ===

    FIELD-SYMBOLS:
      <SOURCE_FIELDS>    TYPE _ty_s_SC_1.

    DATA:
      RESULT_FIELDS      TYPE _ty_s_TG_1.


*$*$ begin of routine -
* insert your code only below this line *-*
... "insert your code here
*$*$ end of routine -
* insert your code only before this line *-*
  ENDMETHOD.      "expert_routine
*---------------------------------------*
```

```
*        Method inverse_expert_routine
*----------------------------------------*
*
* This subroutine needs to be implemented only for
* direct access (for better performance) and for the
* report-report interface (drill through). The inverse
* routine should transform a projection and a selection for
* the target to a projection and a selection for the
* source, respectively. If the implementation remains empty,
* all fields are filled, and all values are selected.
*
*----------------------------------------*
*
*----------------------------------------*
  METHOD inverse_expert_routine.

*$*$ begin of inverse routine -
* insert your code only below this line *-*
... "insert your code here
*$*$ end of inverse routine -
* insert your code only before this line *-*

  ENDMETHOD.    "inverse_expert_routine
ENDCLASS.       "routine IMPLEMENTATION
```

Listing 4.7 Generated Method of an Expert Routine

Here again, you can see that the method interface is relatively simple. The request ID REQUEST and the data package ID DATAPACKID are transferred as well as the source characteristics table SOURCE_PACKAGE. These elements are then used to fill the RESULT_PACKAGE table and the LOG object, which is used to return the error records. The LOG data object isn't a simple table here, as it usually is in these routines. In this case, you must build up the entire structure of the message tree yourself.

Once again, you can define global data structures. You'll probably ask yourself why this is necessary; after all, you only use one routine in the entire transformation. However, when defining global data structures, you can transfer data from one data package to another. This is particularly useful when using customizing tables and derivation tables that must be imported from the database.

In general, the `INVERSE_EXPERT_ROUTINE` method doesn't need to be implemented. This method only makes sense if you need the transformation for a VirtualProvider or for the report-report interface in the source system. If you use the `INVERSE_EXPERT_ROUTINE` method in the routine, you can derive selections for the DataSource from the selections in the data target.

The interface used for this is rather complex because several classes are transferred that contain the selection conditions in a very abstract form. The implementation can be even more difficult if the transformation to be used can't be inverted cleanly in the source system. For this reason, you should first find out what happens if you don't implement the routine.

An empty selection implies that no restrictions are transferred to the source system. This is important in these two situations:

▸ In the case of a RemoteCube, all of the data that is available in the source system is first imported and then transformed using the `EXPERT_ROUTINE` method. Finally, the data is processed by the OLAP processor for the query output. The result is the same as in a correct implementation of the `INVERSE_EXPERT_SELECTION` method. However, it can take much longer to obtain this result if you don't implement the method because then all data records of the source system must be read. Especially when using a VirtualProvider to access line items tables without implementing the method, the system performance would be intolerable.

▸ The result is different if you call a transaction in the source system via a report-report interface and use the query selections in the source system. In that case, the lack of the method implementation means that either all existing data is displayed (a line-items report in the source system would then either display all existing data records or abort with an authorization error), or the user must re-enter all selections in a selection screen.

Consequently, the goal of the implementation must be to select a superset of the actual result set in the return parameters. This superset should be as small as possible.

Because the routine doesn't have much relevance in practice, we won't provide any detailed description of the parameters here. If you need to use the routine, look at the transfer parameters in Transaction RSRT in the Debugger. There you can see that you must fill the C_R_SELSET_INBOUND and C_TH_FIELDS_INBOUND parameters like the OUTBOUND importing parameters.

Sample Expert Routine

You would typically use an expert routine for the transformation from a key figure model into the account model in the profitability analysis module, CO-PA. A typical CO-PA scenario contains several characteristics and key figures: the so-called *key figure model*. However, in SAP NetWeaver BI, it's often more useful to use a data modeling, which, in addition to the characteristics from CO-PA, contains only two key figures: a quantity (0QUANTITY) and an amount (0AMOUNT). Apart from those two key figures, it also contains a characteristic (KEY FIGURE) that indicates the exact key figure being dealt with.

In the expert routine, you'll search through all key figure fields of the source structure, and if the relevant field is unequal to zero, a corresponding entry is written to the data target. Listing 4.8 shows a possible implementation of this.

```
  METHOD expert_routine.
*=== Segments ===
   FIELD-SYMBOLS:
     <SOURCE_FIELDS>      TYPE _ty_s_SC_1.
   DATA:
     RESULT_FIELDS        TYPE _ty_s_TG_1.

*$*$ begin of routine -
* insert your code only below this line *-*
* Here the data fields of the source system are examined
* field by field. Each value that is <> 0 generates an
* entry in the RESULT_TABLE.
TYPES: ty_w_dfies TYPE dfies.
TYPES: ty_t_dfies TYPE STANDARD TABLE
          OF ty_w_dfies
          INITIAL SIZE 0.
DATA: l_t_dfies_tab TYPE ty_t_dfies,
      l_t_dfies_wk  TYPE ty_t_dfies,
      l_s_wa_dfies  TYPE ty_w_dfies,
      l_d_tablename TYPE ddobjname
*       Name of the communication structure of the InfoSource
          VALUE ,/BIC/CSCOPA_DATA',
      l_d_currency TYPE dynptype
```

```
*      Key for identifying the currency fields
                 VALUE ‚CURR' .

* Field symbol for dynamic determination of source values
FIELD-SYMBOLS: <fw> LIKE /BIC/VCOPACUBET-amount.
DATA: l_d_field(40) TYPE c.

* First the SOURCE_PACKAGE structure is determined.
* This happens dynamically because the source structure can
* change. This way the routine does not need to be adjusted
    CALL FUNCTION ‚DDIF_FIELDINFO_GET'
      EXPORTING
        tabname        =    l_d_tablename
      TABLES
        dfies_tab      = l_t_dfies_tab
      EXCEPTIONS
        not found      = 1
        internal error = 2
        others         = 3.
  IF sy-subrc <> 0.
    l_s_message-MSGID = ‚ZDEMO'.
    l_s_message-MSGNO = ‚101'.
    l_s_message-MSGTY = ‚E'.
    l_s_message-MSGV1 = ‚DDIF_FIELDINFO_GET'.
    l_s_message-MSGV2 = l_d_tablename.
    l_s_message-MSGV3 = sy-subrc.
*   l_s_message-MSGV4 = .
    CALL METHOD LOG->ADD_MSG
      EXPORTING
        I_S_MSG = l_s_message
      .
*   Return code &3 when calling &1 for &2.
  ENDIF.

* Only the value fields of type amount= ‚CURR'
* are included.
  l_t_dfies_wk[] = l_t_dfies_tab[].
  DELETE l_t_dfies_wk WHERE datatype ne l_d_currency.

  LOOP AT SOURCE_PACKAGE
    ASSIGNING <SOURCE_FIELDS>.
*   Determine the value field name for each currency field
*   in the data record and set the amount.
```

```
    LOOP AT l_t_dfies_wk INTO l_s_wa_dfies.
*     Concatenate field names
      CONCATENATE .<SOURCE_FIELDS>-'
                  wa_dfies-fieldname
                  INTO l_d_field.
      ASSIGN (l_d_field) TO <fw>.
*     If value field 0, then no transfer
      CHECK <fw> NE 0.
*       Transfer all characteristics that are identical
        MOVE-CORRESPONDING <SOURCE_FIELDS>
                         TO RESULT_FIELDS.
*     Set characteristic for cube
      RESULT_FIELDS-/bic/kennzahl = l_s_wa_dfies-fieldname.
      RESULT_FIELDS-AMOUNT = <fw>.
      APPEND RESULT_FIELDS TO RESULT_PACKAGE.
    ENDLOOP. "th_dfies_wk
  ENDLOOP.
*$*$ end of routine -
* insert your code only before this line *-*
  ENDMETHOD. "expert_routine
```
Listing 4.8 Account Model in the Expert Routine

You should generally use the expert routine only in exceptional cases. But it has its advantages, and after an experienced programmer becomes familiar with the structure of the log, he will regularly use the routine.

The disadvantage of the routine is that only an SAP NetWeaver BI expert with the relevant ABAP knowledge can change it at a later stage. So the integration of a new field in the source or target structure can entail quite a bit of modification work. Also, it's no longer possible to see in the graphical display which field in the target structure depends on which other images.

Due to the complexity of the implementation in the expert routine, the SAP development team is currently designing an appropriate support interface. However, more details aren't available right now.

4.2   Routines in the Data Transfer Processes

In addition to the transformation, with Release 7.0, SAP has also introduced the data transfer process (DTP), which supports the distribution of data within the BI system if transformations are used. InfoPackages are still used to load data into other systems.

In DTP, you can also use routines. Within DTP, you can use two routines that work like the corresponding routines in the InfoPackage, that is, for the file name and for the value selection.

4.2.1 Selecting a File Name in the Data Transfer Process

The aim of the file name determination is to load a file, which has an ever-changing name that can be determined using an algorithm, by means of DTP without having to adapt the file name in DTP each time.

> **Note**
>
> Note that this is only the exception. Usually, the files are loaded via an InfoPackage into the PSA; DTP requires no file name then.

Because regular loading of files is usually implemented via a process chain, you shouldn't use this exit in a properly modeled process. If you still want to do so, you can create the exit as follows:

1. First, make sure that DTP is available with the FULL extraction mode.

2. On the EXTRACTION tab, you can then activate the DO NOT EXTRACT FROM PSA BUT ACCESS DATA SOURCE (FOR SMALL AMOUNTS OF DATA) flag (see Figure 4.6).

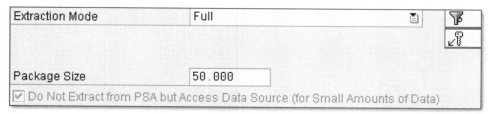

Figure 4.6 Prerequisites for File Name Selection

3. Some lines appear below the flag. You can find a CREATE ROUTINE button behind the file name (see Figure 4.7). To go to the code shown in Listing 4.9, you must click this button.

Adapter	Load Text-Type File from Local Workstation	📃	🔗	Properties

File Name	O:\BW\SAP\V_Upload\Stammdaten\FDL\Aktionsnummer…	⟳📧📃
Header Rows to be Ignored	1	
Character Set Settings	Default Setting 📃	
System Codepage	1100 SAP internal, like ISO 8859-1 (00697/00819)	
Data Format	Separated with Separator (for Example, CSV) 📃	

Figure 4.7   Button for the Routine for File Determination

```
PROGRAM filename_routine.
* Global code
*$*$ begin of global -
* insert your declaration only below this line   *-*
* Enter here global variables and type declarations as well
* as additional form routines, which you may call from the
* main routine COMPUTE_FLAT_FILE_FILENAME below
*TABLES: ...
* DATA:    ...
*$*$ end of global -
* insert your declaration only before this line   *-*
* -----------------------------------------------------------
FORM compute_flat_file_filename
  USING     p_infopackage  TYPE rslogdpid
            p_datasource   TYPE rsoltpsourcer
            p_logsys       TYPE rsslogsys
  CHANGING  p_filename     TYPE RSFILENM
            p_subrc        LIKE sy-subrc.
*$*$ begin of routine -
* insert your code only below this line        *-*
* This routine will be called by the adapter when the
* infopackage is executed.
          p_filename =
*....
          p_subrc = 0.
*$*$ end of routine -
* insert your code only before this line        *-*
ENDFORM.
```

Listing 4.9   Routine for Determining the File Name

SAP has provided some more parameters than are available in the InfoPackage (InfoPackage, DataSource, source system); still this routine doesn't make sense from the data modeling point of view. Users who execute a load process for files regularly should use the correct procedure and load the data into PSA via the InfoPackage. If you still want to use the routine, you should define the file names based on CONCATENATE commands. The current date SY-DATE should be particularly useful for determining time-dependent parts of the file name.

4.2.2 Determining a Characteristics Selection in the Data Transfer Process

Like in InfoPackages, selections in the data transfer process are very critical—or even more critical in some parts. An InfoPackage requires you to update a delta in all data targets simultaneously. DTP enables you to write deltas from the same DataSource in different data targets at different points in time. This allows you to use different filter conditions for the various data targets in the various DTPs.

To create a filter:

1. On the EXTRACTION tab, select the filter list (see Figure 4.8).

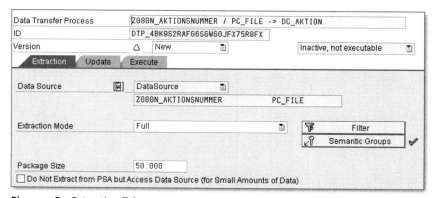

Figure 4.8 Extraction Tab

2. Click on the right button with the blue round-cornered rectangle (see Figure 4.9).

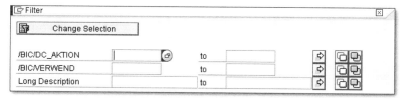

Figure 4.9 Button for the Routine for Filter Determination

The code shown in Listing 4.10 is then shown.

```
*&----------------------------------------------------------*
*&  Include              RSBC_SEL_ROUTINE_TPL
*&----------------------------------------------------------*

PROGRAM conversion_routine.
* Type pools used by conversion program
TYPE-POOLS: rsarc, rsarr, rssm.
TABLES: rssdlrange.
* Global code used by conversion rules
*$*$ begin of global -
* insert your declaration only below this line  *-*
* TABLES: ...
* DATA:   ...
*$*$ end of global -
* insert your declaration only before this line  *-*
* ---------------------------------------------------------
*    Fieldname       =
*    data type       =
*    length          = 000000
* ---------------------------------------------------------
FORM compute_
  TABLES l_t_range STRUCTURE rssdlrange
  CHANGING p_subrc LIKE sy-subrc.
*        Insert source code to current selection field
*$*$ begin of routine -
* insert your code only below this line        *-*
DATA: l_idx LIKE sy-tabix.
        READ TABLE l_t_range WITH KEY
            fieldname = ' '.
        l_idx = sy-tabix.
*....
* At this point, you can fill in the filter values
        IF l_idx <> 0.
          MODIFY l_t_range INDEX l_idx.
        ELSE.
          APPEND l_t_range.
        ENDIF.
        p_subrc = 0.

*$*$ end of routine -
```

```
* insert your code only before this line          *-*
ENDFORM.
```

Listing 4.10 Routine for Determining the Filter Value

The interface of the routine is simple:

▶ Table L_T_RANGE contains all selections of the data transfer process and must be adapted accordingly; parameter P_SUBRC must be filled with a value that isn't equal to 0 if DTP is supposed to be canceled, for example, because data is missing in the control tables.

▶ In table L_T_RANGE, you must fill the fields, FIELDNAME, IOBJNM, and the typical fields of a RANGES table (SIGN, OPTION, LOW, and HIGH).

If, for example, the data of the previous month is to be loaded in the data transfer process, and the month is defined in InfoObject OCALMONTH, the routine looks like Listing 4.11.

```
*$*$ begin of routine -
* insert your code only below this line          *-*
DATA: l_idx LIKE sy-tabix.
data: l_d_datum  type d.
        READ TABLE l_t_range WITH KEY
            fieldname = 'CALMONTH'.
        l_idx = sy-tabix.
*....
        l_t_range-fieldname = 'CALMONTH'.
        l_t_range-iobjnm    = 'OCALMONTH'.
        l_t_range-sign = 'I'.
        l_t_range-option = 'EQ'.
* Now the last day of the the previous month is determined
        l_d_datum = sy-datum.
        l_d_datum+6(2) = '01'.
        l_d_datum  = l_d_datum - 1.
        l_t_range-low = l_d_datum(6).
        IF l_idx <> 0.
          MODIFY l_t_range INDEX l_idx.
```

```
      ELSE.
        APPEND l_t_range.
      ENDIF.
      p_subrc = 0.

*$*$ end of routine -
* insert your code only before this line          *-*
```

Listing 4.11 Example of Filter Value Determination

4.3 Importing a Hierarchy from an Unstructured Excel Sheet

Now let's explore the strengths of the transformation by using a more comprehensive example. The goal is to upload into SAP NetWeaver 7.0 a hierarchy created in Microsoft Excel.

This scenario frequently occurs whenever the hierarchies are defined in different departments of a company, particularly with regard to financial statement hierarchies for annual reports but also concerning sales and distribution structures. Often, the Excel table doesn't have the required structure NODE ID • CHARACTERISTIC • ATTRIBUTE • PARENT ID. Instead, the tables contain hierarchies in a structure that's typically used in Excel, as shown in Figure 4.10.

	A	B	C	D	E
1	Level 01	Level 02	Level 03	Level 04	Text
2	100000000				Total Hierarchy
3		10100000			Node 1
4			10101000		Subnode 1.1
5				10101010	Subnode 1.1.1
6				10101020	Subnode 1.1.2
7				10101030	Subnode 1.1.3
8			10102000		Subnode 1.2
9				10102010	Subnode 1.2.1
10				...	
11					

Figure 4.10 Typical Excel Hierarchy

Individual child nodes must also be sorted; that is, they must be arranged in the same sequence as they appear in the Excel file. For this purpose, you need a *sorted hierarchy* in SAP NetWeaver BI. In this sorted hierarchy, you must specify the parent node ID as well as the node ID of the first child and the node ID of the successor on the same level. To do that, you must use some logical rules that are checked in SAP NetWeaver BI when the hierarchy file is loaded. Note that it's possible to program this entire logic in Excel by using macros, but that's not very easy.

In one bank's IAS implementation project (*International Accounting Standards*), for example, these calculations were performed in SAP NetWeaver BI, and a report was generated that could be used as a source file for the hierarchy upload. An important reason for this decision was that additional master data attributes were required that could be entered into the same Excel sheet. However, in this example, the focus is exclusively on the hierarchy structure.

Note: Structure of a BI Hierarchy

For a better understanding of the example, you should be familiar with the basic logic of SAP NetWeaver BI. The actual hierarchy structure that's created here consists of the following information: NODEID, PARENTID, CHILDID, NEXTID, and LINKNODE.

▶ NODEID represents a simple identification of the nodes. The node IDs don't necessarily have to be continuous or ascending, but if possible, you should make sure that they are arranged in ascending order because that makes troubleshooting much easier.

▶ PARENTID is the NODEID of the parent node in the hierarchy. The PARENTID of the root nodes (there can be several root nodes) is 0.

▶ CHILDID is the NODEID of the first child. For child node 1.1 in the example in Figure 4.10, that's the NODEID of child node 1.1.1. During the hierarchy upload, the system checks if the PARENTID of the node that's specified in the CHILDID is actually the NODEID of the current node. If that isn't the case, an error message is output.

▶ NEXTID is the NODEID of the next node on the same level that has the same PARENTID. If another node exists with the same parent, the NEXTID is assigned the value 0. In the example shown in Figure 4.10, this applies to child node 1.1.3.

The system also checks if the hierarchy contains circular references. A circular reference occurs if you trace the path from a node in a hierarchy up to its root, and somewhere on the way, you end up at the original node again. Furthermore, the system checks if each node in the hierarchy is integrated. With the exception of the top-level root node, each node must have its NODEID either in the CHILDID or in the NEXTID of another node.

This example uses a start and an end routine to demonstrate the basic differences. The start routine will be used to derive the key and hierarchy level from the distribution into several source columns and also to integrate the node ID as simple numbering. The end routine, on the other hand, will be used for a complex algorithmic derivation of the additionally required fields PARENTID, CHILDID, NEXTID, and LINKNODE.

This example also assumes that the hierarchy is small enough to fit into a data package. The newly implemented DTP in SAP NetWeaver 7.0 enables you to make the necessary settings without having to change all customizing settings for the load processes.

4.3.1   Creating the DataStore Object

In SAP NetWeaver 7.0, "DataStore object" is the new name for the ODS object. The creation of the object is almost identical to the process used in SAP BW 3.x. The data model used in this case is relatively simple.

1. You define a DataStore object, HIERUPLD, that contains the data structure shown in Table 4.1.[4]

InfoObject	Key Field	Type	Description
NODEID	X	NUMC(8)	Node ID
NODENAME		CHAR(60)	Contents of the node
IOBJNM		CHAR(20)	Name of the InfoObject
NODETEXT		CHAR(60)	Text of the node
PARENTID		NUMC(8)	Node ID of the parent
CHILDID		NUMC(8)	Node ID of the first child
NEXTID		NUMC(8)	Node ID of the next node on the same level
HIERLVL		NUMC(2)	Hierarchy level
LINKNODE		CHAR(1)	Node doesn't appear for the first time in the hierarchy

Table 4.1   InfoObjects in DataStore Object HIERUPLD

4.3.2   Creating the DataSource

Next you create a DataSource called DS_HIERDATA. In this example, the DataSource contains the structure shown in Table 4.2.

InfoObject	Type	Description
NODE01	CHAR(20)	Key, level 1
NODE02	CHAR(20)	Key, level 2
. . .		
NODE12	CHAR(20)	Key, level 12

Table 4.2   Structure of the DataSource

---

4 For hierarchy nodes, we would use 0HIER_NODE here.

InfoObject	Type	Description
NODETEXT	CHAR(60)	Node text
HIERLVL	NUMC(2)	Hierarchy level
NODEID	NUMC(8)	Node ID
NODENAME	CHAR(20)	Key of the level

Table 4.2 Structure of the DataSource (Cont.)

Here, the fields `HIERLVL`, `NODEID`, and `NODENAME` aren't filled from the file but in the start routine; the file only comprises the columns up to and including `NODETEXT`.

The process of creating a DataSource has completely changed in SAP NetWeaver 7.0:

1. Select DATASOURCES in the navigation column on the left. Then select the SOURCE SYSTEM; in this case, that's PC_FILE. The application component tree that is defined for the respective source system appears. Right-click on an application component, and the CREATE DATASOURCE option can be selected, among other things (see Figure 4.11).

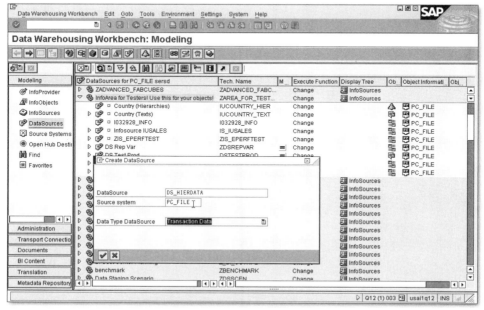

Figure 4.11 The Create DataSource Dialog Box

2. Enter the name and type of the DataSource (in this case, it's a TRANSACTION DATA DataSource). Go to the GENERAL INFO tab to store a description and some additional information, for instance, regarding the currency conversion. The EXTRACTION tab allows you to enter information on the source file, the file type, and so on. Note that it's important that you store the fields specified in Table 4.2 in the FIELDS tab (see Figure 4.12).

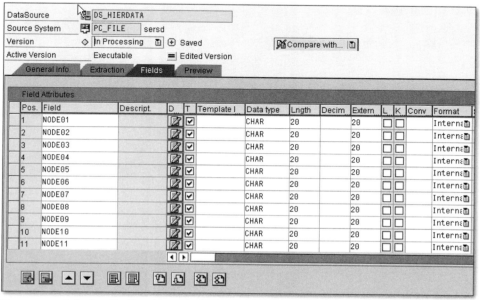

Figure 4.12 Selecting the DataSource Fields

3. If a file has already been stored — you can also do that later in the InfoPackage or DTP — you can check the data formats in the PREVIEW tab.

4.3.3   Creating the Transformation

To create the transformation:

1. Right-click on the DataStore object HIERUPLD, and select CREATE TRANSFORMA-TION. The screen shown in Figure 4.13 appears.

Figure 4.13 Creating a Transformation

2. In this screen, you must select a DataSource and choose the name DS_HIER-DATA. When you press ENTER to continue, the system automatically suggests a possible transformation (see Figure 4.14). In this transformation, those fields are automatically linked that are contained in both the DataSource and the DataStore, namely NODEID, HIERLVL, NODENAME, and NODETEXT. Because you don't want to transfer any other fields from the DataSource, you don't need to change anything at this point.

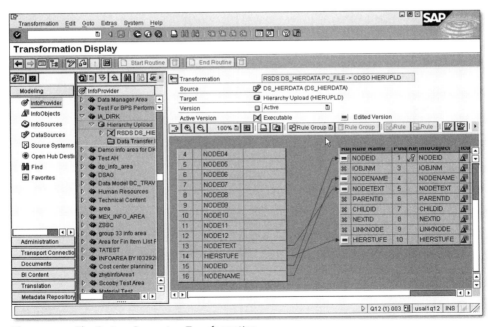

Figure 4.14 The System Suggests a Transformation

4.3.4 Creating the Start Routine

You can create a start routine via EDIT • CREATE START ROUTINE or by clicking on the corresponding button. In this start routine, we want to derive the fields NODEID, NODENAME, and HIERLVL. This can be easily done using the code shown in Listing 4.12. You only need to enter the bolded lines because all other lines are automatically generated by the system.

```
  METHOD start_routine.
*=== Segments ===
    FIELD-SYMBOLS:
      <SOURCE_FIELDS>      TYPE _ty_s_SC_1.
    DATA:
      MONITOR_REC      TYPE rstmonitor.
*$*$ begin of routine -
* insert your code only below this line *-*
... "insert your code here
*-- fill table "MONITOR" with values of structure
*- "MONITOR_REC" to make monitor entries
  DATA: l_d_nodeid type /bic/oinodeid.
 *       Counter for node ID
  l_d_nodeid = 1.
  LOOP AT source_package
    ASSIGNING <source_fields>.
* First the field to be filled must be determined.
    IF <source_fields>-node01 <> ''.
      <source_fields>-hierlvl = '01'.
      <source_fields>-nodename  = <source_fields>-node01.
      <source_fields>-nodeid    = l_d_nodeid.
      ADD 1 TO l_d_nodeid.
    ELSEIF <source_fields>-node02 <> ''.
      <source_fields>-hierlvl = '02'.
      <source_fields>-nodename  = <source_fields>-node02.
      <source_fields>-nodeid    = l_d_nodeid.
      ADD 1 TO l_d_nodeid.
    ELSEIF <source_fields>-node03 <> ''.
 *    ...
    ELSEIF <source_fields>-node12 <> ''.
      <source_fields>-hierlvl = '12'.
      <source_fields>-nodename  = <source_fields>-node12.
      <source_fields>-nodeid    = l_d_nodeid.
      ADD 1 TO l_d_nodeid.
    ELSE.
```

```
*     All fields are empty, delete record
      DELETE source_package.
   ENDIF.
ENDLOOP.
... "to cancel the update process
*    raise exception type
*         CX_RSROUT_ABORT.
*$*$ end of routine -
* insert your code only before this line *-*
  ENDMETHOD.       "start_routine
ENDCLASS.          "routine IMPLEMENTATION
```

Listing 4.12 Start Routine for Hierarchy Transformation

4.3.5   Creating the End Routine

After the start routine has been created, you can create the end routine. After the transformation is complete, you obtain a table in which only NODEID, HIERLVL, NODENAME, and NODETEXT are filled. This complies with the suggested rule. Now you need to fill the other fields of the DataStore: IOBJNM, PARENTID, CHILDID, NEXTID, and LINKNODE. To do that, you must create the end routine shown in Listing 4.13.

> **Note**
>
> The purpose of Listing 4.13 is to demonstrate the functionality of the end routine. For this reason, the number of fields is strictly limited to 12, and the routine doesn't contain any dynamic assigns for field determination. This enhances the readability.

```
  METHOD end_routine.
*=== Segments ===

    FIELD-SYMBOLS:
      <RESULT_FIELDS> TYPE _ty_s_TG_1.

    DATA:
      MONITOR_REC      TYPE rstmonitor.

*$*$ begin of routine -
* insert your code only below this line *-*
... "insert your code here
*-- fill table "MONITOR" with values of structure
*- "MONITOR_REC" to make monitor entries
... "to cancel the update process
```

```
*     raise exception type
*     CX_RSROUT_ABORT.


* Data definitions
  TYPES: BEGIN OF current_parent_line,
           parent_level TYPE
             /bic/oihierlvl,
           parent_node  TYPE
             /bic/oinodeid,
         END OF current_parent_line,
         current_parent_table TYPE
             SORTED TABLE OF
             current_parent_line
             WITH UNIQUE KEY
                 parent_level
             INITIAL SIZE 0.
  DATA: parent_line TYPE
          current_parent_line,
        parent_tab  TYPE
          current_parent_table,
        dp_line     LIKE
          LINE OF DATA_PACKAGE,
        dp_buffer   LIKE
          LINE OF DATA_PACKAGE,
        parent_lvl  TYPE
          /bic/oihierlvl,
        curr_line   LIKE sy-tabix,
        curr_lvl    TYPE /bic/oihierlvl,
        leveldiff   TYPE i.
  DATA: used_nodes  TYPE
         HASHED TABLE OF /bic/oinodename
         WITH UNIQUE KEY TABLE_LINE
         INITIAL SIZE 0.
  DATA: begin of last_node,
          101    type sy-tabix,
          102    type sy-tabix,
          103    type sy-tabix,
          104    type sy-tabix,
          105    type sy-tabix,
          106    type sy-tabix,
          107    type sy-tabix,
          108    type sy-tabix,
          109    type sy-tabix,
```

```
          l10    type sy-tabix,
          l11    type sy-tabix,
          l12    type sy-tabix,
        end of last_node.
  DATA: next_id_found  LIKE sy-tabix,
        parent_is_link TYPE C,
        davon_found    type c.
  DATA: ld_debug LIKE sy-subrc,
        ld_record_all like sy-tabix.
  DATA: ld_monitor type rsmonitors,
        ld_lvl_diff type i.

  SORT RESULT_PACKAGE BY /bic/nodeid.
  ld_record_all = lines( RESULT_PACKAGE ).
* Shorter and more simple than DESCRIBE TABLE
  curr_lvl = 0.

* Determine parent ID, InfoObject, and link node
  LOOP AT RESULT_PACKAGE
      ASSIGNING <RESULT_FIELDS>.
* 0. Determine InfoObject
    IF <RESULT_FIELDS>-/bic/nodename
       co '0123456789'.
      <RESULT_FIELDS>-/bic/iobjnm
         = '0ACCOUNT'.
    ELSE.
      <RESULT_FIELDS>-/bic/iobjnm
         = '0HIER_NODE'.
    ENDIF.
*   Level difference too big?
    curr_line = sy-tabix.
    ld_lvl_diff =
       <RESULT_FIELDS>-/bic/hierlvl
       - curr_lvl.
    IF ld_lvl_diff > 1.
*     Child node more than one level lower
*     than parent node
      ld_monitor-MSGID = 'ZDEMO'.
      ld_monitor-MSGTY = 'I'.
      ld_monitor-MSGNO = '001'.
      ld_monitor-MSGV1 = curr_line.
      ld_monitor-MSGV2 =
              dp_line-/bic/hierlvl.
```

```
        ld_monitor-MSGV3 = curr_lvl.
*       ld_monitor-MSGV4
        ld_monitor-DETLEVEL = 1.
        ld_monitor-RECNO = curr_line.
        append ld_monitor to MONITOR.
     ENDIF.
     curr_lvl =
        <RESULT_FIELDS>-/bic/hierlvl.


* 1. Determine parent ID
    IF <RESULT_FIELDS>-/bic/hierlvl = 1.
       <RESULT_FIELDS>-/bic/parentid = 0.
       parent_line-parent_level =
          <RESULT_FIELDS>-/bic/hierlvl.
       parent_line-parent_node  =
          <RESULT_FIELDS>-/bic/nodeid.
       MODIFY TABLE parent_tab
              FROM parent_line.
       IF SY-SUBRC <> 0.
*        New level
         INSERT parent_line
              INTO TABLE parent_tab.
         IF sy-subrc <> 0.
*          Level already existing? Then MODIFY
*          should have worked.
           RAISE CX_RSROUT_ABORT.
         ENDIF. "SY-SUBRC <> 0
       ENDIF. "SY-SUBRC <> 0
     ELSE.  "Level <> 1
       parent_lvl =
       <RESULT_FIELDS>-/bic/hierlvl - 1.
       READ TABLE parent_tab
          into parent_line
          with table key
              parent_level = parent_lvl.
       IF SY-SUBRC <> 0.
*        NO parent node is not allowed.
         RAISE CX_RSROUT_ABORT.
       ELSE. "sy-subrc = 0.
         <RESULT_FIELDS>-/bic/parentid =
              parent_line-parent_node.
         parent_line-parent_level =
            <RESULT_FIELDS>-/bic/hierlvl.
```

```
        parent_line-parent_node  =
          <RESULT_FIELDS>-/bic/nodeid.
        MODIFY TABLE parent_tab
              FROM parent_line.
        IF SY-SUBRC <> 0.
*         New level
          INSERT parent_line INTO
                TABLE parent_tab.
          IF sy-subrc <> 0.

*             Is not allowed
              RAISE CX_RSROUT_ABORT.
          ENDIF. "sy-subrc <> 0
        ENDIF. "sy-subrc <> 0
      ENDIF. "sy-subrc <> 0
    ENDIF.  "Stufe = 1

* 2. Determine link node
    INSERT <RESULT_FIELDS>-/bic/nodename
          INTO TABLE used_nodes.
    IF sy-subrc <> 0.
*     Node already exists
      <RESULT_FIELDS>-/bic/linknode
        = 'X'.
      <RESULT_FIELDS>-/bic/childid = 0.
      parent_is_link = 'X'.
    ELSE.
      <RESULT_FIELDS>-/bic/linknode
        = ' '.
      parent_is_link = ' '.
    ENDIF.

* 3. Dertermine child ID
    IF curr_line =  ld_RECORD_ALL.
*   The last line cannot contain a child.
      <RESULT_FIELDS>-/bic/childid = 0.
      <RESULT_FIELDS>-/bic/nextid  = 0.
    ELSE.
      IF parent_is_link is initial.
*       Parent node is not a link so
*       the children are considered.
        sy-tabix = curr_line + 1.
        READ TABLE RESULT_PACKAGE
```

```
          INTO dp_buffer
          index sy-tabix.
      leveldiff =
       dp_buffer-/bic/hierlvl -
       <RESULT_FIELDS>-/bic/hierlvl.
      IF leveldiff = 1.
        <RESULT_FIELDS>-/bic/childid =
          dp_buffer-/bic/nodeid.
      ELSE.
      <RESULT_FIELDS>-/bic/childid = 0.
      ENDIF.
    ELSE. "parent_is_link is initial
*     Now the case is considered that the
*     parent node is a link node. All children
*     nodes must be deleted.
      sy-tabix = curr_line + 1.
      leveldiff = 1.
      WHILE ( leveldiff >= 1 ) and
        ( curr_line < ld_record_all ).
        READ TABLE RESULT_PACKAGE
            INTO dp_buffer
            index sy-tabix.
        check sy-subrc = 0.
        leveldiff =
          dp_buffer-/bic/hierlvl
       - <RESULT_FIELDS>-/bic/hierlvl.
        IF leveldiff >= 1.
*     Link node contains items, these are
*     deleted.
          DELETE RESULT_PACKAGE
              INDEX sy-tabix.
          ld_record_all =
            ld_record_all - 1.
        ENDIF.
      ENDWHILE.
    ENDIF.
  ENDIF.

* 4. Determine next ID
  <RESULT_FIELDS>-/bic/nextid = 0.
  CLEAR next_id_found.
  case <RESULT_FIELDS>-/bic/hierlvl.
    when 1.
```

```
      if last_node-l01 <> 0.
        next_id_found = last_node-l01.
      endif.
  when 2.
    if last_node-l02 > last_node-l01.
      next_id_found = last_node-l02.
    endif.
  when 3.
    if last_node-l03 > last_node-l02.
      next_id_found = last_node-l03.
    endif.
  when 4.
    if last_node-l04 > last_node-l03.
      next_id_found = last_node-l04.
    endif.
  when 5.
    if last_node-l05 > last_node-l04.
      next_id_found = last_node-l05.
    endif.
  when 6.
    if last_node-l06 > last_node-l05.
      next_id_found = last_node-l06.
    endif.
  when 7.
    if last_node-l07 > last_node-l06.
      next_id_found = last_node-l07.
    endif.
  when 8.
    if last_node-l08 > last_node-l07.
      next_id_found = last_node-l08.
    endif.
  when 9.
    if last_node-l09 > last_node-l08.
      next_id_found = last_node-l09.
    endif.
  when 10.
    if last_node-l10 > last_node-l09.
      next_id_found = last_node-l10.
    endif.
  when 11.
    if last_node-l11 > last_node-l10.
      next_id_found = last_node-l11.
    endif.
```

```
      when 12.
        if last_node-l12 > last_node-l11.
          next_id_found = last_node-l12.
        endif.
    endcase.
    IF next_id_found > 0.
      READ TABLE RESULT_PACKAGE INTO
           dp_buffer index next_id_found.
      dp_buffer-/bic/nextid =
             <RESULT_FIELDS>-/bic/nodeid.
      MODIFY RESULT_PACKAGE
             FROM dp_buffer
             INDEX next_id_found.
    ENDIF.
    case <RESULT_FIELDS>-/bic/hierlvl.
      when 1.
        last_node-l01 = curr_line.
      when 2.
        last_node-l02 = curr_line.
      when 3.
        last_node-l03 = curr_line.
      when 4.
        last_node-l04 = curr_line.
      when 5.
        last_node-l05 = curr_line.
      when 6.
        last_node-l06 = curr_line.
      when 7.
        last_node-l07 = curr_line.
      when 8.
        last_node-l08 = curr_line.
      when 9.
        last_node-l09 = curr_line.
      when 10.
        last_node-l10 = curr_line.
      when 11.
        last_node-l11 = curr_line.
      when 12.
        last_node-l12 = curr_line.
    endcase.
  ENDLOOP.
```

Listing 4.13 End Routine for Hierarchy Derivation

In this end routine, the provided hierarchy data is used to derive additional information that's necessary for SAP NetWeaver BI. These are in particular:

▸ Name of the InfoObject

▸ Parent ID

▸ Child ID

▸ Next ID

▸ Link nodes

In this context, the following requirements must be met:

▸ All nodes have a unique, continuous node ID.

▸ If nodes occur several times, the first node is the original node; all other nodes are the link nodes.

▸ The numbering of levels starts at 1.

The process is as follows:

1. The first step in Listing 4.13 – "0. Determine InfoObject" – determines the InfoObject. In this example, purely numerical accounts have the InfoObject 0ACCOUNT, whereas other accounts have InfoObject 0HIER_NODE.

2. This step is followed by the determination of the parent ID. For this purpose, a PARENT_TAB table is managed that stores the node that has been read last for each level. Because of the hierarchy structure in Excel, a level 3 node, for example, must have the parent that is entered with level 2 in the PARENT_TAB table.

3. The step "2. Determine link node" then determines whether the node is a link node. To do that, we use table USED_NODES, which stores all nodes that have been used up to this point. So, if a node already exists in this table, it's a link node. For the link nodes, all children must be deleted. This is done in step 3.

4. This step determines the child ID, that is, the ID of the first child. Because of the sorting principle, the first child must immediately follow the node. This means that the line that follows the current line is imported, and the level is checked. If the level of the subsequent line is exactly one level higher than the current level, the node is a child. The child ID is always set to 0 for link nodes because they automatically use the children of the node that is used first. If children are delivered, they will be deleted.

5. Finally, the fourth step determines the next ID. For this purpose, the last occurrence (index) per level is stored in the last_node structure. For a new record of level n, the program checks whether the last index of level n is bigger than the last index of level n-1. If that is the case, the current node and the last node of level n belong to the same parent. Then the next ID for the last node is set to the current index. For better readability, we implemented this algorithm without an ASSIGN statement.

4.3.6 Creating a Data Transfer Process

The *data transfer process* (DTP) has been newly developed for SAP NetWeaver 7.0. The purpose of the DTP is to permit a more comprehensive control of the data flow than is possible with the InfoPackage. But apart from that, you'll recognize many familiar features from the InfoPackage.

1. To create a DTP, right-click on the DataStore object HIERUPLD, and select CREATE DATA TRANSFER PROCESS. The system first displays the extraction information (see Figure 4.15).

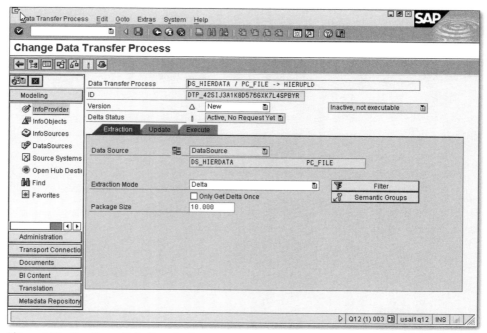

Figure 4.15 Creating a Data Transfer Process

The important innovation compared to the InfoPackage is that you can set individual package sizes. Even more important, however, are the POSTING settings (see Figure 4.16).

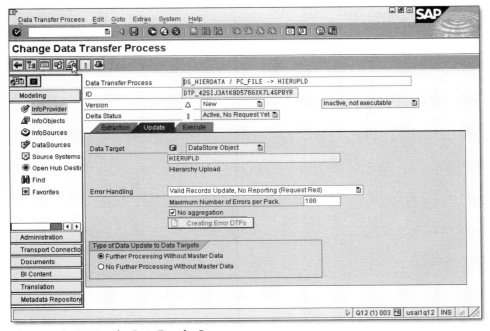

Figure 4.16 Posting the Data Transfer Process

2. Here you'll come across the error-handling process that you already know from the InfoPackage. The SEMANTIC GROUPS button is a new element that enables you to control which data records must be processed in a data package. To do that, you're provided with a list that contains all InfoObjects.

   If, for instance, you select only NODEID, all lines with the same NODEID are processed in a data package. Because you don't load NODEID but calculate it in the start routine, all lines will be processed in a data package.

3. The EXECUTE tab (see Figure 4.17) contains several settings that you could only set globally in previous versions, particularly the settings for the technical status and overall status. This is essential if you expect a different data quality and tolerance from different systems. The program flow feature is another useful innovation that provides an essential troubleshooting support because it allows you to set specific default breakpoints.

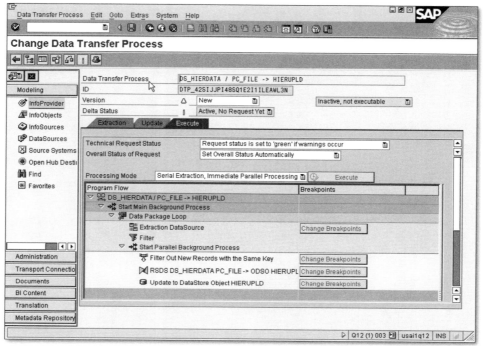

Figure 4.17 Executing the Data Transfer Process

4.3.7 Creating a Query

Finally, we must create a query on the HIERUPLD DataStore. The query contains the columns NODEID, NODENAME, IOBJNM, PARENTID, CHILDID, NEXTID, and LINKNODE, all next to each other. If you run the query now, you can save the result as a CSV file (*comma-separated values*) and then load it directly from there as a hierarchy from a flat file.

4.3.8 Implementation in SAP BW 3.x

If you find the example useful but don't have an installation of SAP NetWeaver 7.0 available yet, you shouldn't worry too much: The entire implementation already has been successfully developed in SAP BW 3.5. So if you want to implement the example, you can simply transfer the start routine into the transfer rules, and the end routine into the update rules.

The only problem is that due to the lack of a DTP, you must use the global data package settings to make sure the data package is processed in one single run.

4.4   Transfer Rules in SAP BW 3.x

SAP BW 3.x doesn't yet contain any transformations. Instead, it uses transfer rules between DataSource and InfoSource, and update rules between the InfoSource and the data target. Although both types of rules seem to have similar functions — namely, to transform certain data packages into a target structure — there are some differences between them. For example, update rules allow you to create a return table in a routine to make several data records out of one. That's not possible in a transfer rule. The reason for this can be found in the essentially different requirements of the two rule types.

Transfer rules are used essentially to standardize the data that can originate from different source systems. For this purpose, the data records that originate from the source system are usually directly assigned to those records that finally end up in the InfoSource. Routines are only needed to enrich information that isn't provided or is insufficiently provided in the source system. For this reason, you shouldn't include fields in the InfoSource that can't be populated from any of the source systems, unless you definitely have to do so for reasons of compounding.

Of course, there's an exception to every rule. The most frequent exceptions are constants that are necessary to obtain a data relationship that makes sense. Typical examples of this are the controlling area, the fiscal year variant, and so on. Another example is the use of InfoObjects that are integrated into the InfoSource in order to use them in the transfer rules, either because you want to derive master data attributes from them or because you need the InfoObject for several other routines, and you don't want to recalculate it every time.

The main purpose of update rules is to format the business data transported in the InfoSource in such a way that an optimal reporting process is enabled for the respective application. Whereas in the transfer rules, the target structure is determined by the terms that are related to each other regarding business, the determining factor in the update rules are the reporting demands of the users and hence the data model of the InfoProvider. This means you can delete the data as per your requirements, split it up, convert it into different units, duplicate records, make several lines out of one, or make one line out of several. All this depends on the reporting requirements and the data model. Usually the data model is denormalized; that is, the data records are complemented with information that is actually redundant to accelerate the reporting process and enable additional reporting requirements.

Example: Data Model in SAP NetWeaver BI versus Data Model in SAP ERP

The production order (0PRODORDER) contains the plant (0PLANT) in which the order is produced as an attribute. The plant, in turn, contains the country (0COUNTRY) in which the plant is located as an attribute.

In a normal database, you only include the production order in the table. This type of modeling, however, doesn't allow you to carry out a selection according to the country in SAP NetWeaver BI. For this reason you at least include the plant, if not the country, in the InfoProvider in SAP NetWeaver BI.

In real life, people usually don't bother about what they program in the transfer rules and what is programmed in the update rules. Most people aren't aware of the differences between the two types of rules, and in both routines, the exits are so flexible that nearly all requirements can be handled in both rules. Nevertheless, you should stick to the distinction made here and carry out data-cleaning processes only in the transfer rules, and make adjustments to the contents in the update rules.

The reason for this is simple. If the reporting requirements increase or if new projects require the same data, you may want to add an InfoSource that has already been used to another InfoProvider. But, if you've already carried out too many derivations and transformations in the transfer rules, the new InfoProvider will receive the previously transformed data, which may not contain all of the information required. In the worst case, this may cause the data flow into the original InfoProvider to be completely reprocessed, which involves a lot of testing work. That can be avoided by carrying out as few adjustments in the transfer rules as possible.

The transfer rule contains two types of routines: the start routine and the routine that's needed to derive InfoObject values.

4.4.1 Start Routine in the Transfer Rule

In the transfer rule, you can find the start routine in the TRANSFER RULES tab above the table that contains the communication structure (see Figure 4.18).

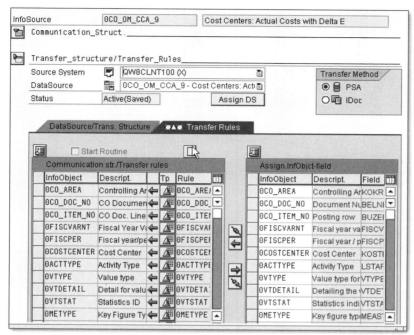

Figure 4.18 Creating a Start Routine

By clicking on the CREATE or CHANGE button — depending on whether a routine already exists or not — you can navigate to the ABAP Editor that contains the predefined code (see Listing 4.14).

```
PROGRAM CONVERSION_ROUTINE.

* Type pools used by conversion program
TYPE-POOLS: RS, RSARC, RSARR, SBIWA, RSSM.

* Declaration of transfer structure (selected fields only)
TYPES: BEGIN OF TRANSFER_STRUCTURE ,
*    InfoObject 0CO_AREA: CHAR - 000004
     KOKRS(000004) TYPE C,
*    InfoObject 0CO_DOC_NO: CHAR - 000010
     BELNR(000010) TYPE C,
* ... Other InfoObjects ...
*    InfoObject ZAUTYP: CHAR - 000004
     AUART(000004) TYPE C,
END OF TRANSFER_STRUCTURE .
```

```
* Declaration of Data Package
TYPES: TAB_TRANSTRU type table of TRANSFER_STRUCTURE.

* Global code used by conversion rules
*$*$ begin of global -
* insert your declaration only below this line *-*
* TABLES: ...
* DATA:    ...
*$*$ end of global -
* insert your declaration only before this line *-*

FORM STARTROUTINE
  USING    G_S_MINFO TYPE RSSM_S_MINFO
  CHANGING DATAPAK type TAB_TRANSTRU
           G_T_ERRORLOG TYPE rssm_t_errorlog_int
           ABORT LIKE SY-SUBRC. "set ABORT <> 0 to
                                " cancel datapackage
*$*$ begin of routine -
* insert your code only below this line *-*
* DATA: l_s_datapak_line type TRANSFER_STRUCTURE,
*       l_s_errorlog TYPE rssm_s_errorlog_int.

* abort <> 0 means skip whole data package!!!
  ABORT = 0.
*$*$ end of routine -
* insert your code only before this line *-*
ENDFORM.
```

Listing 4.14 Predefined Code of a Start Routine

The first part of the program code can't be modified. It informs the developer about the type groups that can be used and, above all, about the transfer structure and the fields it contains.

After that, you can declare global variables. These variables are not only available in the start routine but also in all other routines of the transfer rule. If you want to import and enrich specific data from the database, you should insert a SELECT statement at this point in the start routine to populate an internal table (often a hashed table), which then can be referenced in the individual routines.

After that, the actual code of the start routine begins. The start routine contains the USING parameter G_S_MINFO and the CHANGING parameters DATAPAK, G_T_ERRORLOG, and ABORT; the most important parameter is DATAPAK. This parameter is actually a table that contains the transfer structure as data structure as well as all data records of a data package. The start routine isn't called once per loading process but once per data package. Therefore, you should program a clean code because it's run through more than once.

The other parameters can be described quickly. The parameter G_S_MINFO has the structure RSSM_S_INFO and contains, among other things, the request number (REQUNO), the data package ID (DATAPAKID), the source system (LOGSYS), the Data-Source (ISOURCE), and some other fields that aren't used often. The request number and data package ID are rather useful. Using the data package ID, you can ensure that calls which are to be carried out only once, such as writing log entries in custom database tables, are carried out only once.

Example: Logging Data Transfers

For evaluation purposes, you want to log the time at which a data transfer was started. This could be implemented in the start routine as shown in Listing 4.15.

```
FORM STARTROUTINE
  USING     G_S_MINFO TYPE RSSM_S_MINFO
  CHANGING DATAPAK type TAB_TRANSTRU
           G_T_ERRORLOG TYPE rssm_t_errorlog_int
           ABORT LIKE SY-SUBRC. "set ABORT <> 0 to cancel
                              " data package
*$*$ begin of routine -
* insert your code only below this line *-*
* DATA: l_s_datapak_line type TRANSFER_STRUCTURE,
*       l_s_errorlog TYPE rssm_s_errorlog_int.
* Now follows the assumed structure of
* the log table.

  DATA: begin of l_s_transfer_log,
          REQUNR  TYPE RSREQUNR,
          DATUM   LIKE SY-DATUM,
          UZEIT   LIKE SY-UZEIT,
          LOGSYS  TYPE RSLOGSYS,
        end of l_s_transfer_log.


  IF G_S_MINFO-DATAPAKID = 1.
```

```
* Fill log only once.
    L_S_TRANSFER_LOG-REQUNR = G_S_MINFO-REQUNR.
    L_S_TRANSFER_LOG-DATUM  = SY-DATUM.
    L_S_TRANSFER_LOG-UZEIT  = SY-UZEIT.
    L_S_TRANSFER_LOG-LOGSYS = G_S_MINFO-LOGSYS.
    INSERT L_S_TRANSFER_LOG INTO Z_TRANSFER_LOG.
  ENDIF.
* abort <> 0 means skip whole data package !!!
  ABORT = 0.
*$*$ end of routine -
* insert your code only before this line *-*
ENDFORM.
```

Listing 4.15 Sample Log Function in the Start Routine

Table G_T_ERRORLOG enables you to return messages that can later be displayed in the monitor. For this purpose, you can create our own messages and message classes via Transaction SE91. Regarding the message return, you should note that the messages can affect the status of the data package. So you should return messages of message type E only if the error is so serious that it would abort the data import process.

In general, you should be economical with your messages. If you comment every successful record with a corresponding message, the message table will become very big, and this will affect the performance of the import process and of the monitor. Even if the error case is different, you should try to avoid a message.

For example, if during the data-import process, you derive a financial statement item using a routine, and this routine returns an error item in case of an error, you should create a corresponding number of different error items to control the errors rather than output a message in addition to the error item. The message may be ignored in the monitor because the user thinks everything is okay because the color of the request is green. This depends on what percentage of the data is erroneous and how many messages would be generated as a result. Depending on the data quantity, 50 to 100 error messages per import process are certainly acceptable. But if the number is significantly higher, a standard case is made an exception, which unnecessarily increases the error log.

Practical Tip: Error Handling in InfoPackages

Appropriate options available for the ERROR HANDLING in the InfoPackage enable you to systematically return error messages and to prevent the InfoPackage from aborting (see Figure 4.19).

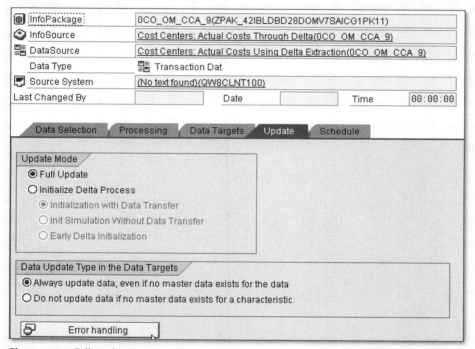

Figure 4.19 Calling the Error-Handling Function

Here you can define the number of permitted errors and the status of the InfoPackage (see Figure 4.20). You must make sure that the data package isn't posted when the number of permitted errors is exceeded. So, if you always want to post the data records that don't contain any errors, you should set a correspondingly high error tolerance. However, this involves the risk of overlooking potential errors or method changes in the source system.

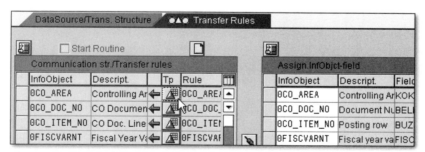

Figure 4.20 Error-Handling Options

Finally, there's the ABORT parameter. This parameter aborts the entire data package. This should happen only in absolutely exceptional cases, for example, if required customizing tables haven't been filled.

4.4.2 Routine for InfoObject Derivation

The transfer rules don't distinguish between routines for characteristics and routines for key figures. Instead, they use a uniform routine that is structured as shown in Listing 4.16. To create the routine, you must first click on the INFOOB-JECT symbol in the left-hand table of the transfer rules (see Figure 4.21).

Figure 4.21 Button for Creating a Routine

```
PROGRAM CONVERSION_ROUTINE.
* Type pools used by conversion program
TYPE-POOLS: RS, RSARC, RSARR, SBIWA, RSSM.
* Declaration of transfer structure (selected fields only)
TYPES: BEGIN OF TRANSFER_STRUCTURE ,
*    InfoObject 0CO_AREA: CHAR - 000004
     KOKRS(000004) TYPE C,
*    InfoObject 0CO_DOC_NO: CHAR - 000010
```

```
*    BELNR(000010) TYPE C,
*    InfoObject 0CO_ITEM_NO: NUMC - 000003
*    BUZEI(000003) TYPE N,
*    InfoObject 0FISCVARNT: CHAR - 000002
*    FISCVAR(000002) TYPE C,
*    ... all fields of the transfer structure ...
END OF TRANSFER_STRUCTURE .
* Global code used by conversion rules
*$*$ begin of global -
* insert your declaration only below this line *-*
* TABLES: ...
* DATA:    ...
*$*$ end of global -
* insert your declaration only before this line *-*
*---------------------------------------*
*        FORM COMPUTE_CO_AREA
*---------------------------------------*
* Compute value of InfoObject 0CO_AREA
* in communication structure
* /BIO/CS0CO_OM_OPA_6
* Technical properties:
*     field name      = CO_AREA
*     data element    = /BIO/OICO_AREA
*     data type       = CHAR
*     length          = 000004
*     decimals        = 000000
*     ABAP type       = C
*     ABAP length     = 000004
*     reference field =
*---------------------------------------*
* Parameters:
*   -->  RECORD_NO       Record number
*   -->  TRAN_STRUCTURE  Transfer structure
*   <--  RESULT          Return value of InfoObject
*   <->  G_T_ERRORLOG    Error log
*   <--  RETURNCODE      Return code (to skip one record)
*   <--  ABORT           Abort code (to skip whole data
*                        package)
*---------------------------------------*
FORM COMPUTE_CO_AREA
  USING    RECORD_NO LIKE SY-TABIX
```

```
             TRAN_STRUCTURE TYPE TRANSFER_STRUCTURE
             G_S_MINFO TYPE RSSM_S_MINFO
   CHANGING RESULT TYPE /BIO/OICO_AREA
             G_T_ERRORLOG TYPE rssm_t_errorlog_int
             RETURNCODE LIKE SY-SUBRC
             ABORT LIKE SY-SUBRC. "set ABORT <> 0 to cancel
                                   " data package
*$*$ begin of routine -
* insert your code only below this line *-*
* DATA: l_s_errorlog TYPE rssm_s_errorlog_int.

   RESULT = .
* returncode <> 0 means skip this record
   RETURNCODE = 0.

* abort <> 0 means skip whole data package!!!
   ABORT = 0.
*$*$ end of routine -
* insert your code only before this line *-*
ENDFORM.
*---------------------------------------*
*        FORM INVERT_CO_AREA
*---------------------------------------*
* Inversion of selection criteria for
* InfoObject 0CO_AREA. This subroutine
* needs to be implemented only for SAP
* RemoteCubes (for better performance)
* and for the report-report interface
* (drill through).
*---------------------------------------*
*   -->  I_RT_CHAVL_CS: Ranges table for
*                       current InfoObject
*   -->  I_THX_SELECTION_CS: Selection
*                       criteria for
*                       all other
*                       InfoObjects
*   <--  C_T_SELECTION: Selection criteria
*                       for fields of
*                       transfer structure
*   <--  E_EXACT: Flag Inversion was exact
*---------------------------------------*
FORM INVERT_CO_AREA
   USING    I_RT_CHAVL_CS       TYPE RSARC_RT_CHAVL
```

```
          I_THX_SELECTION_CS TYPE RSARC_THX_SELCS
  CHANGING C_T_SELECTION      TYPE SBIWA_T_SELECT
          E_EXACT            TYPE RS_BOOL.
*$*$ begin of inverse routine -
* insert your code only below this line *-*
  DATA:
    L_S_SELECTION LIKE LINE OF C_T_SELECTION.
* An empty selection means all values
  CLEAR C_T_SELECTION.
  L_S_SELECTION-FIELDNM = 'CO_AREA'.
* ...

* Selection of all values may be not exact
  E_EXACT = RS_C_FALSE.
*$*$ end of inverse routine -
* insert your code only before this line *-*
ENDFORM.
```

Listing 4.16 Generated Code of the Routine in the Transfer Rule

In the dialog box that displays next, you must select the routine and click on CRE-
ATE (see Figure 4.22).

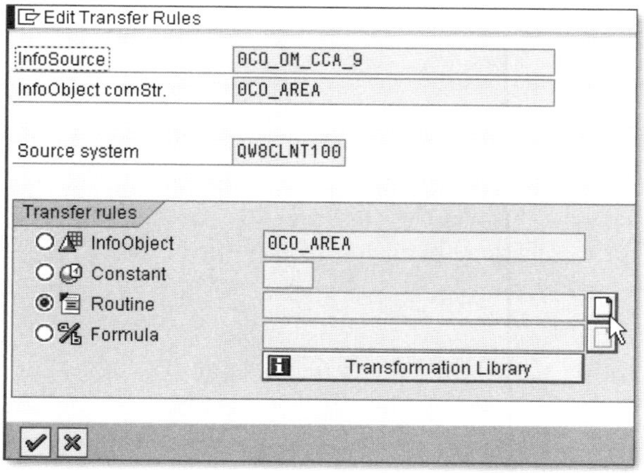

Figure 4.22 Creating a Routine

After you've entered a name for the routine, you must select those fields of the
transfer structure that you want to use in the routine. As shown in Figure 4.23,
you have the following options to select from: NO FIELD, ALL FIELDS, and SELECTED
FIELDS.

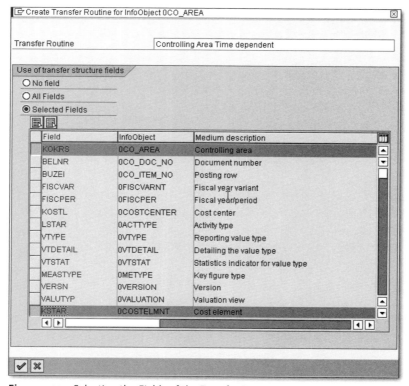

Figure 4.23 Selecting the Fields of the Transfer Structure

If you need fields from the transfer structure for derivation purposes, you should always select Selected Fields and only select those fields in the table that are really required. Selecting the All Fields option may seem to be convenient, but it can affect the performance and, in some cases, even result in typos or other errors in the routine going unnoticed until it's too late. As a matter of fact, it happens rather often that many InfoObjects with similar names are summarized in one DataSource, and a typo can suddenly cause a different field of the transfer structure to be used. You can avoid this situation by selecting only the required fields right from the start.

After you have selected the fields, the code shown in Listing 4.16 is displayed. First the transfer structure is defined. This includes only those fields that were selected for use in the routine in the previous step. If you selected No field in the previous step, the transfer structure automatically contains a DUMMY field that is only generated into the structure so that the structure isn't empty, a situation that would lead to syntax errors. A section for global data follows next. This section is identical to a global section that may be defined in the start routine or in other routines, and changes to it are automatically copied to all other routines of this transfer rule. In particular, you can access internal tables here that were populated in the start routine.

This is followed by the actual routine for determining the return value. This routine contains the following parameters. The `TRAN_STRUCTURE` parameter contains the fields of the transfer structure that were selected in the previous step exactly as they are delivered from the source system. This parameter is the most important parameter for calculating the values. The most important return parameter is `RESULT`, which returns the value calculated in the routine. Then there's the `G_T_ERRORLOG` table that can be used to return error messages, as well as the two error flags `RETURNCODE` and `ABORT`. The value of both flags is 0 if the process did not contain any errors. Their value is different from 0 if either the data record (`RETURNCODE`) or the entire data package (`ABORT`) wasn't processed.

Note: Error Handling in SAP BW 3.x

In SAP BW 3.x, the error-handling process in the transfer rules differs slightly from that in the update rules. The transfer rules comprise a `G_T_ERRORLOG` table that contains all important information, whereas there are two tables, `MONITOR` and `MONITOR_RECNO` in the update rules, whose functions are slightly different. In the start routine, the `MONITOR` table only contains error messages that aren't associated with a specific row, such as missing customizing tables. The `MONITOR_RECNO` table, on the other hand, provides the row where the error occurred in addition to the error message itself. However, this requires you to populate the row yourself from the relevant field in the data package. The individual rules of the update rule only contain the `MONITOR` table, which is completed with the row number after the process.

Table 4.3 provides an overview of the table fields in the routines.

Field	G_T_ERROR_LOG	MONITOR	MONITOR_RECNO
Row number	RECNO	Not available	RECNO
Message class	MSGID	MSGID	MSGID
Message number	MSGNO	MSGNO	MSGNO
Message type	MSGTY (I, W, E, A)	MSGTY	MSGTY
Message field 1-4	MSGV1 - MSGV4	MSGV1 - MSGV4	MSGV1 - MSGV4

Table 4.3 Fields in the Error-Handling Tables

All entries that you insert into the table are displayed in the monitor. Unfortunately, the performance decreases with a growing number of messages. You should therefore not use the monitor for debugging purposes or have intermediate results of the calculations output in each line. This can lead to serious performance problems when displaying the results in the monitor, especially when you expand the individual nodes.

You can create new messages in Transaction SE91. The new messages may contain up to four placeholders, which can be included in the message text as &1 through &4.

The routine for calculation is followed by the inversion routine. This routine is almost obsolete today except for RemoteCubes that import data from source systems. In that case, a selection for the characteristic is made up of selections in the query in the source system. For example, if the fields Fiscal Year and Period exist in the source system, and if you restrict the characteristic Fiscal Year/Period in the report to 012.2005 through 001.2006, you use this data to build up the selection 2005 through 2006 for the fiscal year, as data from both 2005 and 2006 is needed. For the period, you must set the selection 001 and 012 because those two periods are contained in the interval. However, this includes more than the original specification indicated, namely the periods 001.2005, 012.2005, 001.2006, and 012.2006. For this reason, you would set the `E_EXACT` parameter to `RS_C_FALSE`.

4.4.3 Implementing the InfoObject Derivation

As mentioned earlier in this chapter, the transfer rule should mainly be used for data-cleaning purposes. For this reason, there are only a few patterns that are always implemented in the transfer rules in addition to an actual derivation. These patterns predominantly involve the setting of default values.

Example: Setting a Currency

In Listing 4.17, different flat files are imported via the same DataSource. Some of the files don't contain any currency. In this case, we want to use the currency of the controlling area.

```
*$*$ begin of global -
* insert your declaration only below this line *-*
* TABLES: ...
  DATA: g_t_co_area TYPE SORTED TABLE OF /bi0/qco_area
          WITH UNIQUE KEY
              CO_AREA
              OBJVERS
              DATETO
```

```
        INITIAL SIZE 0,
        g_w_co_area TYPE /bi0/qco_area.
*$*$ end of global -
* insert your declaration only before this line *-*

FORM COMPUTE_CURRENCY
* ...
*$*$ begin of routine -
* insert your code only below this line *-*
* DATA: l_s_errorlog   TYPE rssm_s_errorlog_int.
  DATA: l_d_check_date TYPE d.
* Is currency empty?
  IF TRAN_STRUCTURE-CURRENCY IS INITIAL.
* Read controlling areas if that hasn't been done yet
    IF LINES( g_t_co_area ) = 0.
      SELECT * FROM /BI0/QCO_AREA
            INTO TABLE g_t_co_area.
    ENDIF.
    CALL FUNCTION 'FIRST_DAY_IN_PERIOD_GET'
      EXPORTING
        GJAHR = TRAN_STRUCTURE-fiscyear
        PERIV = TRAN_STRUCTURE-fiscvarnt
        POPER = TRAN_STRUCTURE-fiscper3
      IMPORTING
        DATUM = l_d_check_date.
    LOOP AT TABLE g_t_co_area
        INTO g_w_co_area
        WHERE co_area  = TRAN_STRUCTURE-co_area
        AND   objvers  = 'A' "active master data only
        AND   datefrom <= l_d_check_date
        AND   dateto   >= l_d_check_date.
* There can only be one valid record in the table, otherwise
* the master data of 0CO_AREA is inconsistent.
      RESULT = g_w_co_area-currency.
    ENDLOOP.
  ELSE.
* Copy value from file
    RESULT = TRAN_STRUCTURE-currency.
  endif.
* returncode <> 0 means skip this record
    RETURNCODE = 0.
* abort <> 0 means skip whole data package!!!
  ABORT = 0.
```

```
*$*$ end of routine -
* insert your code only before this line *-*
ENDFORM.
```

Listing 4.17 Sample Implementation of a Characteristics Derivation

The code shown in Listing 4.17 is used so often that sometimes it would be useful if the standard attribute derivation could handle this variant. The second variant doesn't occur as often in everyday life, and it isn't very convenient either. Often, this variant must be used when a data-loading process aborts for the first time because no attribute could be found for a specific master record. The code is almost identical to the previous example except that the table is read first, and a default value is returned if a record doesn't exist. Listing 4.18 shows a possible excerpt from a corresponding implementation.

```
*...
  READ TABLE l_t_posfind INTO l_w_posfind
    WITH TABLE KEY
      value_type =
        TRAN_STRUCTURE-/bic/value_type
      costelemt  =
        TRAN_STRUCTURE-costelemt.
  IF SY-SUBRC = 0.
    RESULT = l_w_posfind-position.
  ELSE.
    RESULT = const_default_pos.
  ENDIF.
*...
```

Listing 4.18 Setting a Condition Default Value Example

Because both routines are used often, it's preferable to have a standard solution available.

4.5 Update Rules in SAP BW 3.x

As described in Section 4.4, Transfer Rules in SAP BW 3.x, you should use the update rule to format the business data in such a way that you can generate the required reports. You should therefore always bear this aspect in mind during the data-modeling process. Each calculation that you can carry out in the update rules no longer needs to be performed at the time of reporting. This way, you can avoid performance problems when running a report.

In contrast to the transfer rules, you can't simply provide schemas here with regard to what can and cannot be done. The rule of thumb is everything the user department can describe using an algorithm can actually be implemented. You must consider the following aspects:

▶ The algorithms should not require any parameters that the user wants to enter in the report.

▶ Particularly with regard to daily processes, it's significant that the actual data be imported even if individual entries are missing in control or derivation tables. Nothing is more annoying to the IT department than a loading process that must be checked on at least three days out of five.

▶ The results should be comprehensible. In complex derivations, all input fields from the data record should therefore be included in the cube. This helps you to analyze errors.

Apart from that, the update rule is the place where you can "make things happen." Here you can implement the entire logic that is usually handled manually in the user departments, which takes hours and requires hundreds of Excel sheets.

Example: Update Rules

In former releases — particularly in Release 2.0A in which the only available data target was the InfoCube — complex implementations of the update rule were handled in a particular way. If, for instance, a file was created each quarter that contained accumulated values, but you only wanted to load the delta compared to the last file into the InfoCube, the start schema was read out in the update rules across several selects in the database. In this way, the existing value in the InfoCube was determined for previous periods. This value could then be subtracted from the newly provided value.

This procedure is no longer advisable, and fortunately we can use the DataStore object today to solve such problems more easily. Nevertheless, there are a lot of things we can learn from this past practice, especially from the recurring surprise that the differences were not correct.

There are some important rules you should consider.

▶ When building differences, you must take into account that one key can include several data records. In this case, you can build the difference only once. For example, if cost center XYZ has two data records — one with the value 100 and one with value 50 — while the InfoCube contains the value 30:

> ▶ You must correct the first value to 70 (= 100 – 30), and leave the second value at 50; that is, you must not correct the second value.
>
> ▶ This becomes even more complicated if you must maintain a cross-process buffer because the data arrives in several data packages, so you should save the buffer table using the following call:
>
> `EXPORT ... TO BUFFER / IMPORT ... FROM BUFFER.`
>
> ▶ If you must access data from other cubes, you should make sure that each cube contains two fact tables: the `F` table (`/BIC/F<CUBENAME>`) containing the uncompressed requests and the `E` table (`/BIC/E<CUBENAME>`) containing the compressed values. However, this procedure isn't advisable. Section 5.3, VirtualProviders, describes a better way to import content from InfoProviders via VirtualProviders.
>
> Note that selects always affect performance, which is why you should carry out as few selects as possible. In any event, you shouldn't store the entire contents of a fact table in memory, particularly because you usually don't notice the resulting memory problems until you carry out the import process in the live system with the relevant data quantities.

In addition, we regularly come across some usual suspects in the update rules, including complex derivation formulas such as financial statement item determinations, the distribution of data records across several rows, the transfer from the account model to the key figure model and vice versa[5], as well as key figure calculations, and aggregations. The problems are always the same, in particular, the problem that when carrying out cross-record calculations, you must take into account that the data records can be contained in different InfoPackages.

The following sections provide useful tricks that help you solve these problems. The update rule contains three different types of routines: the start routine, the routine that determines key figures and data fields, and the routine used to determine the key fields.

4.5.1 Start Routine

The start routine in the update rule is created above the actual update rules (see Figure 4.24).

---

5 The difference between the account model and the key figure model is described in detail in SAP Note 407563.

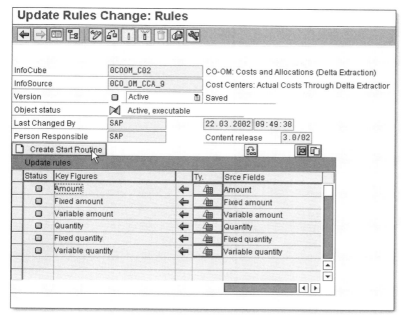

Figure 4.24 Calling the Start Routine in the Update Rule

If you open the start routine, a code is generated automatically that is similar to the one shown in Listing 4.19.

```
PROGRAM UPDATE_ROUTINE.
*$*$ begin of global -
* insert your declaration only below this line *-*
* TABLES: ...
* DATA:   ...
*$*$ end of global -
* insert your declaration only before this line *-*

* The following definition is new in SAP BW 3.x
TYPES:
  BEGIN OF DATA_PACKAGE_STRUCTURE.
     INCLUDE STRUCTURE /BIC/CS80FIAR_O03.
TYPES:
     RECNO   LIKE sy-tabix,
  END OF DATA_PACKAGE_STRUCTURE.
DATA:
  DATA_PACKAGE TYPE STANDARD TABLE OF DATA_PACKAGE_STRUCTURE
     WITH HEADER LINE
```

```
        WITH NON-UNIQUE DEFAULT KEY INITIAL SIZE 0.

FORM startup
  TABLES   MONITOR STRUCTURE RSMONITOR "user defined
                                        "monitoring
           MONITOR_RECNO STRUCTURE RSMONITORS "monitoring
                                        "with record n
           DATA_PACKAGE STRUCTURE DATA_PACKAGE
  USING    RECORD_ALL LIKE SY-TABIX
           SOURCE_SYSTEM LIKE RSUPDSIMULH-LOGSYS
  CHANGING ABORT LIKE SY-SUBRC. "set ABORT <> 0 to
                                        "cancel update
*$*$ begin of routine -
* insert your code only below this line *-*
* fill the internal tables "MONITOR" and/or "MONITOR_RECNO"
* to make monitor entries

* if abort is not equal to zero, the update process will be
* canceled
  ABORT = 0.
*$*$ end of routine -
* insert your code only before this line *-*
```

Listing 4.19 Generated Code of the Start Routine in the Update Rule

Like the start routine of the transfer rule, the start routine of the update rule begins with a block in which the developer can define global variables. These variables are then made available in all other routines of the update rule. This block is followed by the definition of the data package structure. Here, however, you can't select the fields you want to transfer because all fields of the InfoSource are transferred.

In addition, each data record contains the corresponding record ID. This ID matches the record ID in the PSA. This means you should always use this record ID instead of a sy-tabix when populating the MONITOR_RECNO table because the data package already may have changed in the transfer rule. The next part of the program code contains the definition of the actual form routine, which is called STARTUP in this example. In the generated program, the routine is called routine_9998. You can view the generated program in the overview screen of the update rule via EXTRAS • DISPLAY ACTIVATED PROGRAM.

In addition to the tables MONITOR and MONITOR_RECNO that have already been described in the error-handling note in Section 4.4, Transfer Rules in SAP BW 3.x, and the actual data package, DATA_PACKAGE, the interface only contains the ABORT parameter that aborts the entire data package, and the RECORD_ALL parameter that contains the number of data records.

4.5.2 Filling of Fields in a Data Structure

A typical scenario for applying the start routine is the simultaneous filling of several fields in the data structure. The following example shown in Listing 4.20 contains an ODS object, COMPONENT, which stores the planned input quantity (PLQUANT) and the actual input quantity (ACTQUANT) for the individual components of production orders. Instead of creating separate routines that read the same data records from one table, we'll implement the whole process in the start routine. Depending on the application, this can have significant performance benefits, especially if many intermediate results must be calculated in several routines.

```
FORM startup

   TABLES    MONITOR STRUCTURE RSMONITOR "user defined
                                         "monitoring
             MONITOR_RECNO STRUCTURE RSMONITORS "monitoring
                                                "with record n
             DATA_PACKAGE STRUCTURE DATA_PACKAGE
   USING     RECORD_ALL LIKE SY-TABIX
             SOURCE_SYSTEM LIKE RSUPDSIMULH-LOGSYS
   CHANGING ABORT LIKE SY-SUBRC. "set ABORT <> 0 to
                                 "cancel update
*$*$ begin of routine -
* insert your code only below this line *-*
* Data package header
   DATA: l_s_dp_line TYPE data_package_structure.
* The comp type contains the structure of the ODS object.
   types: BEGIN OF comp,
       plant      TYPE /bi0/oiplant,
       prodorder TYPE /bi0/oiprodorder,
       component type /bi0/oicomponent,
       /bic/plquant  TYPE /bic/oiplquant,
       /bic/actquant TYPE /bic/oiactquant,
       BASE_UOM      type /BI0/OIBASE_UOM,
         END OF comp.
* Structures for importing ODS data
   data:  l_s_comp  type comp.
   statics: l_th_comp type hashed table of comp
```

```
            with unique key plant prodorder component.
* Has ODS data been read yet?
  if l_th_comp[] is INITIAL.
* /BIC/ACOMPONENT00 is the table with active data of the
* ODS component.
    SELECT * FROM /bic/acomponent00
      appending CORRESPONDING FIELDS
      OF table l_th_comp.
  endif.
* Perform loop across the data package.
  loop at DATA_PACKAGE INTO l_s_dp_line.

* Read components from hashed table
  read table l_th_comp into l_s_comp
        with table key  plant = l_s_dp_line-plant
        prodorder = l_s_dp_line-prodorder
        component = l_s_dp_line-component.

  if sy-subrc = 0.
    l_s_dp_line-/BIC/plquant   = l_s_comp-/bic/plquant.
    l_s_dp_line-/bic/actquant  = l_s_comp-/bic/actquant.
    l_s_dp_line-UNIT           = l_s_comp-BASE_UOM.
*   If no record was found, the fields remain empty.
*   You could also insert an error message into the
*   MONITOR_RECNO table if the process does not provide
*   for this.
    MODIFY DATA_PACKAGE from l_s_dp_line.
  endif.
  endloop.
* if abort is not equal to zero, the update process will be
* canceled
  ABORT = 0.
*$*$ end of routine -
* insert your code only before this line *-*
```

Listing 4.20 Sample Start Routine

4.5.3 Characteristic Calculation

The characteristic calculation in the update rule is essentially identical to the characteristic calculation in the transfer rule. The only difference can be found in the parameters. The following sections describe a sample implementation.

The problem in the project described here was that specific commitment data could only be loaded once per month in a full upload process. The data could then be assigned to the respective period. However, the aggregation across the different periods produced incorrect results. For this reason, it was decided that after the data was loaded, the value of the last period was to be updated with an inverted mathematical sign into the subsequent period (with the exception of period 12). This way, it became possible to report the various commitment changes in the different periods. For this purpose, an additional value type was introduced, and the assignment between the original value type and the delta value type was stored in a database table, Z_VTYPE_CHNG. In controlling, a value type indicates whether the values are planned values, actual values, commitment values, and so on.

The program code in Listing 4.21 determines the new value type from the table. If no corresponding entry exists, the record won't be updated. Moreover, this example deviates from the usual logic because it's possible for the table to be empty.

```
FORM compute_key_field
  TABLES    MONITOR STRUCTURE RSMONITOR "user defined
                                        "monitoring
  USING     COMM_STRUCTURE LIKE
                /BIC/CS8DATACUBE
            RECORD_NO LIKE SY-TABIX
            RECORD_ALL LIKE SY-TABIX
            SOURCE_SYSTEM LIKE
                    RSUPDSIMULH-LOGSYS
  CHANGING RESULT LIKE
                  /BIC/VDATACUBET-VTYPE
            RETURNCODE LIKE SY-SUBRC
            ABORT LIKE SY-SUBRC. "set ABORT <> 0 to
                                 "cancel update

*$*$ begin of routine -
* insert your code only below this line *-*
* fill the internal table "MONITOR", to make monitor
* entries
* ST_VTYPE_CHNG contains the value types to be changed.
  STATICS : ST_VTYPE_CHNG
            LIKE SORTED TABLE OF
                Z_VTYPE_CHNG
            INITIAL SIZE 0
            WITH UNIQUE KEY VTYPE.
* SD_DATA_READ is used to check if the data has been read.
```

```
                    SD_DATA_READ TYPE C VALUE ' '.

    DATA:     LD_VTYPE_CHNG
                LIKE LINE OF ST_VTYPE_CHNG.

* result value of the routine
  IF SD_DATA_READ IS INITIAL.
* No data read, then initialization
    SELECT * FROM Z_VTYPE_CHNG
            INTO TABLE ST_VTYPE_CHNG.
    SD_DATA_READ = 'X'.
  ENDIF.
  READ TABLE ST_VTYPE_CHNG
*    Does the value type have to be implemented?
        WITH TABLE KEY
            VTYPE = COMM_STRUCTURE-VTYPE
        INTO LD_VTYPE_CHNG .
  IF SY-SUBRC = 0.
*    Yes, change value type
    RESULT = LD_VTYPE_CHNG-VTYPETO.
* if the returncode is not equal to zero, the result will not
* be updated
    RETURNCODE = 0.
  ELSE.
* If no entry has been found, then do not update record
    RETURNCODE = 4.
  ENDIF.
* if abort is not equal to zero, the update process will be
* canceled
  ABORT = 0.

*$*$ end of routine -
* insert your code only before this line *-*
ENDFORM.
```

Listing 4.21 Typical Characteristic Derivation in the Update Rule

You can see that, compared to the start routine, the only additional parameters are the record ID RECORD_NO and the return value RESULT. This example contains some typical elements that can usually be found in update rules. For one thing, new characteristic attributes are generated here that don't occur as such in the source system. For another, data records that won't be used for reporting are eliminated from the data package. Typically, those two types of elements are implemented in the update rules, not in the transfer rules.

4.5.4 Key Figure Derivation

At best, the key figure or data field derivation in the update rules is almost identical to the characteristic value derivation. The interesting things here are the two checkboxes that are located below the radio button for the creation of a routine (see Figure 4.25).

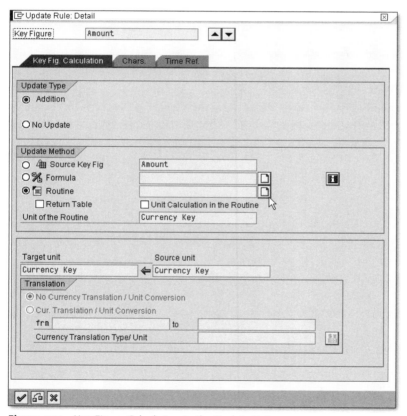

Figure 4.25 Key Figure Calculation in the Update Rule

You can use these two checkboxes either to carry out the UNIT CALCULATION IN THE ROUTINE or — instead of outputting a single key figure — to output a RETURN TABLE containing data records.

4.5.5   Unit Calculation

The unit calculation in the routine is required when the DataSource delivers the values in a quantity unit or currency that's different from the one to be used in the data target. The conversion types in SAP NetWeaver BI are powerful tools for having the system carry out the currency conversion, whereas the conversion of quantity units is practically not supported by SAP NetWeaver BI. For this reason, you should use the unit calculation in the routine for quantity conversions.

Tip

Due to legal requirements, the currency conversion function in the various SAP systems is very complex, in particular since the extension that was caused by the introduction of the Euro. For this reason, you should not read the exchange rates from the corresponding TCUR* tables and instead use the conversion types or, if need be, the standard function modules CONVERT_TO_LOCAL_CURRENCY and CONVERT_TO_FOREIGN_CURRENCY.

In Listing 4.22, we'll determine the default quantity unit (0BASE_UOM) on the basis of the master data attributes of the material. After that, we'll convert the delivered quantity unit (0UNIT) into the default quantity unit.

```
PROGRAM UPDATE_ROUTINE.
*$*$ begin of global -
* insert your declaration only below this line *-*
* TABLES: ...
* DATA:    ...
*$*$ end of global -
* insert your declaration only before this line *-*

FORM compute_data_field
  TABLES    MONITOR STRUCTURE RSMONITOR "user defined
                                        "monitoring
  USING     COMM_STRUCTURE LIKE
                    /BIC/CSABSATZMG
            RECORD_NO LIKE SY-TABIX
            RECORD_ALL LIKE SY-TABIX
            SOURCE_SYSTEM LIKE
                    RSUPDSIMULH-LOGSYS
  CHANGING  RESULT LIKE
                    /BIC/VABSATZT-QUANTITY
            UNIT LIKE
                    /BIC/VABSATZT-UNIT
```

```
                RETURNCODE LIKE SY-SUBRC
                ABORT LIKE SY-SUBRC. "set ABORT <> 0 to
                                     "cancel update

*$*$ begin of routine -
* insert your code only below this line *-*
* fill the internal table "MONITOR," to make monitor
* entries
DATA: l_s_material TYPE /bi0/pmaterial,
      l_th_material TYPE hashed table
          OF /bi0/pmaterial
          WITH UNIQUE KEY material objvers
          INITIAL SIZE 0,
      l_d_quantity TYPE /bi0/oiquantity.


* result value of the routine
  IF l_th_material[] IS INITIAL.
    SELECT * FROM /bi0/pmaterial
        INTO TABLE l_th_material
        WHERE objvers = 'A'.
  ENDIF.
* First determine the basic quantity unit.
  READ TABLE l_th_material INTO
      l_s_material WITH TABLE KEY
      material = COMM_STRUCTURE-material
      objvers  = 'A'.
  IF sy-subrc = 0.
*    Then convert the quantity
    CALL FUNCTION
        'UNIT_CONVERSION_SIMPLE'
      EXPORTING
        INPUT = COMM_STRUCTURE-quantity
        UNIT_IN = COMM_STRUCTURE-unit
        UNIT_OUT = l_s_material-base_uom
      EXPORTING
        OUTPUT = l_d_quantity
      EXCEPTIONS
        OTHERS = 1
      .
    IF sy-subrc = 0.
*    Conversion successful
      RESULT = l_d_quantity.
      UNIT   = l_s_material-base_uom.
```

```
     ELSE.
*        If conversion not possible, copy original values
         RESULT = COMM_STRUCTURE-quantity.
         UNIT   = COMM_STRUCTURE-unit.
     ENDIF.
   ELSE.
* If no basic quantity unit available copy
* quantity and unit
     RESULT = COMM_STRUCTURE-quantity.
     UNIT   = COMM_STRUCTURE-unit.
   ENDIF.
* if the returncode is not equal to zero, the result will not
* be updated
   RETURNCODE = 0.
* if abort is not equal to zero, the update process will be
* canceled
   ABORT = 0.

*$*$ end of routine -
* insert your code only before this line *-*
ENDFORM.
```

Listing 4.22 Sample Unit Conversion

The example has been programmed as very error-tolerant, in that it ignores all errors, be they missing master data or incompatible quantity units. This leads back to the fact that the original values are written to the InfoCube. This procedure is often used, particularly if it's clear that because of the nature of the business process, no data consistency can be guaranteed. If the quantity data is only used for reporting purposes and not as input data for other algorithms such as cost distributions, a consistent supply of units is no longer required. And if the processes are redesigned in such a way that the source system provides only quantity units that can be converted, and the master data is available on time, the data quality in SAP NetWeaver BI is improved.

In practice, you should always output error messages during the test phase to evaluate the data quality. In a live system, you only extend those error messages if you find out that almost every loading process contains erroneous data. Otherwise, you should at least output information messages (I messages).

If the information is needed consistently in subsequent steps or downstream systems, the update process in the InfoProvider must be stopped here. You can do that by setting the return code to 4.

4.5.6 Return Table

The return table differs from all other routines in that it's the only routine that allows you to return the data records in the data-target structure. Note, however, that you must make sure to use only the key figure or data field for which the routine was actually created.

This option is particularly interesting if you want to calculate the entire result to be written into the InfoCube in the start routine and store this result in the global data. In the return table, you then can copy the global data in Record 1, while the data remains empty for all other records. In this way, you can directly calculate the cube results.

The routine that's now generated contains the familiar parameters `MONITOR`, `COMM_STRUCTURE`, `RECORD_NO`, `RECORD_ALL`, `SOURCE_SYSTEM`, `RETURNCODE`, and `ABORT`. Additionally, it contains two new parameters: the `RESULT_TABLE` table, which replaces the return value `RESULT`, and the structure `ICUBE_VALUES`. The `ICUBE_VALUES` structure contains the results of the data field derivations. This demonstrates the logic SAP BW 3.x uses to calculate the update rules. First it calculates the characteristic values and then the key figure. However, in case of doubt, it's safer to rely on the communication structure and build up the entire table from there.

The return table isn't included in the transformation of SAP NetWeaver 7.0; however, it's supposed to be delivered as of SAP NetWeaver 7.1.

5   User Exits and BAdIs in Reporting

The exits described so far are very efficient and enable you to format the data so that it meets many typical reporting requirements. However, there frequently is a requirement to make the reports more flexible by using variables. For example, no BI consultant would recommend that you define separate reports per cost center within your company. Instead, he would ask you to define the cost center as an input variable.

On the other hand, this flexibility should not be attained at the cost of the users by overloading them with a multitude of variables. For this reason, it's useful for the user to get suggestions from the program regarding cost center(s) the user will probably want to see in the report, depending on his position and area of responsibility.

The following sections describe how you can derive variable values and set default values by employing the right programming technique. You then will be introduced to virtual characteristics and key figures as well as to the topic of Virtual-Providers. Whereas the variables make the value selection at the time a report is analyzed more flexible, both virtual InfoObjects and VirtualProviders go one step further and enable you to customize the data at the time of reporting. As you might guess, the implementation of this is more complex. Finally, the chapter provides a brief description of all other techniques that employ ABAP to customize the reporting process.

5.1   Variable Exit RSR00001

At its core, the user exit RSR00001 contains function module EXIT_SAPLRRS0_001, which performs several different functions related to the input of variables. This exit poses the same problem as the user exit for extractor extension described in Section 3.3, User Exit RSAP0001. In a typical BI system, the user exit grows steadily. For this reason, you should make sure right from the start that you don't carry out the implementation in include ZXRSRU01. Instead, you should separate the implementation from the include, for instance, by deriving the name of a function module from the variable name.

The interface of the user exit contains two central parameters. In addition to the variable name, I_VAR, the call step I_STEP is very important. This call step is a counter because the user exit is called several times at up to four different places. You can implement different functions at those different points in time. For this reason, we should describe the I_STEP parameter before we continue with the actual implementation.

▶ I_STEP = 1

The first call of the user exit is used to calculate default values. For this purpose, the exit is called once per customer-exit-type variable. This is actually one of the biggest weaknesses of the exit. If you want to assign a default value to an existing input variable, you can do so only by creating a new variable of the customer exit type and then making it ready for input. It would be very useful if in this step you were able to assign default values to other variables that are ready for input.

Even though this step is used for determining default values, you can also fill variables that aren't ready for input. That only makes sense, however, if you need the values later in Step 2 to derive other variables.

▶ I_STEP = 2

This step isn't called for all variables of the user exit type but only for those not ready for input. In this step, you define the final variable values. To do that, you must call the user exit once for each variable that isn't ready for input. So, you can't overwrite any user input in this step. That's generally impossible because it often leads to misunderstandings by the user. For this reason, you should either forbid any user input or reject the user entry by returning an error message.

▶ I_STEP = 3

In contrast to the first two steps, the third step isn't called for each variable but only once. When it's called, all variable content is transferred for validation purposes. So, you can check if "Period from" is smaller or equal to "Period to," provided that the two periods aren't entered as an interval but in two different variables. This technique is indispensable for a flexible validation. However, it obstructs a clear separation by queries—or at least by projects—because variables should preferably be used across several projects to keep the total number of variables as small as possible. For this reason, you should use a different field to obtain a separation in the implementation.

▶ I_STEP = 0

Step 0 is used very rarely. It's used for all calls that aren't related to the variables. SAP NetWeaver 7.0 and SAP BW 3.x contain three applications in this context.

▸ First, the step is used when you use variables in the InfoPackage for selection purposes.

▸ Second, it's used to determine the filter values in the navigation block of the query.

▸ Third, and possibly most importantly, it's used to fill variables that are used in authorizations. This is particularly useful if authorizations are to be filled from tables that have been imported into a DataStore object, or if the authorizations are to be derived from master data.

This book focuses only on the latter case because all other cases occur only rarely in practice.

5.1.1 Interface of Function Module EXIT_SAPLRSR0_001

Now that we have clarified the meaning of the I_STEP parameter, we'll describe the complete interface. The header of the function module has the structure shown in Listing 5.1.

```
FUNCTION EXIT_SAPLRRSO_001.
*"--------------------------------------
*"*"Local interface:
*"  IMPORTING
*"    VALUE(I_VNAM)    LIKE   RSZGLOBV-VNAM
*"    VALUE(I_VARTYP)  LIKE   RSZGLOBV-VARTYP
*"    VALUE(I_IOBJNM)  LIKE   RSZGLOBV-IOBJNM
*"    VALUE(I_S_COB_PRO) TYPE
*"                       RSD_S_COB_PRO
*"    VALUE(I_S_RKB1D)  TYPE
*"                       RSR_S_RKB1D
*"    VALUE(I_PERIV) TYPE
*"                   RRO01_S_RKB1F-PERIV
*"    VALUE(I_T_VAR_RANGE) TYPE
*"                       RRSO_T_VAR_RANGE
*"    VALUE(I_STEP) TYPE  I DEFAULT 0
```

```
*" EXPORTING
*"   VALUE(E_T_RANGE) TYPE   RSR_T_RANGESID
*"   VALUE(E_MEEHT) LIKE   RSZGLOBV-MEEHT
*"   VALUE(E_MEFAC) LIKE   RSZGLOBV-MEFAC
*"   VALUE(E_WAERS) LIKE   RSZGLOBV-WAERS
*"   VALUE(E_WHFAC) LIKE   RSZGLOBV-WHFAC
*" CHANGING
*"   VALUE(C_S_CUSTOMER) TYPE
*"             RRO04_S_CUSTOMER OPTIONAL
*"- - - - - - - - - - - - - - - - - - - - - - - - - - - - - - - - - - - - - -
```

Listing 5.1 Interface of Function Module EXIT_SAPLRSRO_001

The various parameters have the following meanings:

▶ I_VNAM

In Steps 0, 1, and 2, this parameter contains the variable name to be calculated.

▶ I_VARTYP

This parameter specifies which variable type is being used in Steps 1 and 2; that is, it determines whether the return value to be expected is a characteristic value, a text, a formula value, a hierarchy node, or a hierarchy.

▶ I_IOBJNM

This parameter specifies the InfoObject to which the variable refers.

▶ I_S_COB_PRO

This parameter contains various pieces of information about the InfoObject to which the variable refers. ATRNAVFL, for instance, specifies whether the variable is a navigation attribute, whereas ATRTIMFL tells you if the navigation attribute is time-dependent. Furthermore, the parameter provides information that is only needed in special situations because that information is usually fixed at the time of programming, after which it isn't changed. For this reason, the parameter isn't used frequently.

▶ I_S_RKB1D

This parameter contains information such as the query name, the calling program, and so on. It's particularly important in Step 3 to determine which validations are to be carried out. Important fields for this are INFOCUBE (this is the name of the InfoProvider on which the report is run) and COMPID (the name of the query that's currently executed).

▶ I_PERIV

This parameter contains the fiscal year variant, provided it can be uniquely determined in the query. This is important whenever you must determine a period based on a date, for instance, if you want to present the current posting period as a default value. However, because it's rare that several different fiscal year periods exist in the same system, the parameter isn't used very often.

▶ I_T_VAR_RANGE

This parameter contains a table, which in turn contains all other variable values. This is particularly useful for Steps 2 and 3.

▶ I_STEP

The step for variable determination has already been described in detail.

▶ E_T_RANGE

In this table, the return values in Steps 0, 1, and 2 must be returned. Basically, the table is structured like a ranges table; all other fields can be ignored. Depending on the type of variable, you must take into account the following constraints.

  ▶ For characteristic values, the field LOW contains the value or the lower value limit (for intervals). For text variables, it contains the text; for hierarchy variables, the hierarchy; for node variables, the node; and for formula variables, the calculation value.

  ▶ The field HIGH contains the upper limit of the interval for characteristic value variables for intervals or selection options. For hierarchy-node variables, this field contains the InfoObject of the hierarchy node. This can be omitted if the node is a leaf of the hierarchy. For other variables, it's empty.

  ▶ The field SIGN usually contains an I (include). The only exception can be selection options, which also allow an E (exclude).[1]

  ▶ The OPT field is usually filled with EQ (equal). For intervals, you also can use BT (between) or NB (not between). For selection options, you can use all operators that are allowed in ranges tables. Those operators can, for instance, be found in the ABAP documentation for the key word IF.

▶ E_MEEHT, E_MEFAC, E_WAERS, E_WHFAC, C_S_CUSTOMER

These parameters are specified in the interface, but they aren't queried.

---

1 SAP NetWeaver BI also allows an E for intervals. However, because this doesn't correspond to the logic of intervals, you should implement such variables as selection options.

Based on the different meanings of the individual steps, you can also define the implementation of the exit accordingly. If you want to make a generic definition that calls individual function modules, as described in Listing 3.2, you can use the implementation shown in Listing 5.2.

```
DATA: l_d_fname(30) TYPE c.
CASE i_step.
  WHEN 1.
    CONCATENATE 'Z_VAR_PRE_POPUP_'
      i_vnam INTO l_d_fname.
  WHEN 2.
    CONCATENATE 'Z_VAR_POST_POPUP_'
      i_vnam INTO l_d_fname.
  WHEN 0.
    CONCATENATE 'Z_VAR_AUTHORITY_'
      i_vnam INTO l_d_fname.
  WHEN 3.
    l_d_fname = 'Z_VAR_CHECK_VALIDITY'.
ENDCASE.
CALL FUNCTION l_d_fname IF FOUND
  EXPORTING
    I_VNAM        = i_vnam
    I_VARTYP      = i_vartyp
    I_IOBJNM      = i_iobjnm
    I_S_COB_PRO   = i_s_cob_pro
    I_S_RKB1D     = i_s_rkb1d
    I_PERIV       = i_periv
    I_T_VAR_RANGE = i_t_var_range
    I_STEP        = i_step
  IMPORTING
    E_T_RANGE     = e_t_range
    E_MEEHT       = e_meeht
    E_MEFAC       = e_mefac
    E_WAERS       = e_waers
    E_WHFAC       = e_whfac
  CHANGING
    C_S_CUSTOMER = c_s_customer
  EXCEPTIONS
    OTHERS = 1.
IF SY-SUBRC <> 0.
  MESSAGE ID SY-MSGID TYPE SY-MSGTY
          NUMBER SY-MSGNO
          WITH
```

```
                  SY-MSGV1 SY-MSGV2
                  SY-MSGV3 SY-MSGV4
              RAISING ERROR_IN_VARIABLE.
ENDIF.
```

Listing 5.2 Sample Implementation for Variable Exit ZXRSRU01

If you take a closer look at the RSVAREXIT_* function modules, you can see that the SAP development implements variables with an SAP exit in almost the same way as shown in Listing 5.2, the only difference being that SAP development doesn't make any distinction based on I_STEP. However, you should make a distinction here because you then can tell the purpose of a function module by its name.

If you have already worked in larger BI systems, you've noticed that the exit ZXRSRU01 is one of the biggest exits in the entire system. Apart from that, all changes to this exit are critical because those changes may affect all reports. You'll probably know what I'm talking about if you've ever transported into a live system an exit that wasn't free of syntax errors.

For this reason, you should use the sample implementation right from the start to avoid an annoying problem: a transport separated by content to enable different variable implementations. This frequently doesn't occur until several projects are running concurrently in the live system. Naturally, the question of who will be responsible for function module Z_VAR_CHECK_VALIDITY will arise. But in case of doubt, you can call a central function module from any project in this function module and collect the check results there.

5.1.2   Implementation for I_STEP = 1

Let's now discuss the actual implementation of the variable logic. Because I_STEP = 1 is supposed to set the default values, you can only implement algorithms that don't require any input by the user. So, there are two main types of algorithms available:

- ▶ Date-dependent default value determination
- ▶ Table-controlled default value determination

Example 1: Date-Dependent Default Value Assignment

We want to implement a variable called WEEK6F for InfoObject OCALWEEK. This variable is a characteristic value variable of the interval type, and we want to assign it the interval that starts in the current week and lasts for six weeks. The code appears as shown in Listing 5.3:

```
   DATA: l_d_datum TYPE d,
         l_d_woche TYPE /bi0/oicalweek.
   DATA: l_s_range TYPE rsr_s_rangesid.
CASE i_vnam.
  WHEN 'WEEK6F'.
    IF i_step = 1. "Prior to popup
*     determine current week
      CALL FUNCTION 'DATE_GET_WEEK'
        EXPORTING
          DATE        = sy-date
        IMPORTING
          WEEK        = l_d_week
          .
      l_s_range-low = l_d_week.
      l_s_range-sign = 'I'.
      l_s_range-option = 'EQ'.
*     Now determine six weeks later
      l_d_date = sy-date + 42.
                    "42 days = 6 weeks
      CALL FUNCTION 'DATE_GET_WEEK'
        EXPORTING
          DATE        = l_d_date
        IMPORTING
          WEEK        = l_d_week
          .
      l_s_range-high = l_d_week.
      APPEND l_s_range TO l_t_range.
```

Listing 5.3 Example of a Date-Dependent Variable Pre-Assignment

Example 2: Table-Dependent Default Value Assignment

In the second example, the variable LASTCPER is supposed to contain the last closed period from the source system. To avoid having to call the source system via Remote Function Calls (RFCs) all the time, a table Z_BEX_VAR was created that consists of the fields KEY (CHAR 20) and VALUE (CHAR 60). KEY is the only key field in the table.

The last closed period is maintained in the entry that contains the string KEY = 'LASTCPER'. The code that's used to query the table is shown in Listing 5.4.

```
DATA: l_s_bex_var TYPE z_bex_var,
      l_s_range TYPE rsr_s_rangesid.
CASE i_vnam.
  WHEN 'LASTCPER'.
    IF i_step = 1. "Prior to variable popup
      SELECT SINGLE * FROM z_bex_var
        INTO l_s_bex_var
        WHERE key = 'LASTCPER'.
      IF SY-SUBRC = 0.
        l_s_range-low = l_s_bex_var-value.
      ELSE.
        clear l_s_range-low.
      ENDIF.
      l_s_range-sign = 'I'.
      l_s_range-opt  = 'EQ'.
    ENDIF.
ENDCASE.
```

Listing 5.4 Example of a Table-Dependent Pre-Assignment

The type of pre-assignment you choose determines the type of implementation to be used. A typical use of the table-dependent default value pre-assignment is to make the assignment dependent on the user name or even on specific user rights.

Because it isn't easy to handle reporting authorizations, the following example demonstrates how to read RSR class reporting authorizations without having to perform an AUTHORITY-CHECK for each master record.

Example 3: Pre-Assignment Based on Authorizations

You want to implement a two-dimensional authorization object that merges the external company structure (InfoObject 0COMPANY) and the internal business area (InfoObject 0BUS_AREA) in one authorization object.[2] Depending on the report that is chosen, the respective owners should see either all costs incurred within the

---

2 The fact that two InfoObjects are used in one reporting authorization is rather unusual, and many developers certainly don't know that this is possible. But both the reporting process and BPS run without any problem in the system, and they check the authorizations correctly.

entire company or all costs incurred within their business area. For this reason, many employees have two values for their authorization objects, such as:

▶ 0COMPANY = 100 and 0BUS_AREA = *

▶ 0COMPANY = * and 0BUS_AREA = 1000

There's a big problem involved in this concept. If an employee calls a report in the external view, the default value for his company, 100, should be automatically displayed. However, if the variable is filled with information from the authorization, the system always displays the extended value, *, which represents an empty selection in this case.

The implementation shown in Listing 5.5 reads the authorizations and populates the default value accordingly.

```
DATA: v_tsx_auth_values_user   TYPE
                               rssb_tsx_auth_values_user,
      w_sx_auth_values_user    TYPE  line of
                               rssb_tsx_auth_values_user,
      w_sx_auth_values_auth    TYPE
                               rssb_sx_auth_values_user_auth,
      w_sx_auth_values_iobjnm TYPE
                               rssb_sx_auth_values_user_iobj,
      w_sx_auth_values_range   LIKE  rrrange,
      v_ts_authnode            TYPE  rssbr_ts_authnode,
      w_s_authnode             TYPE  line of
                               rssbr_ts_authnode,
      v_authhieruid            TYPE  rssauthhieruid.

CONSTANTS: c_zcomp_bus TYPE rssb_sx_auth_values_user-object
              VALUE 'ZCOMP_BUS',
           c_attrinm_company TYPE
                      rssb_sx_auth_values_user_iobj-iobjnm
              VALUE '0COMPANY',
           c_attrinm_busarea TYPE
                      rssb_sx_auth_values_user_iobj-iobjnm
              VALUE '0BUS_AREA'.

  IF i_step  = 1.

* Read all reporting authorizations of user
  CALL FUNCTION 'RSSB_AUTHORIZATIONS_OF_USER'
    EXPORTING
```

```
      I_IOBJNM                   = 'OBUS_AREA'
      I_INFOPROV                 = 'DEMOCUBE'
      I_UNAME                    = sy-uname
      I_HIENM                    = 'DEMOHIER'
      I_DATETO                   = sy-datum
      I_VERSION                  = '000'
    IMPORTING
*     E_T_RANGESID               =
      E_TSX_AUTH_VALUES_USER     = v_tsx_auth_values_user
*     E_NIOBJNM                  =
*     E_NODE                     =
*     E_TS_NODE                  =
*     E_TS_AUTH_VALUES_HIERARCHY =
*     E_T_MSG                    =
    EXCEPTIONS
      NOT_AUTHORIZED             = 1
      INTERNAL_ERROR             = 2
      USER_DOESNT_EXIST          = 3
      X_MESSAGE                  = 4
      OTHERS                     = 5
            .
  IF sy-subrc <> 0.
    MESSAGE ID SY-MSGID TYPE SY-MSGTY
            NUMBER SY-MSGNO
            WITH SY-MSGV1 SY-MSGV2 SY-MSGV3 SY-MSGV4
            RAISING not_authorized.
  ENDIF.

* LOOP across all reporting authorizations of user
  LOOP AT v_tsx_auth_values_user
       INTO w_sx_auth_values_user.
*   Which authorization object?
    CHECK w_sx_auth_values_user-object = c_zcomp_bus.
*   Double authorization object LOOP across all values for
*   authorization object
    LOOP AT w_sx_auth_values_user-auth
         INTO w_sx_auth_values_auth.
*     Read company value
      READ TABLE w_sx_auth_values_auth-values_iobjnm
           INTO  w_sx_auth_values_iobjnm
           WITH KEY iobjnm = c_attrinm_company.
      IF sy-subrc = 0.
*       Company found
```

```
            LOOP AT w_sx_auth_values_iobjnm-ranges
                INTO w_sx_auth_values_range.
             IF  ( w_sx_auth_values_range-sign = 'I' )
            AND ( w_sx_auth_values_range-opt = 'CP' )
            AND ( w_sx_auth_values_range-low = '*' ).
*   Does an authorization exist for OCOMPANY?
*   Determine business area.
               READ TABLE w_sx_auth_values_auth-values_iobjnm
                   INTO  w_sx_auth_values_iobjnm
                   WITH KEY iobjnm = c_attrinm_busarea.
               IF sy-subrc = 0.
*          Authorization for business area
                 LOOP AT w_sx_auth_values_iobjnm-ranges
                    INTO w_sx_auth_values_range.
                    MOVE-CORRESPONDING w_sx_auth_values_range
                                   TO l_s_range.
                    APPEND l_s_range TO e_t_range.
                 ENDLOOP. "w_sx_auth_values_iobjnm_range
               ENDIF.   "sy-subrc = 0
             ENDIF.   "* authorization for OCOMPANY
           ENDLOOP.  " w_sx_auth_values_iobjnm-ranges
        ENDIF.  "sy-subrc = 0
      ENDLOOP.   "w_sx_auth_values_user-auth
    ENDLOOP.    "v_tsx_auth_values_user
```

Listing 5.5 Derivation of Authorizations from Specific Authorization Objects

5.1.3   Implementation for I_STEP = 2

The implementation of Step 2 is essentially the same as that of Step 1. However, there's one significant difference: In Step 2, you can use the values that have previously been entered in the dialog box. This is often necessary if the user enters a specific time, and derivations are made based on that point in time. This scenario is explained in the following example.

Example 4: Time-Dependent Versions

The user wants to enter a reporting period in the variable, REP_PER. Depending on the time of variable REP_PER, the variable REP_VERS is to get the values listed in Table 5.1.

REP_PER Time	REP_VERS Value
Period is closed.	ACT (actual version)
Period is in the current year, but not closed	PRE (preview)
Period is in a subsequent year.	PLN (planned version)

Table 5.1 Version Implementation

The implementation for this is shown in Listing 5.6.

```
DATA: l_s_range TYPE rsr_s_rangesid.
DATA: l_s_var_range LIKE rrrangeexit,
      l_d_date LIKE sy-date,
      l_d_year  TYPE /bi0/oifiscyear,
      l_d_per3  TYPE /bi0/oifiscper3.
CASE i_vnam.
  WHEN 'CUMMONTH'.
    CLEAR l_s_range.
    IF i_step = 2.    "Read entries
*       of REP_PER variable after dialog popup
        READ TABLE i_t_var_range INTO l_s_var_range
            WITH KEY vnam = 'REP_PER'.
        IF sy-subrc = 0.
          l_d_year = l_s_var_range-low(4).
          l_d_per3 = l_s_var_range-low+4(3).
          CALL_FUNCTION 'LAST_DAY_IN_PERIOD_GET'
            EXPORTING
              I_GJAHR  = l_d_year
              I_PERIV  = i_periv
              I_POPER  = l_d_per3
            IMPORTING
              E_DATUM  = l_d_datum
            EXCEPTIONS
              OTHERS   = 1.
          IF SY-SUBRC <> 0.
*           Cannot be determined (fiscal year
*           variant missing?) => set default
            l_s_range-low = 'ACT'.
          ELSE.
            IF l_d_date <= sy-date.
*             Period closed
              l_s_range-low = 'ACT'.
            ELSE.
```

```
                    CALL_FUNCTION 'FIRST_DAY_IN_YEAR_GET'
                      EXPORTING
                        I_GJAHR   = l_d_year
                        I_PERIV   = i_periv
                      IMPORTING
                        E_DATUM   = l_d_datum
                      EXCEPTIONS
                        OTHERS    = 1.
                    IF sy-subrc <> 0.
*                      Cannot be determined (but could period
*                      be determined?) => set default
                      l_s_range-low = 'ACT'.
                    ELSE.
                      IF l_d_date > sy-date.
*                        Fiscal year has not yet started
                        l_s_range-low = 'PLN'.
                      ELSE.
                        l_s_range-low = 'PRE'.
                      ENDIF.
                    ENDIF.
                  ENDIF.
                ENDIF.
              ELSE.
*                Variable was used in error, set useful
*                default (e.g., ACT)
                l_s_range-low = 'ACT'.
              ENDIF.
              l_s_range-sign = 'I'.
              l_s_range-opt  = 'EQ'.
              APPEND l_s_range TO e_t_range.
```

Listing 5.6 Sample Variable Determination Based on Input Variables

Here are typical examples of a variable determination that depends on input variables.

▶ Derivation of a formula variable from an input period to extrapolate annual forecasts or to distribute annual values.

▶ Derivation of a comparison group (e.g., a hierarchy node variable) for an input characteristic such as a profit center.

▶ Derivation of upper and lower limits of a time interval that isn't defined by a fixed number of periods but by other constraints, such as the beginning or end of a quarter.

▶ Determination of an authorization-dependent formula variable to display periods that have not yet been released. Based on the specified period, a check is carried out as to whether the period has already been released. If not, an authorization check is performed. If the authorization check fails, 0 is returned; otherwise, 1. The query then multiplies the actual value by the result of the formula variable.

▶ Derivation of variables for MultiProviders. For example, you can query a variable for a cost center. You then derive the profit center that's assigned to the cost center because one of the involved InfoProviders doesn't contain any cost center, only the profit center.

5.1.4   Implementation for I_STEP = 0

Step 0 can be used, among other things, to derive variables in authorizations. In a reporting authorization, you can simply use a variable by inserting a variable name that begins with a dollar sign ($). This variable must be defined up front in the Query Designer. When running the report, the exit is called, and you can implement the authorization in ABAP.

When you determine authorizations, the return table is treated like an authorization so that all restrictions for authorizations must also be accounted for with regard to the return table. Accordingly, SIGN must always have the value I, and the value of OPT must either be EQ or BT. Excluding authorizations such as "all salaries except those of the executive board" aren't allowed.

Possible and typical applications for these authorizations are authorization derivations from tables or master data. You also can use the excluding authorizations to assign an authorization dependent on the current date. The following demonstrates a typical example.

Example 5: Changing Authorizations in the Quiet Period

In this example, we want to implement the time-dependent control of an authorization for a regional hierarchy. All employees have authorizations for all regions except during the so-called *quiet period,* which lasts from the 25th of a quarter-end month until the 15th of the following month (in January until the 25th of January). During that time, the employees are allowed to view only those regions that are stored in a table. For this purpose, their authorization contains the variable QREGION. We'll now fill this variable in Listing 5.7.

```
DATA: L_S_RANGE TYPE RSR_S_RANGESID.
CASE i_vnam.
  WHEN 'QREGION'.
*    Date in quiet period?
    DATA: l_d_tag(4) TYPE n,
          l_s_region TYPE z_user_region.
    l_d_tag = sy-date+4(4).
    IF    ( l_d_tag <= '0125' )    OR
       ( ( l_d_tag >= '0325' ) AND
         ( l_d_tag <= '0415' ) ) OR
       ( ( l_d_tag >= '0625' ) AND
         ( l_d_tag <= '0715' ) ) OR
       ( ( l_d_tag >= '0925' ) AND
         ( l_d_tag <= '1015' ) ) OR
         ( l_d_tag >= '1225' ).
      l_s_range-sign = 'I'.
      l_s_range-opt  = 'EQ'.
      SELECT * FROM z_user_region
        INTO  l_s_region
        WHERE uname = sy-uname.
        l_s_range-low =
                      l_s_region-region.
        APPEND l_s_range TO e_t_range.
      ENDSELECT.
    ELSE.
      l_s_range-sign = 'I'.
      l_s_range-opt  = 'CP'.
      l_s_range-low  = '*'.
      APPEND l_s_range TO e_t_range.
    ENDIF.
```

Listing 5.7 Implementing an Authorization Variable

The IF query in Listing 5.7 normally is stored in a separate check function or even in a customizing table. Otherwise, those lines would have to be changed regularly in practice.

5.1.5   Implementation for I_STEP = 3

The implementation for I_STEP = 3 is different and a little more complicated than the implementation of the other steps. This is because you must make sure that not every query uses the same variables, and also because not all checks are restricted to one variable.

Nevertheless, some typical patterns recur regularly in variable checks. Before these can be examined, you should try to minimize the problems by using a clever variable-handling strategy.

> **Note: Variable Handling in SAP NetWeaver Business Intelligence**
>
> The definition of variables in SAP NetWeaver BI always causes problems because you must take into account two opposing trends. In an ideal scenario, you want to reuse the variables, but you also want to use individual texts and default values for the individual reports. Moreover, the definition of variables is very easy, so that many report developers prefer to define a new variable instead of searching through the existing ones to check if a variable exists that meets the requirements of a specific report. This attitude is perfectly clear to those of you who have seen what happens if a variable is redefined, and the users complain about sudden occurrences of incorrect default values in live reports.
>
> Because there's no way to solve this problem, you should come up with a strategy that specifies how you want to use the variables. There are as many possible strategies as there are data warehouses, so the following suggestion is particularly intended for those readers who don't yet have any strategy.
>
> Regarding variables, there is a simple rule of thumb. You must assign an owner to each variable. This is an easy way to resolve all usage problems. The rule could be implemented as follows.
>
> The owner of the system is responsible for all business content variables and defines central variables that can be used by everyone, such as time variables and variables for central company concepts.
>
> Each project[3] is assigned a prefix and can define any variable within this namespace. Furthermore, each project can use all central variables without restriction. If a project wants to use variables from other projects, the use must be announced. In addition, the project must inform those users who have announced the use about changes to variables. If this strategy is adhered to, various central variables will be widely used, while an even greater number of project-specific variables are used outside of the respective projects in exceptional cases. Those who don't comply with this strategy will probably do so when they see that one of their variables has been changed several times without prior announcement.

---

3 By "project," we mean an entity that defines one or several InfoProviders that are separated based on their contents, including their reports. In large BI projects, this corresponds to the subproject level.

A consistent variable strategy has the following invaluable advantages for Step 3.

▶ It's immediately clear who is responsible for the implementation of the exit. If the validation is centrally defined, it's centrally implemented. If not, it's implemented in the project.

▶ Each project knows where its variables are being used and can adjust the implementation accordingly. This holds true especially for combination checks because in those checks, it's clear where and in which combinations the variables are used.

▶ It's clear who must be informed about changes to the exit.

If you use the example described in Listing 5.2 for implementing the variable exit, you'll probably ask yourself how you can implement the function module Z_VAR_CHECK_VALIDITY to meet these requirements. At this point, you can call a central function module and a function module for each project to carry out the validation. This way, you can make sure that each project can validate its own variables so that identical validations don't need to be implemented several times. On the other hand, if you do implement the identical validations, you can transport the validations separately.

In general, you must distinguish between two different cases:

▶ You can validate individual variables. The variant should not be query-dependent.

▶ You can validate combinations of variables. The second variant is often query-dependent because you can't be sure that other queries don't use the same variables.

5.1.6 Validating an Individual Variable

The validation of an individual variable is relatively simple. Step 3 of the variable exit determines the variable input and checks if the value entered by the user is permitted.

Probably the most frequent use you'll find in practice is the validation of time entries. In this context, the check must determine whether specific intervals must have a minimum or maximum size or whether specific reports can be executed only once per quarter.

Example 6: Specifying a Quarter

A quarterly report is defined in an InfoProvider that contains the InfoObjects OFISCPER and OFISCPER3 as its only time characteristics. Because certain postings are only made at the end of the quarter, the report would provide incorrect results if it wasn't run at the end of the quarter. For this reason, we define a variable, FP_QUART, this is supposed to output an error if the user enters a value other than 3, 6, 9, or 12 for the period. Listing 5.8 describes the implementation.

```
DATA: l_s_var_range LIKE rrrangeexit.
READ TABLE i_t_var_range
     INTO l_s_var_range
     WITH KEY vnam = 'FP_QUART'.
IF sy-subrc = 0.
  IF ( l_s_var_range-low = '003' ) OR
     ( l_s_var_range-low = '006' ) OR
     ( l_s_var_range-low = '009' ) OR
     ( l_s_var_range-low = '012' ).
*    Everything OK, don't do anything
  ELSE.
*   The actual exception can be freely selected here.
    RAISE wrong_entry.
  ENDIF.
ELSE.
* If variable does not exist, do not perform any action
ENDIF.
```

Listing 5.8 Sample Validation of a Variable

At this point, you can see that the validation you want to implement should be error-tolerant. Each line you implement here is run through for all queries irrespective of the variables that are actually used in the query, provided that at least one variable is used. For this reason, you shouldn't constantly output error messages but only react if you're sure the overall combination is wrong.

You can't easily check if the query contains certain characteristics. You obtain the name of the query, but the exit doesn't contain any definition. So, it's usually impossible to check at this point whether a variable was used for a specific characteristic or if the characteristic exists without any constraint in the query.

5.1.7 Checking Characteristic Combinations in Step 3

The validation of multiple variables in the exit is a much more specific case. The reasons for a combination check are often as specific as the algorithms those checks are based on. Examples are characteristic values that are only valid in specific periods or variable inputs for compounded characteristics.

A frequent scenario is the validation of time intervals if those aren't entered as intervals but as individual variables. This scenario is described in the following example.

Example 7: Validating Period Entries

In the following example, four variables are queried: two for "Period from and to," and two for "Fiscal year from and to." The exit checks whether "Fiscal year from" is smaller than "Fiscal year to" or if "Fiscal year from" and "Fiscal year to" are equal, and if "Period from" is smaller than or equal to "Period to." This is implemented as shown in Listing 5.9.

```
DATA: l_s_var_range TYPE rrrangeexit,
      l_d_year_from TYPE /bi0/oifiscyear,
      l_d_year_to   TYPE /bi0/oifiscyear,
      l_d_per3_from TYPE /bi0/oifiscper3,
      l_d_per3_to   TYPE /bi0/oifiscper3.
IF i_step = 3.
  READ TABLE i_t_var_range INTO l_s_var_range
      WITH KEY vnam = 'YEARFROM'.
  IF sy-subrc = 0.
    l_d_year_from = l_s_var_range-low(4).
  ELSE.
*   If the variable does not exist, the value is set to
*   0000 to make the final validation always valid.
    l_d_year_from = '0000'.
  ENDIF.
  READ TABLE i_t_var_range INTO l_s_var_range
      WITH KEY vnam = 'YEARTO'.
  IF sy-subrc = 0.
    l_d_year_to   = l_s_var_range-low(4).
  ELSE.
*   If the variable does not exist, the value is set to
*   9999 to make the final validation always valid.
    l_d_year_to   = '9999'.
```

```
ENDIF.
READ TABLE i_t_var_range INTO l_s_var_range
    WITH KEY vnam = 'PER3FROM'.
IF sy-subrc = 0.
  l_d_per3_from = l_s_var_range-low(4).
ELSE.
*   If the variable does not exist, the value is set to 000
*   to make the final validation always valid.
  l_d_per3_from = '000'.
ENDIF.
READ TABLE i_t_var_range INTO l_s_var_range
    WITH KEY vnam = 'PER3TO'.
IF sy-subrc = 0.
  l_d_year_from = l_s_var_range-low(4).
ELSE.
*   If the variable does not exist, the value is set to 999
*   to make the final validation always valid.
  l_d_year_from = '999'.
ENDIF.
IF l_d_year_from > l_d_year_to.
  RAISE wrong_value.
ELSEIF l_d_year_from = l_d_year_to.
  IF l_d_per3_from > l_d_per3_to.
    RAISE wrong_value.
  ENDIF.
ENDIF.
ENDIF.
```

Listing 5.9 Sample Validation of Characteristic Combinations

The example in Listing 5.9 shows how conscientiously you must make sure that an error message is only returned if an error really occurs. Here, the validation check is only carried out if the query uses all four variables. Otherwise, the setting of default values makes sure that the lower IF queries never cause an error.

You can also see the problems involved in those queries. If only one query developer uses the variables YEARFROM, PER3FROM, and PER3TO and expects that the system will automatically check whether PER3FROM is smaller than or equal to PER3TO, the developer will see that this isn't the case.

For this reason, you must either modify the query in such a way that different conditions are validated depending on the variables being used, or you must limit the query to specific queries. To do that, you must query the field, I_S_RKB1D-COMPID. The disadvantage of this variant is that new queries must be released via a corresponding specific customizing for the validation to work properly.

Note: Returning Error Messages

The validation types described previously all work, but they have one essential drawback: The user receives only a vague error message saying that the values of the variables are invalid. However, the user doesn't obtain any information on those variables that actually caused the error. This is why, if possible, you should store a corresponding message in the message collector in addition to the actual **RAISE EXCEPTION** statement.

The exit can't return error messages by itself because this would be possible in data staging. Nor is it possible to use a MESSAGE...RAISING... call to return an adequate message because that message would simply be ignored. For this reason, you must use the same message collector used by the OLAP processor: the function module RRMS_MESSAGE_HANDLING. This function module contains the typical interface for a message collector (see Listing 5.10).

```
FUNCTION rrms_message_handling.
*"----------------------------------------
*"*"Local interface:
*"  IMPORTING
*"     VALUE(I_CLASS)  LIKE  SMESG-ARBGB
*"                     DEFAULT 'BRAIN'
*"     VALUE(I_TYPE)   LIKE  SMESG-MSGTY
*"                     DEFAULT 'S'
*"     VALUE(I_NUMBER) LIKE  SMESG-TXTNR
*"                     DEFAULT '000'
*"     VALUE(I_MSGV1)  OPTIONAL
*"     VALUE(I_MSGV2)  OPTIONAL
*"     VALUE(I_MSGV3)  OPTIONAL
*"     VALUE(I_MSGV4)  OPTIONAL
*"     VALUE(I_INTERRUPT_SEVERITY)
*"        LIKE SY-SUBRC DEFAULT 16
*"     VALUE(I_LANGU)  LIKE SY-LANGU
*"                     DEFAULT SY-LANGU
*"     VALUE(I_SAPGUI_FLAG) DEFAULT SPACE
*"     VALUE(I_SUPPRMESS)
*"        TYPE RSRSUPPRMESS OPTIONAL
*"  EXCEPTIONS
*"     DUMMY
```

Listing 5.10 Interface of Function Module RRMS_MESSAGE_HANDLING

If you want to output only plain text, you can use message 000 of message class RSBBS. However, if possible, you should create your own messages in Transaction SE91 to be able to specify a long text.

If you use this function module, the final part of the example in Listing 5.9 can then be implemented as shown in Listing 5.11.

```
IF l_d_year_from > l_d_year_to.
  CALL FUNCTION 'RRMS_MESSAGE_HANDLING'
    EXPORTING
      I_CLASS  = 'RSBBS'
      I_TYPE   = 'I'
      I_NUMBER = '000'
      I_MSGV1  = 'Year from bigger than year to'.
  RAISE WRONG_VALUE.
ELSEIF l_d_year_from = l_d_year_to.
  IF l_d_per3_from > l_d_per3_to.
  CALL FUNCTION 'RRMS_MESSAGE_HANDLING'
    EXPORTING
      I_CLASS  = 'RSBBS'
      I_TYPE   = 'I'
      I_NUMBER = '000'
      I_MSGV1  = 'Month from bigger than month to'.
    RAISE WRONG_VALUE.
  ENDIF.
ENDIF.
```

Listing 5.11 Example of Using Messages

Of course, you can also use the function module RRMS_MESSAGE_HANDLING to return messages in the other steps of the exit.

5.2   Virtual Key Figures and Characteristics

Another exit frequently used in SAP NetWeaver BI is the exit for virtual key figures and characteristics. Virtual key figures and characteristics are InfoObjects that are contained in the InfoProvider, but whose values aren't read from the InfoProvider. Instead, the values are determined at the time the query is run. There are many reasons for this; the most frequent are the following:

▶ You want to carry out calculations that are too complex for query formulas and for which you don't have all necessary information available at the time of loading.

153

▶ You want to integrate data from several InfoProviders, but the results provided by the MultiProvider are insufficient.

▶ You must carry out calculations at a level that is more detailed than the query. This happens, for example, if costs are calculated as a product of quantity and price at purchase-order level, while the query presents the results at sales department level.

▶ You want to carry out complex calculations based on user input.

▶ You want to display specific values based on the time the query is executed or hide those values (during the quiet period).

In all those cases, you'll have to use virtual key figures and characteristics.

5.2.1 Advantages and Disadvantages

The advantage of virtual key figures and characteristics is that they make reporting much more flexible. The ability to generate values at the time a query is run provides simple solutions to various problems that otherwise would have to be calculated manually.

However, this method also has one drawback: Each calculation that's carried out at this point affects the performance during the query execution. For this reason, you must consider two factors: First, you should try and avoid any kind of database access. Second, the exit enables you to read additional characteristics from the database. This means that existing queries no longer access existing aggregates.

This can have a substantial impact, particularly because the exit is called once per data record, and the data record in turn is read from the database. If the records are read from an aggregate, the number of records read from the database is significantly smaller. For this reason, it's important to always test the exit by using (almost) live data, particularly with regard to the number of data records when you use virtual key figures and characteristics.

> **Example: Testing the Use of Virtual Key Figures**
>
> In a customer system, the exit for virtual key figures was run in a test system with approximately 500 data records without any error and then transported into the live system. When the respective report was called in the live system, it took two hours before the report returned the required data. In this case, the data was wrong because not all combinations were tested in the test system.

5.2.2   Implementation

Those of you who have experience with virtual key figures and characteristics may remember the user exit RSR00002, which allowed you to implement virtual InfoObjects. This user exit was very difficult to implement because it required the creation of specific form routines with fixed naming conventions in certain includes. Consequently, it was as easy to make mistakes as it was difficult to find those mistakes.

This is why we want to focus on describing how to implement virtual key figures and characteristics using the BAdI RSR_OLAP_BADI. Compared to the old implementation, this BAdI has the following three advantages.

▶ You can create different implementations that can even be restricted to different InfoProviders.

▶ You only need to implement two methods. A relatively simple pattern is available for both of these. This pattern facilitates the implementation. A third method that is available in the BAdI can be copied unmodified from the sample implementation.

▶ There are no large confusing includes.

These three factors make it easier to implement virtual key figures and characteristics in such a way that after you have implemented the BAdI once or twice, you'll be able to quickly create more.

The following describes an example in which you would want to implement the display of customer contacts. An InfoProvider contains purchase orders that include customer numbers and sales offices. A DataStore object, CCONTACT, (current contact) contains one contact (CONTACT) per sales office (SALESOFF) and customer number (0CUSTOMER). The sales office and customer number aren't compounded. You want to create a report that displays the current contact depending on the sales office. To do that, the DataStore must be read at report runtime because it's impossible to reload the complete purchase order InfoProvider if the contacts change.

Step 1: Creating the BAdI Implementation

1. Call Transaction SE19 to create a BAdI implementation. This transaction was completely revised for Release SAP NetWeaver 7.0.

2. In SAP NetWeaver 7.0, go to the Create Implementation section, and choose the Classic BAdI radio button (see Figure 5.1).

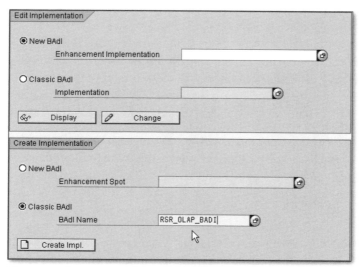

Figure 5.1 Creating a BAdI in SAP NetWeaver 7.0

3. Enter the name of the BAdI definition. For virtual key figures and characteristics, that's RSR_OLAP_BADI. Click on the CREATE IMPL. button.

4. Use a corresponding name in the dialog box that follows, for example, ZANPART (see Figure 5.2).

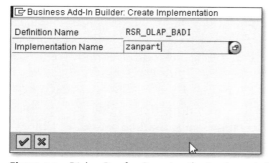

Figure 5.2 Dialog Box for Querying the Implementation

5. In SAP BW up to Release 3.5, the transaction looks as shown in Figure 5.3 where you first enter the name of the implementation and then click on the CREATE button.

6. The dialog box that follows prompts you for the BAdI definition. The BAdI definition for virtual key figures and characteristics is called RSR_OLAP_BADI.

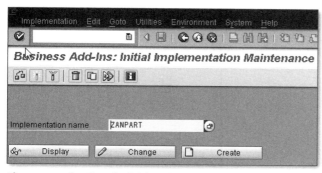

Figure 5.3 Creating the BAdI in SAP BW 3.x

7. After you have confirmed your entry by pressing the ENTER key, the attributes of the BAdI implementation are displayed. Assign an IMPLEMENTATION SHORT TEXT, and select in the lower part of the screen the InfoProvider for which you want to create the implementation. Masked entries are also allowed. In our example, the InfoProvider is called ORDER (see Figure 5.4).

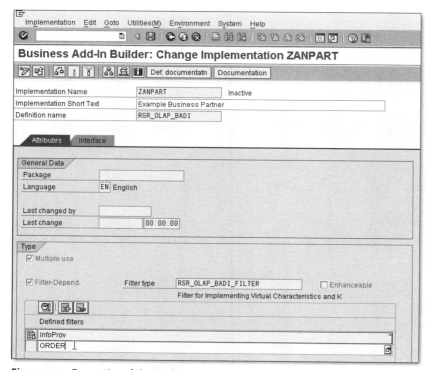

Figure 5.4 Properties of the BAdI

8. Then, save the BAdI implementation prior to copying the sample code provided by SAP via GOTO • SAMPLE CODING • COPY. This step is important because the sample code contains the complete INITIALIZATION method, which means you don't need to change that.

9. Go to the INTERFACE tab (see Figure 5.5), and you'll see that the BAdI contains three methods for implementation: DEFINE, INITIALIZATION, and COMPUTE. You will soon realize, though, that you only need to implement the first and the last one.

Moreover, at this point, you can still change the name of the class to be implemented. But you should only do that in exceptional cases. The class name suggested by the system can be clearly derived from the name of the implementation so that the class name clearly indicates that the implementation is a BAdI implementation.

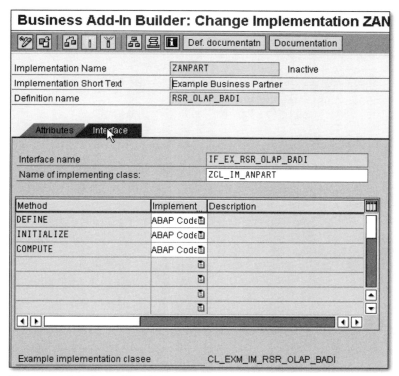

Figure 5.5 Interface of the BAdI

Step 2: Implementing the DEFINE Method

In the next step, you implement the DEFINE method. The DEFINE method is called at the time the query is generated, and it tells the system which characteristics and key figures are virtual and which ones are required for calculating the virtual characteristics.

The method contains the interface shown in Table 5.2.

Type	Parameter	Type	Description
I	FLT_VAL	RSR_OLAP_ BADI_FLT	FLT_VAL specifies the filter that is defined in the interface.
I	I_S_RKB1D	RSR_S_RKB1D	I_S_RKB1D is the same parameter that is also used in the interface for user exit EXIT_SAPLRRS0_001. It contains information on the query being used, particularly on the InfoProvider that is used.
I	I_TH_ CHANM_ USED	RRKE_TH_CHANM	I_TH_CHANM_USED contains all characteristics used in the query. Characteristics that don't exist in the query don't need to be calculated.
I	I_TH_ KYFNM_ USED	RRKE_TH_KYFNM	I_TH_KYFNM_USED contains all key figures used in the query. This is important in ensuring that key figures that don't exist in the query don't need to be calculated.
C	C_T_CHANM	RRKE_T_CHANM	C_T_CHANM and C_T_KYFNM must be filled in the method. That's where the characteristics and key figures are included that are to be filled and are required as a precondition. In addition to the InfoObject, C_T_CHANM contains the read mode in the MODE field. This field has two values: RRKE_C_MODE- READ makes sure the InfoObject is read from the database, while RRKE_C_ MODE-NO_SELECTION makes sure that the InfoObject isn't read from the database and that it can be filled in the COMPUTE method instead.
C	C_T_KYFNM	RSD_T_KYFNM	

Table 5.2 Signature of the DEFINE Method

Type	Parameter	Type	Description
X	CX_RS_ ERROR		In case of a severe error, the exception CX_RS_ERROR can be triggered.

I = Importing, E = Exporting, C = Changing, X = Exception

Table 5.2 Signature of the DEFINE Method (Cont.)

1. Double-click on the method name DEFINE to go to the ABAP Editor where you want to implement the method. For this example, you should enter the code shown in Listing 5.12.

```
METHOD IF_EX_RSR_OLAP_BADI~DEFINE .
  DATA: l_s_chanm        TYPE rrke_s_chanm,
        l_s_chanm_used TYPE rschanm,
        l_kyfnm          TYPE rsd_kyfnm.
  CASE i_s_rkb1d-infocube.
    WHEN ,ORDER'.
      LOOP AT i_th_chanm_used INTO l_s_chanm_used.
        CASE l_s_chanm_used.
*           Here the required InfoObjects are queried.
          WHEN ,CONTACT'.
            l_s_chanm-chanm = ,CONTACT'.
            l_s_chanm-mode  = rrke_c_mode-no_selection.
            APPEND l_s_chanm TO c_t_chanm.
            l_s_chanm-chanm = ,SALESOFF'.
            l_s_chanm-mode  = rrke_c_mode-read.
            APPEND l_s_chanm TO c_t_chanm.
            l_s_chanm-chanm = ,OCUSTOMER'.
            l_s_chanm-mode  = rrke_c_mode-read.
            APPEND l_s_chanm TO c_t_chanm.
        ENDCASE.
      ENDLOOP.
*     LOOP AT i_t_kyfnm_used into l_kyfnm.
*       CASE l_kyfnm.
*         WHEN ,...'.
*           APPEND l_kyfnm TO c_t_kyfnm.
*       ENDCASE.
*     ENDLOOP.
  ENDCASE.
```

Listing 5.12 Implementing the DEFINE Method

It usually makes sense to have the DEFINE method begin with a CASE query on InfoProvider I_S_RKB1D-INFOCUBE, even though you can only use one InfoProvider. If you do that, you can already see in the code which InfoProvider the definition runs on.

2. Then the required characteristics must be inserted in table C_T_CHANM. A decisive factor regarding functionality is the read mode, L_S_CHANM-MODE.

Two read modes are available:

▶ RRKE_C_MODE-READ reads the characteristic from the database in any case, even if it isn't used in the query. For this reason, you may no longer be able to use existing aggregates.

▶ RRKE_C_MODE-NO_SELECTION doesn't read the characteristic from the database. Instead, it marks the characteristic as being virtual. This means it can be modified in the BAdI.

3. If the contact is contained in the query, the sales office and the customer number must also be read so that the contact can be derived. So the query only uses aggregates that contain SALESOFF and OCUSTOMER. After that, the key figures follow. The key figures don't require a read mode.

4. Finally, you must save and activate the method.

Step 3: Creating the Instance Attributes

> **Note**
>
> At this point, it's inevitable that you will take a quick look at object-oriented programming, because you will have to create attributes for a class. But we'll focus only on the required technique without going into the theoretical details. You should simply regard the instance attributes as a kind of global variable.

1. If you double-click on the INITIALIZATION method to take a look at it, you can see a complete implementation that doesn't need to be changed. This method is used to facilitate the implementation of the COMPUTE method. However, you must first do some preparatory work to get there.

2. Double-click on the name of the implementing class in the INTERFACE tab of the BAdI to go to the class definition (see Figure 5.5). Then select the ATTRIBUTES tab (see Figure 5.6).

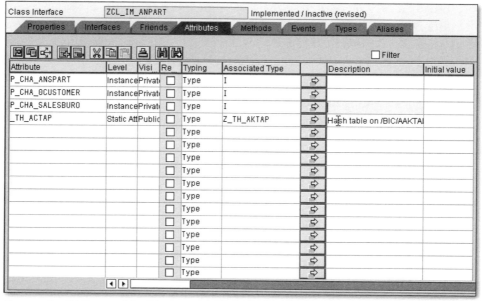

Figure 5.6 Attributes of the ZCL_IM_CONTACT Class

3. Now you must include an attribute for each InfoObject that you inserted into the C_T_CHANM and C_T_KFNM tables in the DEFINE method. For characteristics, this attribute is called P_CHA_<InfoObject>; for key figures, P_KYF_<InfoObject>. All attributes are instance attributes that have the visibility PUBLIC of type I.

For this case, you must create three public instance attributes: P_CHA_CONTACT, P_CHA_OCUSTOMER, and P_CHA_SALESOFF. These attributes are necessary because the structure that is transferred to the COMPUTE method doesn't contain any typical field names such as /BIC/CONTACT. Instead, it contains field names such as K_022.

To access the correct fields, the INITIALIZATION method fills the attributes as follows. If the InfoObject is contained in the query, the attribute P_CHA_<InfoObject> is assigned a value greater than 0. This value indicates the position of the InfoObject within the structure. If the InfoObject isn't contained in the query, the value is 0. These attributes are used in the COMPUTE method to access the appropriate field via an ASSIGN COMPONENT.

4. In addition, you need another attribute that buffers the data of the DataStore object. For this purpose, you need a Z_TH_CCONTACT table type that references a hashed table with the structure /BIC/ACCONTACT00.

5. Create a static attribute, _TH_CCONTACT, that has the corresponding table type. The result is displayed in Figure 5.6.

Step 4: Implementing the COMPUTE Method

Now you can implement the COMPUTE method:

1. Double-click on the method name COMPUTE in the INTERFACE tab of the BAdI implementation to go to the implementation of the method that contains the interface from Table 5.3.

Type	Parameter	Type	Description
I	FLT_VAL	RSR_OLAP_BADI_FILTER	FLT_VAL specifies the filter that is stored in the BAdI.
I	I_PARTCUBE	RSD_INFOCUBE	I_PARTCUBE specifies the subprovider of a MultiProvider from which the current data record originates.
I	I_S_RKB1D	RSR_S_RKB1D	I_S_RKB1D is the same parameter that is also used in the interface for user exit EXIT_SAPLRRS0_001. It contains information on the query being used, particularly on the InfoProvider that is used.
I	I_NCUM	RS_BOOL	I_NCUM specifies whether the InfoProvider contains inventory values.
C	C_S_DATA	ANY	C_S_DATA is the structure that contains the values from the database in the structure that's necessary for the query. This structure also contains the fields that were included in the C_T_CHANM and C_T_KYFNM tables in the DEFINE method. However, the field names don't correspond to the usual field names in database tables.

I = Importing, C = Changing

Table 5.3 Signature of the COMPUTE Method

2. In this method, you will implement the actual calculation of the virtual characteristics. The implementation of the method consists of two parts. The first part is basically standardized and is used to assign input and output values to field symbols. The second part contains the actual calculation. Initially, take a look at the first part (see Listing 5.13).

```
METHOD IF_EX_RSR_OLAP_BADI~COMPUTE .
FIELD-SYMBOLS: <l_contact>  TYPE /bic/oicontact,
               <l_customer> TYPE /bi0/oicustomer,
               <l_salesoff>   TYPE /bic/oisalesoff.
* Assign field symbols using instance attributes
  IF p_cha_contact > 0.
     ASSIGN COMPONENT p_cha_contact
       OF STRUCTURE c_s_data
       TO <l_contact>.
  ELSE.
*    If virtual characteristic does not exist, exit routine
     EXIT.
  ENDIF.
  IF p_cha_customer > 0.
     ASSIGN COMPONENT p_cha_customer
       OF STRUCTURE c_s_data
       TO <l_customer>.
  ELSE.
*    If source characteristic does not exist, initialize
*    CONTACT and exit routine
     CLEAR <l_contact>.
     EXIT.
  ENDIF.
  IF p_cha_salesoff > 0.
     ASSIGN COMPONENT p_cha_salesoff
       OF STRUCTURE c_s_data
       TO <l_salesoff>.
  ELSE.
*    If source characteristic does not exist, initialize
*    CONTACT and exit routine
     CLEAR <l_contact>.
     EXIT.
  ENDIF.
```

Listing 5.13 First Part of the Implementation of the COMPUTE Method

The decisive command is always ASSIGN COMPONENT p.... This command must be entered for each InfoObject that is required for the calculation. Because the exit is usually executed for each query on the InfoProvider, you must always be able to react to the fact that certain InfoObjects aren't contained in the query; sometimes you may even skip the entire calculation.

3. After all field symbols have been assigned in this way, the actual calculation can begin (see Listing 5.14).

```
IF _th_contact[] IS INITIAL.
  SELECT * FROM /bic/accontact00
    INTO TABLE _th_ccontact.
ENDIF.
DATA: l_s_ccontact TYPE /bic/acontact00.
READ TABLE _th_ccontact INTO l_s_ccontact
  WITH TABLE KEY
    customer     = <l_customer>
    /bic/salesoff = <l_salesoff>.
IF sy-subrc = 0.
  <l_contact> = l_s_ccontact-/bic/contact.
ELSE.
* No records exists, hence empty return value
  CLEAR <l_contact>.
ENDIF.
```

Listing 5.14 Second Part of the Implementation of the COMPUTE Method

If necessary, the contents of the DataStore are read first. Usually this would be done in a CONSTRUCTOR method. However, we do that here to keep the example simple. After the field symbols have been assigned, the table entry can be read.

Here it's important that you keep the logic as efficient as possible. The ASSIGN calls per data record are already time-consuming enough. For this reason, you should use hashed tables whenever possible, fill these tables in the CONSTRUCTOR, and implement as few database accesses as possible. For the database selection in the CONSTRUCTOR, you must make sure that all SELECT calls in the CONSTRUC-TOR are executed even when the table isn't needed in the COMPUTE method; if, for instance, the virtual characteristic isn't used at all in the query. Otherwise, the performance of those queries would be affected without any reason. Large loops usually also have a negative influence on the query performance, but they are only rarely used because the COMPUTE method only processes individual records.

5.2.3 Other Useful Information

The procedure described in the preceding example is typical of a BAdI implementation. However, you must take some things into account for more complex applications.

▶ First of all, you can't make any statement on the sequence in which the data records arrive. For example, if you try to determine the material range of coverage by first entering the inventory and then running the open orders against the inventory in the exit, you will be faced with the problem that the orders will probably not be received in the correct time sequence.

▶ Because only individual processing is possible, dependencies between individual records can't be evaluated. So standard deviations and variations can't be calculated in this BAdI.

▶ Moreover, you can't create or insert any additional records in this BAdI. If not all characteristic combinations are available in the InfoProvider, you can't generate any additional ones.

▶ In individual cases, the relationship between virtual characteristics and the elimination of intercompany sales can be important. The elimination of intercompany sales doesn't consider the virtual characteristics; the elimination is based on the values that are originally stored in the InfoCube.[4] This fact prevents us from creating some nice solutions that would use the elimination of intercompany sales to adjust the hierarchy aggregation.

5.2.4 Transferring Variable Values to the BAdI

Another option to make the BAdI more flexible is the transfer of variables. For this purpose, a static public attribute is created in the implementing class for each variable to be transferred to the BAdI.

---

4 This observation was made in SAP BW 3.x. We don't know how much this was changed in SAP NetWeaver 7.0 Business Intelligence.

The actual transfer of the variable occurs in Step 3 of exit `EXIT_SAPLRRSO_001`. You can use the code shown in Listing 5.15, and in the BAdI, you can simply access the value `ZCL_IM_CONTACT=>MY_VAR`. If you want to transfer intervals and selection options, the query must be modified accordingly.

```
DATA: l_s_var_range LIKE rrrangeexit.
READ TABLE i_t_var_range
     INTO l_s_var_range
     WITH KEY vnam = 'MY_VAR'.
IF SY-SUBRC = 0.
  zcl_im_anpart=>my_var = l_s_var_range-low.
ENDIF.
```

Listing 5.15 Sample Variable Transfer to a BAdI

Variables can be particularly useful in restricting a possible selection right from the start. Instead of reading the entire contents of a DataStore object, only the required records are read. It can also be useful to transfer formula variables or posting periods to the exit if you want to implement specific nonlinear extrapolations.

The virtual key figures and characteristics represent a very efficient way to extend the reporting functionality. Because you can access variables and also add more database tables to the calculation, you can bypass many restrictions of SAP NetWeaver BI.

However, because the BAdI is called at a sensitive point, namely after the data has been read from the database, the implementation must be very clean to avoid problems in reporting performance.

Furthermore, you must always take into account that the BAdI is called for all queries that run on the corresponding InfoProviders even if the virtual characteristics and key figures aren't used. Here you must ensure that calculations and especially database selections are only carried out if they are really required.

5.3 VirtualProviders

If you still think that the exits discussed so far aren't flexible enough to provide the required results, your last resort is the *VirtualProvider*, or rather the VirtualProvider that's based on a function module (in SAP BW 3.x it was called *RemoteCube with services*). By definition, a VirtualProvider is an InfoProvider that doesn't store the data by itself but reads the data from other data sources that aren't InfoProviders (as opposed to MultiProviders). In this context, three DataSources are relevant:

▶ The data is read from a DataSource (e.g., directly from the source system).

▶ The data is read from a table using a BAPI.

▶ The data is calculated using a function module.

The third method, in particular, provides a lot of options for designing the report, but its implementation is rather complex and exceeds the scope of this book. The following sections describe how you can create a VirtualProvider and which interfaces you must implement; however, we won't provide any extensive sample implementations.

Example: Avoiding Rounding Differences

If, in an annual report, certain overview reports are presented in terms of thousands, rounding differences are very likely to occur (e.g., $500,000 + $500,000 = $1,000,000 would be represented as 1+1=1 in terms of thousands). If you try to round off the results during the loading process, the totals would no longer match. For this reason, you could use a VirtualProvider to read the basic data and convert it to thousands, then aggregate both values on the basis of the transferred variables, calculate the difference, and distribute the difference downward. Some developers prefer to correct the rounding differences manually.

Interestingly, it's much easier to include an additional line for the rounding difference into the program code and show the rounding difference there.

5.3.1 Creating a VirtualProvider

You can create a VirtualProvider via the context menu of an InfoProvider. You have three options for a VirtualProvider (see Figure 5.7).

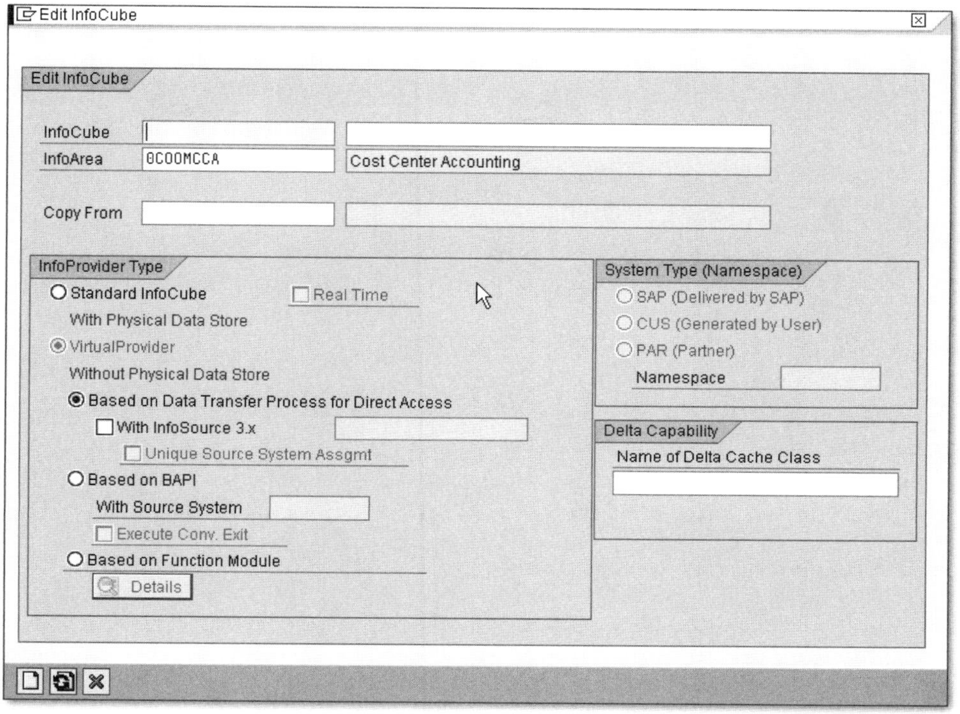

Figure 5.7 Creating a VirtualProvider

From the point of view of an ABAP developer, the most interesting and most flexible VirtualProvider is the one that's BASED ON FUNCTION MODULE. If you select this VirtualProvider and click on the DETAILS button, various control checkboxes are displayed. For the implementation, the check boxes RFC PACKING and SID SUPPORT are of particular importance because the interface of the function module to be implemented changes depending on these switches. The following scenarios are possible.

Case 1: RFC Packing Is Set

If RFC PACKING is set for the VirtualProvider, the interface is structured as shown in Listing 5.16.

```
IMPORTING
  infocube LIKE bapi6200-infocube
  keydate LIKE bapi6200-keydate
```

```
EXPORTING
  return LIKE bapiret2
TABLES
  selection STRUCTURE bapi6200sl
  characteristics STRUCTURE bapi6200fd
  keyfigures STRUCTURE bapi6200fd
  data STRUCTURE bapi6100da
EXCEPTIONS
  communication_failure
  system_failure
```

Listing 5.16 Interface of the VirtualProvider (RFC Packing)

This is the standard case, which should be used whenever possible. The interface is implemented in function module BAPI_INFOCUBE_READ_REMOTE_DATA, which you can use as a template module. It also contains a comprehensive documentation.

Because the parameters can't be derived from the interface without difficulty, we should briefly describe them here.

▶ INFOCUBE is the name of the VirtualProvider.

▶ KEYDATE is the key date on which the query is run and on which the master data should be read. However, you'll see further on that you have to read the navigation attributes by yourself. In doing so, you don't have to adhere to the key date, but you should do this in order not to confuse the reader. You can implement different key dates for different navigation attributes.

▶ RETURN is the standard return structure of each BAPI. You should make sure that the function module to be implemented should behave like a BAPI. In particular, it should not end with an X message, which causes the program to abort. Instead, the function module should always provide a clean return and, if necessary, an abort message. Otherwise, the user will have to wait in front of the Business Explorer (BEx) screen because the system isn't able to detect that the data-retrieval process in SAP NetWeaver BI has terminated.

▶ SELECTION contains the selections that are defined in the query. Variables have already been replaced with input or replacements. The structure of the table is EXPRESSION, INFOOBJECT, SIGN, OPTION, LOW, HIGH.

The most important field here is the EXPRESSION field. If the value of this field is 0, the corresponding restriction is a global filter. If the value isn't 0, the restriction refers to a row, column, or cell reference. This is of decisive importance for data selections that must be implemented. It makes a big difference whether in a query a column is restricted to the country "USA" and the sales channel "Internet," or if a query contains two columns and one of them is restricted to the country "USA" while the other is restricted to the sales channel "Internet."

If several values exist for EXPRESSION, the logic to be implemented requires that all those records from the database are read to which the restriction E0 and at least one of the restrictions E1 through En apply. The documentation for function module BAPI_INFOCUBE_READ_REMOTE_DATA describes this logic in the following way:

```
E0 AND ( E1 OR E2 OR E3 ... OR En )
```

A better way of presenting this logic is to display it as follows:

```
( E0 AND E1 ) OR

( E0 AND E2 ) OR

( E0 AND E3 ) ... OR

( E0 AND En ).
```

This way, you can regard each statement as being a separate line or column of a query.

▶ CHARACTERISTICS and KEYFIGURES are two tables that contain the characteristics and key figures used in the query. Both tables have the same structure: INFOOBJECT, DATATYPE, DECIMALS, SIGN, LENGTH, OFFSET, LOWERCASE. The LENGTH and OFFSET fields are particularly important here. These fields indicate in which position and at what length the InfoObject can be found in the return structure.

As already mentioned, not only are the characteristics transferred in the CHARACTERISTICS table but also the navigation attributes used in the query.

▶ DATA is the table that contains the return values for the OLAP processor. This table only consists of the fields CONTINUATION and DATA. Because it's a BAPI, the length of the DATA field can't be variable; it always consists of 250 characters.

If the return structure contains more than 250 characters, it must be distributed to several rows in the DATA table. To do that, you can use the CONTINUATION field. Each line of a data record except for the last one is assigned the value X in this field. The field remains empty in the last record. So, it must be interpreted as "Data record will continue in the next row."

The class `CL_RSDRV_REMOTE_IPROV_SRV` contains some useful methods and services for implementing this BAPI. This class is predominantly used to implement the BAPI for reading data from a database table.

Case 2: RFC Packing and SID Support Are Not Set

If neither RFC PACKING nor SID SUPPORT is set, the interface is structured as shown in Listing 5.17.

```
IMPORTING
  i_infoprov TYPE rsinfoprov
  i_keydate TYPE rrsrdate
  i_th_sfc TYPE rsdri_th_sfc
  i_th_sfk TYPE rsdri_th_sfk
  i_t_range TYPE rsdri_t_range
  i_tx_rangetab TYPE rsdri_tx_rangetab
  i_first_call TYPE rs_bool
  i_packagesize TYPE i
EXPORTING
  e_t_data TYPE standard table
  e_end_of_data TYPE rs_bool
  e_t_msg TYPE rs_t_msg
```

Listing 5.17 Interface of the VirtualProvider (Neither RFC Packing nor SID Support)

Instead of the BAPI structures, this interface contains the structures that are used internally by SAP NetWeaver BI. Whereas in Case 1, the function module is called only once, the generated function module is called several times in this implementation; that is, it's called until the `E_END_OF_DATA` parameter is set to `RS_TRUE`. For each call, `I_PACKAGESIZE` records are expected. However, this default setting comes from system customizing and can be ignored. If many data records must be returned so that the `DATA` table described in Listing 5.16 would significantly affect system performance or cause the main memory to overflow, you should consider implementing the variant described in Listing 5.17.

Case 3: RFC Packing Is Not Set; SID Support Is Set

In all other cases, that is, if RFC PACKING isn't set and SID SUPPORT is set, the variant is referred to as "internal," and it indicates that the interface can be modified without a warning. For this reason, you should use Case 1. For the intrepid ones among you, however, Listing 5.18 contains the interface for Case 3.

```
IMPORTING
  i_infoprov TYPE rsinfoprov
  i_keydate TYPE rrsrdate
  i_th_sfc TYPE rsdd_th_sfc
  i_th_sfk TYPE rsdd_th_sfk
  i_tsx_seldr TYPE rsdd_tsx_seldr
  i_first_call TYPE rs_bool
  i_packagesize TYPE i
EXPORTING
  e_t_data TYPE standard table
  e_end_of_data TYPE rs_bool
  e_t_msg TYPE rs_t_msg
```

Listing 5.18 Interface of the VirtualProvider (RFC Packing Is Not Set, SID Support Is Set)

When implementing this, you should note that SID SUPPORT doesn't mean you will be supported in defining the SIDs, but that in addition to the characteristic values, you must also return the SIDs for the data records. This variant is used internally, for instance, to implement additional logic in SAP SEM-BCS (*Business Consolidation*). For each InfoProvider that stores data, SAP SEM-BCS creates a VirtualProvider in which reporting takes place. This VirtualProvider also uses a corresponding service that reads the InfoProvider and the SIDs at the same time. This means the OLAP processor doesn't need to further determine the SIDs afterward.

5.3.2 Do's and Don'ts for the Implementation of the Service

Similar to the implementation of virtual key figures and characteristics, the implementation of a VirtualProvider is critical because it's called for each query. For this reason, you should absolutely adhere to the following restrictions:

▶ If your DataSource isn't a small table containing some 1,000 data records, you should only read what has been transferred in the query.

▶ You should only read the requested characteristic values and, if possible, have those records aggregated by the database.

▶ Similarly, you should only read the required key figures from the database. Especially when the query is run, every additional byte is inconvenient, particularly if the query is used by many users. Nothing is more annoying in the BI system than having users wait too long for a query to be run. This would immediately decrease the degree of acceptance of the system as a whole.

It's relatively easy to read data from master data tables and DataStore objects, because this data is stored in flat tables, and every developer can implement the SELECT statements by himself regardless of optimization aspects. But what can you do if the data isn't stored in a DataStore object but in an InfoCube?

Here, you have two options. If you don't need the entire InfoCube but only aggregated data that refers to a relatively small number of data records (in SAP NetWeaver BI, this means approximately 100,000 records, depending on the design of the system and the structure of the data), you can create a DataStore object with the required structure, load the data into the DataStore via a data mart interface, and obtain the required aggregation. For this, however, you need additional hard disk space. But why should you store the data once again when it's already stored in a form that's optimized for database access, namely the star schema of the InfoCube? That's why you must find an efficient way to access the contents of the InfoCube.

One option is to use function module RSDRI_INFOPROV_READ. Although this function module has not been officially released by SAP, it has been used successfully in the past, even for larger quantities of data. This function module has several advantages. You can assign the required characteristics and key figures to it, and the function module automatically carries out a data aggregation. Further, it uses the parameters assigned to it to automatically select an aggregate, which it then uses for data selection. It's this feature, in particular, that enables you to build VirtualProviders that access InfoProviders containing millions of data records and still return a query result within a couple of seconds.

The interface of the function module is described in Listing 5.19.

```
FUNCTION rsdri_infoprov_read .
*"----------------------------------------
*"*"Local interface:
*"  IMPORTING
*"     REFERENCE(I_INFOPROV)
*"             TYPE  RSINFOPROV
*"     REFERENCE(I_TH_SFC)
*"             TYPE  RSDRI_TH_SFC
*"     REFERENCE(I_TH_SFK)
*"             TYPE  RSDRI_TH_SFK
*"     REFERENCE(I_T_RANGE)
*"        TYPE  RSDRI_T_RANGE OPTIONAL
*"     REFERENCE(I_TH_TABLESEL)
```

```
*"          TYPE   RSDRI_TH_SELT OPTIONAL
*"      REFERENCE(I_T_RTIME)
*"          TYPE   RSDRI_T_RTIME OPTIONAL
*"      VALUE(I_REFERENCE_DATE)
*"            TYPE   RSDRI_REFDATE
*"            DEFAULT SY-DATUM
*"      VALUE(I_ROLLUP_ONLY)
*"          TYPE   RS_BOOL DEFAULT RS_C_TRUE
*"      REFERENCE(I_T_REQUID)
*"            TYPE   RSDR0_T_REQUID OPTIONAL
*"      VALUE(I_SAVE_IN_TABLE)
*"            TYPE   RSDRI_SAVE_IN_TABLE
*"            DEFAULT SPACE
*"      VALUE(I_TABLENAME)
*"          TYPE   RSDRI_TABLENAME OPTIONAL
*"      VALUE(I_SAVE_IN_FILE)
*"            TYPE   RSDRI_SAVE_IN_FILE
*"            DEFAULT SPACE
*"      VALUE(I_FILENAME)
*"            TYPE   RSDRI_FILENAME OPTIONAL
*"      VALUE(I_PACKAGESIZE)
*"            TYPE   I DEFAULT 1000
*"      VALUE(I_MAXROWS) TYPE   I DEFAULT 0
*"      VALUE(I_AUTHORITY_CHECK)
*"            TYPE   RSDRI_AUTHCHK DEFAULT
*"            DEFAULT RSDRC_C_AUTHCHK-READ
*"      VALUE(I_CURRENCY_CONVERSION)
*"            TYPE   RSDR0_CURR_CONV
*"            DEFAULT 'X'
*"      VALUE(I_USE_DB_AGGREGATION)
*"            TYPE   RS_BOOL
*"            DEFAULT RS_C_TRUE
*"      VALUE(I_USE_AGGREGATES)
*"            TYPE   RS_BOOL
*"            DEFAULT RS_C_TRUE
*"      VALUE(I_READ_ODS_DELTA)
*"          TYPE RSDRI_CHANGELOG_EXTRACTION
*"          DEFAULT   RS_C_FALSE
*"      VALUE(I_CALLER)
*"            TYPE   RSDRS_CALLER
*"            DEFAULT RSDRS_C_CALLER-RSDRI
*"      VALUE(I_DEBUG)
*"            TYPE   RS_BOOL
```

```
*"              DEFAULT RS_C_FALSE
*"        VALUE(I_CLEAR)
*"              TYPE   RS_BOOL
*"              DEFAULT RS_C_FALSE
*"    EXPORTING
*"        REFERENCE(E_T_DATA)
*"                TYPE   STANDARD TABLE
*"        VALUE(E_END_OF_DATA)
*"              TYPE   RS_BOOL
*"        VALUE(E_AGGREGATE)
*"              TYPE   RSINFOCUBE
*"        VALUE(E_SPLIT_OCCURRED)
*"              TYPE   RSDR0_SPLIT_OCCURRED
*"        REFERENCE(E_T_MSG) TYPE   RS_T_MSG
*"    CHANGING
*"        REFERENCE(C_FIRST_CALL)
*"                TYPE   RS_BOOL
*"    EXCEPTIONS
*"        ILLEGAL_INPUT
*"        ILLEGAL_INPUT_SFC
*"        ILLEGAL_INPUT_SFK
*"        ILLEGAL_INPUT_RANGE
*"        ILLEGAL_INPUT_TABLESEL
*"        NO_AUTHORIZATION
*"        ILLEGAL_DOWNLOAD
*"        ILLEGAL_TABLENAME
*"        TRANS_NO_WRITE_MODE
*"        INHERITED_ERROR
*"        X_MESSAGE
```

Listing 5.19 Interface of Function Module RSDRI_INFOPROV_READ

At first glance, this table appears shocking. What is important in this function module is the IMPORTING parameter I_INFOPROV that contains the name of the Info-Provider plus I_TH_SFC and I_TH_SFK. Those two tables contain the characteristics (I_TH_SFC) and key figures (I_TH_SFK) that are to be read from the InfoProvider. Most of the other parameters are self-explanatory and can be ignored. It's also advisable to set a breakpoint in the function module and to call Transaction LIST-CUBE. Overall, the function module is very powerful; just try it yourself.

If you want to use the function module in the VirtualProvider, you will certainly receive an error message first telling you that the function module must not be called recursively. The reason for this is that the same function module is used to read data from the VirtualProvider. In that case, you should create an RFC-enabled function module that wraps the part of the interface you need. After that, you can call the newly created function module via RFC.

Nevertheless, it's clearly preferable that your users are flexible enough to avoid using VirtualProviders with services. Usually these InfoProviders require more maintenance work, and it's more time-consuming to extend queries than to use normal InfoCubes or MultiProviders. If possible, you should always try to convince your customer of a solution that meets his requirements by using virtual key figures and characteristics. Always remember that it's possible to carry out some of the calculations in a Microsoft Excel worksheet.

5.4 BAdI SMOD_RSR00004

Finally, let's take a look at BAdI SMOD_RSR00004, which originated from user exit RSR00004 and was automatically migrated from it. This BAdI is called in the report-report interface, where it's used to carry out automatic adjustments. You can use this function, for example, to modify an InfoObject.

For instance, if you display those cost centers in a report that services a specific purchase order, and if you want to display a cost report for the cost center, the cost center will be contained in InfoObject 0PCOST_CTR (Partner Cost Center) in the first report. In the second report, it will be located in InfoObject 0COSTCENTER. This kind of mapping can't be stored as such in the report-report interface. For this reason, you can use the BAdI at this point to carry out the jump anyway. Jumps from a current monthly report to a report that shows the cumulative values from the beginning of the year require this BAdI.

The BAdI contains two methods: EXIT_SAPLRSBBS_001 and EXIT_SAPLRSBBS_002. Both methods can be used to individually customize the field mapping, which is defined in Transaction RSBBS in the report-report interface. The only difference between them is the point in time at which the jump is called. The EXIT_SAPLRS-BBS_001 method is called for normal jumps within SAP NetWeaver BI, whereas the EXIT_SAPLRSBBS_002 method is used for jumps within SAP ERP.

The EXIT_SAPLRSBBS_001 method has the signature shown in Table 5.4. The table contains several old friends of ours such as the fiscal year variant I_PERIV, the query information for sender and recipient, `I_S_RKB1D_SENDER` and `I_S_RKB1D`, and the structure `E_S_RETURN` that is used to return status information.

Type	Parameter	Type
I	I_PERIV	RRO01_S_RKB1F-PERIV
I	I_S_RKB1D	RSR_S_RKB1D
I	I_S_RKB1D_SENDER	RSR_S_RKB1D
I	I_THX_RECEIVER	RSBBS_THX_MAPPING
I	I_THX_SENDER	RSBBS_THX_MAPPING
E	E_S_RETURN	BAPIRET2
E	E_THX_MAPPING	RSBBS_THX_MAP_BY_EXIT
I = Importing, E = Exporting		

Table 5.4 Signature of Method EXIT_SAPLRSBBS_001

However, the most important tables are `I_THX_RECEIVER` and `I_THX_SENDER`, which contain the mapping from the definition of the report-report interface and `E_THX_MAPPING` that is supposed to contain the new mapping.

As an example, we now want to implement the jump from a profitability data report (`SALES_COPA`) into a report that contains the corresponding sales orders (`SALESORDERS`). We want to map the posting periods (`0FISCPER`) to the corresponding calendar days (`0CALDAY`). This method then appears as shown in Listing 5.20.

```
METHOD IF_EX_SMOD_RSR00004~EXIT_SAPLRSBBS_001 .
DATA: l_s_thx_sender
      TYPE LINE OF rsbbs_thx_mapping,
      l_s_thx_mapping TYPE LINE OF rsbbs_thx_map_by_exit,
      l_s_range       TYPE rrrangesid,
      l_d_year        TYPE /bi0/oifiscyear,
      l_d_per3        TYPE /bi0/oifiscper3,
      l_d_date_from   LIKE SY-DATE,
      l_d_date_to     LIKE SY-DATE.
* Check queries
  IF i_s_rkb1d_sender-compid <> 'SALES_COPA'.
    EXIT.
  ENDIF.
  IF i_s_rkb1d-compid <> 'SALESORDERS'.
    EXIT.
```

```
      ENDIF.
* Read period in sender
   READ TABLE i_thx_sender
       INTO l_s_thx_sender
       WITH KEY fieldnm = 'OFISCPER'.
   IF SY-SUBRC <> 0.
*    No period found, hence no restriction
     EXIT.
   ENDIF.
* Start of actual mapping: define InfoObject
* in recipient report
   l_s_thx_mapping-fieldnm_to = 'OCALDAY'.
   l_s_thx_mapping-fieldtp_to = RSBBS_C_FIELDTP-INFOOBJECT.
   l_s_thx_mapping-dtelnm     = '/BI0/OICALDAY'.
   l_s_thx_mapping-domanm     = '/BI0/OCALDAY'.
* Transfer data
   LOOP AT l_s_thx_sender-range
       INTO l_s_range.
     IF l_s_range-opt = 'EQ' OR
        l_s_range-opt = 'NE' OR
        l_s_range-opt = 'LT' OR
        l_s_range-opt = 'LE'.
       l_s_range-high = l_s_range-low.
     ENDIF.
*     Convert periods
     l_d_year = l_s_range-low(4).
     l_d_per3 = l_s_range-low+4(3).
     CALL FUNCTION 'FIRST_DAY_IN_PERIOD_GET'
       EXPORTING
         GJAHR  = l_d_year
         PERIV  = i_periv
         POPER  = l_d_per3
       IMPORTING
         DATUM  = l_d_date_from.
     IF NOT ( l_s_range-high IS INITIAL ).
       l_d_year = l_s_range-high(4).
       l_d_per3 = l_s_range-high+4(3).
       CALL FUNCTION 'FIRST_DAY_IN_PERIOD_GET'
         EXPORTING
           GJAHR  = l_d_year
           PERIV  = i_periv
           POPER  = l_d_per3
         IMPORTING
```

```
              DATE  = l_d_date_to.
      ENDIF.
*     Compose correct interval
      CASE l_s_range-opt.
        WHEN 'EQ' OR 'BT'.
          l_s_range-opt = 'BT'.
          l_s_range-low = l_d_date_from.
          l_s_range-high = l_d_date_to.
        WHEN 'NE' OR 'NB'.
          l_s_range-opt = 'NB'.
          l_s_range-low = l_d_date_from.
          l_s_range-high = l_d_date_to.
        WHEN 'LE' OR 'GT'.
*         <= includes the period, thus last day
*         of period analogous >
          l_s_range-low = l_d_date_to.
        WHEN 'LT' OR 'GE'.
*         < does not include period, thus first day
*         of period analogous >=
          l_s_range-low = l_d_date_from.
      ENDCASE.
      APPEND l_s_range TO l_s_thx_mapping-range.
    ENDLOOP.
    INSERT l_s_thx_mapping INTO TABLE e_thx_mapping.
ENDMETHOD.
```

Listing 5.20   Example of Method EXIT_SAPLRSBBS_001

The interface of the second method is slightly different, but it works similarly to the first one. Table 5.5 contains this interface.

Type	Parameter	Type
I	I_COMPID	RSZCOMPID
I	I_INFOCUBE	RSD_INFOCUBE
I	I_S_RECEIVER	RSTIREC
I	I_THX_MAPPING	RSBBS_THX_MAPPING
E	E_THX_MAPPING	RSBBS_THX_MAP_BY_EXIT
I = Importing, E = Exporting		

Table 5.5   Signature of Method EXIT_SAPLRSBBS_002

Contrary to the first method, the mapping here is only exported on the side of the sender. Instead of the entire query information, only the query name (I_COMPID) and the InfoProvider (I_INFOCUBE) are transferred. The information on the source system is contained in structure I_S_RECEIVER, which contains all necessary information such as the field I_S_RECEIVER-RONAM. This contains a transaction name in case it was selected as a jump target. The actual tables used for the original mapping and the return are identical. This means that the example in Listing 5.20 can be used virtually unmodified for a jump into a source system.

In general, these methods are very useful if you need to resolve specific problems when jumping from one report into another. However, because this subject usually doesn't attract as much attention as it deserves, this BAdI is probably abandoned in most BI systems. Even though the actual implementation isn't difficult, you should nevertheless ask yourself—as you should with all exits—if it's worth the implementation effort and, above all, the future maintenance work.

5.5 Implementing Own Read Routines for Master Data

SAP NetWeaver 7.0 also includes a new exit. You can now store your own master data read routines in InfoObjects. This is useful if you have either a lot of master data for which you want to maintain the changes in texts and attributes per upload because this data is already contained in other tables, or because you can read the data from a table, domain, and so on without loading it again. Depending on the user authorizations, you can also display or delete specific attributes.

To implement a master data read routine, you need to enter a master data read class in the InfoObject on the MASTER DATA/TEXTS tab. A master data read class is a class that implements interface IF_RSMD_RS_ACCESS. If interface IF_RSMD_RS_GENERIC is integrated additionally, you can transfer parameters to the master data read class. This is very useful, for example, for the master data read class CL_RSMD_RS_GENERIC_DOMAIN, which is delivered by SAP and which you can use to populate the values and texts of an InfoObject automatically with the fixed values of a domain.

The following sections describe how you can use such a class. For this purpose, you implement a class that reads the master data of the existing InfoObject 0COST-CENTER and hides all cost centers that don't contain 'X' in the attribute IST_HKST. You can then use this class in InfoObject HAUPT_KST, for example, to display only those cost centers in the $\boxed{\text{F4}}$ help during the query execution and creation that are selected as primary cost centers. The benefit of this method is that the data is maintained in duplicate, and you don't require any additional load processes to transfer the data from one InfoObject to the other.

The master data read classes are used at different locations in Release 7.0, in particular to provide master data for InfoObjects that are defined by SAP-specific tables, for example, the master data for the client (0CLIENT) or the fiscal year variant (0FISCVARNT). Moreover, there are numerous InfoObjects that access fixed values of domains or contents of tables via generic master data read classes, for example, 0INM_MFNL or 0RSPL_LOCK. The master data read classes used here, CL_RSMD_RS_GENERIC_DOMAIN or CL_RSMD_RS_GENERIC_TABLE, can also be used for your own InfoObjects, in particular if the contents of the InfoObjects originate from your own tables or other custom developments. You can thus avoid loading data into InfoObjects or double maintenance of data.

5.5.1 Creating a Master Data Read Class

You can create a master data read class in the Object Navigator (Transaction SE80). For this purpose, you need to go to the INTERFACES tab in the class interface and enter interface IF_RSMD_RS_ACCESS in the table. Then, save the class. In the object list, you can now find six methods you can implement (see Table 5.6).

Con. No.	Method	Description
1	CREATE	Static method; returns the reference to the object
2	GET_ATTRIBUTES	Reads the master data attributes
3	GET_CAPABILITIES	Returns information about the texts and time dependencies to be delivered
4	GET_TEXT	Reads texts for master data
5	GET_VALUES	Returns the existing values
6	SET_KEY_DATE	Sets the key data for time-dependent texts and master data

Table 5.6 Methods of Interface IF_RSMD_RS_ACCESS

The following sections describe the individual methods without any examples and then discuss the complete implementation of a class.

Method CREATE

The CREATE method is a static method that is called by the calling program to retrieve a handler to the object. Consequently, the method must generate and return an object of the class. Additionally, you can fill buffer tables if these have not been populated yet. It's usually not necessary to overwrite the standard implementation, which is described in Listing 5.21.

```
METHOD if_rsmd_rs_access~create.
  DATA l_r_rs_bw_spec TYPE REF TO cl_rsmd_rs_bw_spec.
  IF i_clnm IS NOT INITIAL.
    CREATE OBJECT r_r_rs_access TYPE (i_clnm)
      EXPORTING i_chanm = i_chanm
                i_infoprov = i_infoprov
                i_langu = i_langu.
  ELSE.
    CREATE OBJECT l_r_rs_bw_spec
        EXPORTING i_chanm = i_chanm
                  i_infoprov = i_infoprov
                  i_langu = i_langu.
    r_r_rs_access ?= l_r_rs_bw_spec.
  ENDIF.
ENDMETHOD.
```

Listing 5.21 Example of Method IF_RSMD_RS_ACCESS~CREATE

As you can see here, an object of the CL_RSMD_RS_BW_SPEC class is created in case of doubt. This class is delivered by SAP and is used as the standard for all InfoObjects that don't implement their own master data read routines. If required, you can check the implementation of this class to see how the reading from the master data tables is done.

Method SET_KEY_DATE

Method SET_KEY_DATE is called during the execution of a query to transfer the query key date. Here, an instance attribute, P_KEY_DATE, is populated from the called parameter. In principle, a redefinition isn't required; the only exception can be that you want to read different characteristics at different points in time. However, no application is known for which this is required.

Method GET_CAPABILITIES

The only parameter of method GET_CAPABILITIES is a returning parameter R_S_CAPABILITIES. It contains seven individual flags (see Table 5.7) that control the properties of the InfoObject. These must be filled completely.

Name of the Flag	Description	FALSE	TRUE
NOVALFL	Characteristic doesn't contain a check table.	' '	'X'
TXTTABFL	Text table exists.	'0'	'1'
TXTTIMFL	Text table is time-dependent.	'0'	'1'
NOLANGU	Texts are language-independent.	' '	'X'
TXTSHFL	Short text exists.	' '	'X'
TXTMDFL	Medium-length text exists.	' '	'X'
TXTLGFL	Long text exists.	' '	'X'

Table 5.7 Fields of Parameter R_S_CAPABILITIES

For InfoObject 0FISCPER, the method was implemented as shown in Listing 5.22:

```
METHOD IF_RSMD_RS_ACCESS~GET_CAPABILITIES.
  r_s_capabilities-novalfl   = rs_c_false.
  r_s_capabilities-txttabfl  = rsd_c_cnvfl-true.
  r_s_capabilities-txttimfl  = rsd_c_cnvfl-false.
  r_s_capabilities-nolangu   = rs_c_false.
  r_s_capabilities-txtshfl   = rs_c_true.
  r_s_capabilities-txtmdfl   = rs_c_true.
  r_s_capabilities-txtlgfl   = rs_c_false.
ENDMETHOD.
```

Listing 5.22 Example of Method IF_RSMD_RS_ACCESS~GET_CAPABILITIES

You can see the difference between the various flags.

If you don't want to implement the flags directly, you can also fill the corresponding fields from table RSDCHABAS. The implementation could look like the one shown in Listing 5.23.

```
METHOD IF_RSMD_RS_ACCESS~GET_CAPABILITIES.
  SELECT SINGLE * FROM RSDCHABAS
          INTO CORRESPONDING FIEDLS OF r_s_capabilities
          WHERE CHABASNM = 'HAUPT_KST'
          AND    OBJVERS = 'A'.
ENDMETHOD.
```

Listing 5.23 Generic Implementation of Method IF_RSMD_RS_ACCESS~GET_CAPABILITIES

The benefit here is that you can change the individual settings directly in the InfoObject. For this purpose, the following methods must be implemented generically so that the correct values are returned depending on the set switches.

Method GET_VALUES

This is the central method of the interface. In this method, values, texts, and, if necessary, the required attributes are returned. The method's signature is shown in Figure 5.8.

Ty.	Parameter	Type spec.	Description
▶□	I_T_SELOPT	TYPE RSMD_RS_T_SELOPT OPTIONAL	Select options for master data read services
▶□	I_MAXROWS	TYPE INT4 DEFAULT 200	Natural number
▶□	I_T_SORTING	TYPE RSMD_RS_T_SORTING OPTIONAL	Sorting Information for Master Data Read Service
▶□	I_TS_REQ_ATTR	TYPE RSR_TS_IOBJNM OPTIONAL	Table of attributes to be fetched
□▶	E_T_CHAVLINFO	TYPE RSDM_TA_CHAVLINFO	Gives back the chavls and their corresponding text
□▶	E_TX_ATR	TYPE RSDM_TX_ATR	contains the attribute values (optional)
◫	CX_RS_ERROR		BW: General Error Class

Figure 5.8 Signature of Method GET_VALUES

In this method, you must implement three things. First, you must collect all allowed values. For this purpose, SAP usually creates a _VALUES_GENERATE method, which returns the desired values in table E_T_CHAVLINFO. If you implement the class yourself, you should use the same name for the method.

The tables, which must be filled in the method, are an important aspect in the method's interface. E_T_CHAVLINFO contains the characteristic values and the corresponding texts, while E_TX_ATR comprises the corresponding attributes. To maintain performance you should note the following:

▶ Table I_T_SELOPT contains selection options. Only characteristic values meeting the conditions should be returned.

▶ Parameter I_MAXROWS contains the number of values returned. If possible, this number of values should not be exceeded.

▶ Table I_TS_REQ_ATR contains the requested attributes. No additional attributes should be returned.

When the values have been determined, you must enrich them with texts and attributes. To do so, you can call methods GET_ATTRIBUTES and GET_TEXT, which are described in the following. A possible implementation for this is shown in Listing 5.24.

```
METHOD if_rsmd_rs_access~get_values.

* First save the transferred parameters
* to make them available for other methods.
  o_t_selopt         = i_t_selopt.
  o_maxrows          = i_maxrows.
  o_t_sorting        = i_t_sorting.

  TRY.
      CALL METHOD _values_generate
* You must implement this method yourself. You
* must only fill the fields, C_CHAVL and I_READ_MODE.
        IMPORTING
          e_t_chavlinfo = e_t_chavlinfo.
    CATCH cx_rs_error .
      x_message('IF_RSMD_RS_ACCESS~GET_VALUES-01').
  ENDTRY.


**************************************************************
* Now, the texts are read.
**************************************************************

  TRY.
      CALL METHOD if_rsmd_rs_access~get_text
* This method must be implemented/overwritten.
* Create an empty implementation in case of doubt.
        CHANGING
          c_t_chavlinfo = e_t_chavlinfo.
    CATCH cx_rs_error .
      x_message('IF_RSMD_RS_ACCESS~GET_VALUES-02').
  ENDTRY.
```

```
**********************************************************
**   Now, the attributes are read, if they have been
*    requested
**********************************************************

  IF i_ts_req_attr IS NOT INITIAL.
* Have attributes been requested?
    TRY.
        CALL METHOD if_rsmd_rs_access~get_attributes
* This method must be implemented/overwritten.
* Create an empty implementation in case of doubt.
            EXPORTING
              i_ts_req_attr = i_ts_req_attr
              i_t_chavlinfo = e_t_chavlinfo
            RECEIVING
              r_tx_atr      = e_tx_atr.
      CATCH cx_rs_error .
        x_message('IF_RSMD_RS_ACCESS~GET_VALUES-03').
    ENDTRY.
  ENDIF.
ENDMETHOD.
```

Listing 5.24 Example of Method IF_RSMD_RS_ACCESS~GET_VALUES

Method GET_TEXT

In method GET_TEXT, you must enrich the characteristic attributes provided in the table with corresponding texts. Hence, the signature of this method is simple (see Figure 5.9).

Ty.	Parameter	Type spec.	Description
▶□▶	C_T_CHAVLINFO	TYPE RSDM_TA_CHAVLINFO	This will return the text of the Chavls
⚷	CX_RS_ERROR		BW: General Error Class

Figure 5.9 Signature of Method GET_TEXT

The only parameter of this method is table C_T_CHAVLINFO. This table contains all characteristic values, texts, and other information. The corresponding structure is shown in Table 5.8.

Con. No.	Field Name	Type	Description
1	I_SID	RSD_SID	SID of the characteristic value
2	C_CHAVL	RSD_CHAVL	Characteristic value
3	C_NIOBJNM	RSD_IOBJNM	Name of the InfoObject
4	C_HIEID	RSHIEID	Hierarchy ID
5	I_TABIX	I	Row index
6	E_EXIST	RS_BOOL	Indicates whether value exists.
7	E_CHATEXTS	RS_S_TXTSML	Short, medium, or long text
8	C_RC	SYSUBRC	Return value
9	I_READ_MODE	RSDM_READ_MODE	Read mode

Table 5.8 Fields of Table C_T_CHAVLINFO

In method GET_TEXT, it's important to fill structure E_CHATEXTS with the fields TXTSH (short text), TXTMD (medium-length text), and TXTLG (long text). You must fill the fields that were indicated in method GET_CAPABILITIES.

Method GET_ATTRIBUTES

Method GET_ATTRIBUTES fills table R_TX_ATTR. This table is supposed to contain the corresponding attributes for each characteristic value that is transferred in table I_T_CHAVLINFO. The requested attributes are transferred to the method in table I_TS_REQ_ATTR. The method's signature is shown in Figure 5.10.

Ty.	Parameter	Type spec.	Description
▶□	I_TS_REQ_ATTR	TYPE RSR_TS_IOBJNM OPTIONAL	Table of attributes to be fetched
▶□	I_T_CHAVLINFO	TYPE RSDM_T_CHAVLINFO	table containg the list of CHAVLS
◧	VALUE(R_TX_ATR)	TYPE RSDM_TX_ATR	table containing the attribute values of the info object.
◪	CX_RS_ERROR		BW: General Error Class

Figure 5.10 The GET_ATTRIBUTES Method's Signature

The structure of Table I_T_CHAVLINFO is already known from method GET_TEXT. Table I_TS_REQ_ATTR is a simple table that contains an InfoObject for each row. Table R_TX_ATTR contains the characteristic value, CHANM, in each row; the SID and the table of the attribute value, T_ATR, which comprises the attribute name ATTRINM; and the attribute value ATTRIVL in each row.

Method _VALUES_GENERATE

Method _VALUES_GENERATE (or _VALUE_GENERATE) isn't contained in interface IF_RSMD_RS_ACCESS. Nevertheless, it's contained in most classes delivered by SAP; for this reason, it's described in the following.

This method is used to initially fill table E_T_CHAVLINFO, which is the only parameter of the method. C_CHAVL is the only field of the structure that must be filled. The corresponding attributes of method GET_VALUES indicate which characteristic values must be delivered and how many.

5.5.2 Sample Implementation of a Master Data Read Class

The following sections describe how you can implement a class for InfoObject HAUPT_KST that automatically contains all master data of the cost centers 0COST-CENTER for which a specific flag (IST_HKST) was set in their master data. Texts and attributes are automatically read from the existing texts and attributes of 0COSTCENTER.

Creating Class ZCL_READ_HAUPT_KST

1. First, call Transaction SE80.
2. Select CLASS/INTERFACE, and enter the class name, "ZCL_READ_HAUPT_KST" (see Figure 5.11).

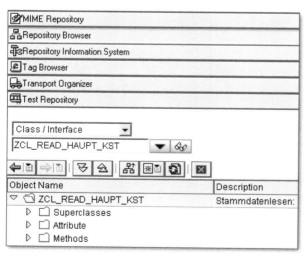

Figure 5.11 Creating Class ZCL_READ_HAUPT_KST

3. Confirm that you want to create a new class.

4. The simplest way to receive all required attributes is to inherit class CL_RSMD_RS_BW_SPEC. For this purpose, right-click the class name, ZCL_READ_HAUPT_KST, select CHANGE, and go to the PROPERTIES tab.

5. Click the SUPERCLASS button, and enter the "CL_RSMD_RS_BW_SPEC" class in the INHERITS FROM field (see Figure 5.12).

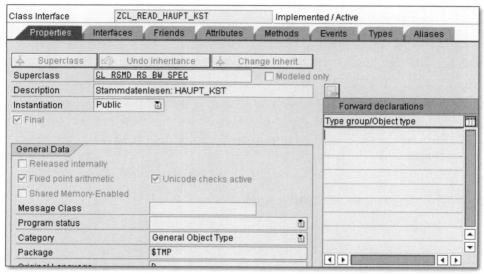

Figure 5.12 Specifying the Inheritance in the Class Properties

Creating Method GET_VALUES

To create method GET_VALUES, proceed as follows:

1. Search method GET_VALUES in the left-hand object list under ZCL_READ_HAUPT_KST • METHODS • INHERITED METHODS • IF_RSMD_RS_ACCESS.

2. Right-click the method, and select REDEFINE (see Figure 5.13).

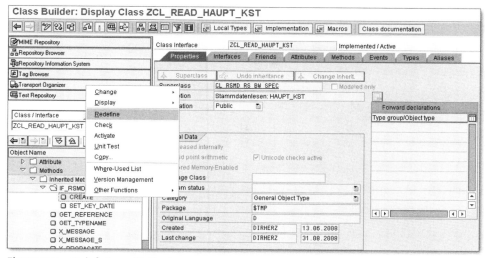

Figure 5.13 Redefining a Method

3. Select method IF_RSMD_RS_ACCESS~GET_VALUES under ZCL_READ_HAUPT_KST
   • METHODS • REDEFINITIONS, and insert the following code (see Listing 5.25).

```
METHOD IF_RSMD_RS_ACCESS~GET_VALUES.

  o_t_selopt        = i_t_selopt.
  o_maxrows         = i_maxrows.
  o_t_sorting       = i_t_sorting.

  TRY.
      CALL METHOD _value_generate
        IMPORTING
          e_t_chavlinfo = e_t_chavlinfo.
    CATCH cx_rs_error .
      x_message('IF_RSMD_RS_ACCESS~GET_VALUES-01').
  ENDTRY.

*************************************************************
* This is for fetching the text for the CHAVLS of
* InfoObject HAUPT_KST
*************************************************************
```

191

```
TRY.
    CALL METHOD if_rsmd_rs_access~get_text
      CHANGING
        c_t_chavlinfo = e_t_chavlinfo.
  CATCH cx_rs_error .
    x_message('IF_RSMD_RS_ACCESS~GET_VALUES-02').
ENDTRY.


**************************************************************
*  This is for the attributes of InfoObject
*  HAUPT_KST
**************************************************************

  IF i_ts_req_attr IS NOT INITIAL.

    TRY.
        CALL METHOD if_rsmd_rs_access~get_attributes
          EXPORTING
            i_ts_req_attr = i_ts_req_attr
            i_t_chavlinfo = e_t_chavlinfo
          RECEIVING
            r_tx_atr      = e_tx_atr.
      CATCH cx_rs_error .
        x_message('IF_RSMD_RS_ACCESS~GET_VALUES-03').
    ENDTRY.

  ENDIF.
ENDMETHOD.
```

Listing 5.25 Comprehensive Example of Method IF_RSMD_RS_ACCESS~GET_VALUES

Creating Method _VALUE_GENERATE

Method _VALUE_GENERATE is copied from class CL_RSMD_RS_BW_SPEC and corresponds to the _VALUES_GENERATE method used in other classes. It must be redefined analogous to method GET_VALUES and is created as described in Listing 5.26.

```
METHOD _VALUE_GENERATE.
  DATA: l_s_costcenter TYPE /bi0/mcostcenter,
        l_s_chavlinfo   TYPE rsdm_s_chavlinfo.
* Read data in buffers. In a real implementation
* Table l_s_costcenter should be created as a
* static attribute to the class.
```

```
  SELECT * FROM /BIO/MCOSTCENTER INTO l_s_costcenter
        UP TO o_maxrows ROWS
    WHERE DATEFROM <= sy-datum
      AND DATETO   >= sy-datum
      AND /BIC/IST_HKST = 'X'.
* Set read mode now
    l_s_chavlinfo-i_read_mode = rsdm_c_read_mode-text.
* Because HAUPT_KST is compounded to 0CO_AREA (analogous to
* 0COSTCENTER), the key must be composed here.
    CONCATENATE l_s_costcenter-co_area
                l_s_costcenter-costcenter
                INTO l_s_chavlinfo-c_chavl.
    INSERT l_s_chavlinfo INTO TABLE e_t_chavlinfo.
  ENDSELECT.
  IF sy-subrc <> 0.
    RAISE EXCEPTION TYPE cx_rs_error.
  ENDIF.
ENDMETHOD.
```

Listing 5.26 *Comprehensive Example of Method _VALUE_GENERATE*

Creating Method GET_ATTRIBUTES

Analogous to the previous methods, method GET_ATTRIBUTES is implemented as follows (see Listing 5.27). Here, the master data of the cost centers is read from the view to attribute table /BIO/MCOSTCENTER. For the sake of simplicity, time-dependency is ignored here, and only the currently valid value is read. Then, the attributes, 0PROFIT_CTR and 0RESP_PERS, are transferred to the return table, R_TX_ATR.

```
METHOD IF_RSMD_RS_ACCESS~GET_ATTRIBUTES.
**TRY.
*CALL METHOD SUPER->IF_RSMD_RS_ACCESS~GET_ATTRIBUTES
*   EXPORTING
**    i_ts_req_attr =
*     I_T_CHAVLINFO =
*   RECEIVING
*     R_TX_ATR      =
*     .
** CATCH cx_rs_error .
**ENDTRY.

  FIELD-SYMBOLS:
```

```
        <f_chavl>  TYPE RSDM_S_CHAVLINFO,
        <f_mcctr>  TYPE /bi0/mcostcenter.

  DATA: l_t_mcctr   TYPE HASHED TABLE
              OF /bi0/mcostcenter
              WITH UNIQUE KEY co_area costcenter
              INITIAL SIZE 0.
  DATA: l_sx_atr TYPE rsdm_sx_atr,
        l_s_atr  TYPE rsdm_s_atr.

* Here as well,  Table l_t_mcctr should be outsourced in a
* static attribute of the class and filled in the
* CREATE routine.
  SELECT * FROM /bi0/mcostcenter INTO TABLE l_t_mcctr
        WHERE dateto   >= sy-datum
            AND datefrom <= sy-datum.

* Now,  all characteristics to be filled are read
  LOOP AT i_t_chavlinfo ASSIGNING <f_chavl>.
    READ TABLE l_t_mcctr ASSIGNING <f_mcctr>
      WITH TABLE KEY co_area    = <f_chavl>-c_chavl(4)
                     costcenter = <f_chavl>-c_chavl+4(10).
    IF sy-subrc = 0.
*      Now, Return Table R_TX_ATR is filled
       l_sx_atr-chavl = <f_chavl>-c_chavl.
       REFRESH l_sx_atr-t_atr.
*      Fill profit center
       l_s_atr-attrinm = 'OPROFIT_CTR'.
       l_s_atr-attrivl = <f_mcctr>-profit_ctr.
       INSERT l_s_atr INTO TABLE l_sx_atr-t_atr.
*      Fill person responsible
       l_s_atr-attrinm = 'ORESP_PERS'.
       l_s_atr-attrivl = <f_mcctr>-resp_pers.
       INSERT l_s_atr INTO TABLE l_sx_atr-t_atr.
       INSERT l_sx_atr INTO TABLE r_tx_atr.

    ENDIF.
  ENDLOOP.
ENDMETHOD.
```

Listing 5.27 Comprehensive Example of Method IF_RSMD_RS_ACCESS~GET_CAPABILITIES

Creating Method GET_TEXT

Method GET_TEXT is implemented as shown in Listing 5.28. For the determined cost centers, the texts from text table /BIO/TCOSTCENTER are read and filled into the fields of structure E_CHATEXTS.

```
METHOD IF_RSMD_RS_ACCESS~GET_TEXT.
**TRY.
*CALL METHOD SUPER->IF_RSMD_RS_ACCESS~GET_TEXT
*   CHANGING
*     C_T_CHAVLINFO =
*       .
** CATCH cx_rs_error .
**ENDTRY.
  FIELD-SYMBOLS:
    <f_chavl>  TYPE RSDM_S_CHAVLINFO,
    <f_tcctr>  TYPE /bi0/tcostcenter.

  DATA: l_t_tcctr  TYPE HASHED TABLE
            OF /bi0/tcostcenter
            WITH UNIQUE KEY co_area costcenter
            INITIAL SIZE 0.

  SELECT * FROM /bi0/tcostcenter INTO TABLE l_t_tcctr
        WHERE dateto   >= sy-datum
          AND datefrom <= sy-datum
          AND langu     = sy-langu.

  LOOP AT c_t_chavlinfo ASSIGNING <f_chavl>.
    READ TABLE l_t_tcctr ASSIGNING <f_tcctr>
      WITH TABLE KEY co_area    = <f_chavl>-c_chavl(4)
                     costcenter = <f_chavl>-c_chavl+4(10).
    IF sy-subrc = 0.
      <f_chavl>-e_chatexts-txtsh  = <f_tcctr>-txtsh.
      <f_chavl>-e_chatexts-txtmd  = <f_tcctr>-txtmd.
    ENDIF.
  ENDLOOP.
ENDMETHOD.
```

Listing 5.28 Comprehensive Example of Method IF_RSMD_RS_ACCESS~GET_TEXT

5.5.3 Entering the Class in the InfoObject

Then, you must change the InfoObject `HAUPT_KST`.

1. Call InfoObject `HAUPT_KST`.
2. The MASTER DATA/TEXTS tab contains the field, MASTER DATA ACCESS. In this field, select OWN IMPLEMENTATION (see Figure 5.14).

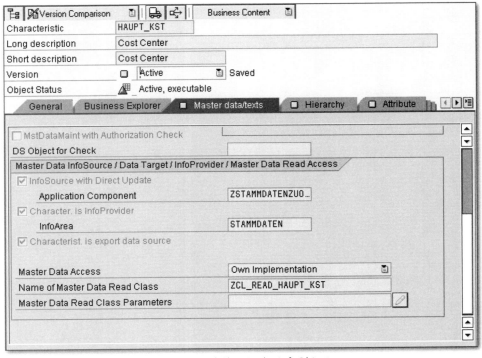

Figure 5.14 Entering the Master Data Read Class in the InfoObject

Select the name of the master data read class, `ZCL_READ_HAUPT_KST`.

> **Note**
>
> InfoObjects with master data read classes can't have *any* navigation attributes. Moreover, the master data maintenance doesn't read the results of the master data read class.

3. After you've activated the InfoObject, you can test the implementation. The simplest way to do this is to call the master data maintenance and use [F4] in the InfoObject.

   At this point, you can set a clean breakpoint to simply debug any possible errors.

In general, creating your own master data read class is a nice alternative to implement effects that would not be possible otherwise, for example, automatic filtering or user-dependent texts. However, you should always check whether it would make more sense to load the InfoObject conventionally.

It's recommended to implement the master data read classes only in exceptional cases. Particularly, the restriction that InfoObjects mustn't contain navigation attributes doesn't allow for widespread use.

6   User Exits in Planning

The biggest strength of planning in SAP NetWeaver BI is the option to manipulate the dataset stored in the InfoProvider by means of the planning function. There are customers who use this option to correct actual data retrospectively if corrections can't be done in the SAP ERP system due to closed periods. The datasets can also be corrected retrospectively if errors were found in the transformations.

In general, there are three different types of exits in planning:

▶ Variables that function analogous to query variables

▶ Characteristic derivations to derive fields that don't exist in the planning interface directly

▶ Specifically written functions

This also indicates the order of complexity. Variables have a relatively simple programming; functions, however, feature a rather complex implementation and are very powerful.

The following sections describe the various types of exits and the examples for their implementations in SAP BW-BPS (Business Planning and Simulation) and in SAP NetWeaver BI Integrated Planning. You'll discover that the actual logic remains unchanged despite completely different interfaces—SAP BW-BPS usually includes function modules, whereas SAP NetWeaver BI Integrated Planning uses classes. This makes it relatively easy to continue to use the existing modules after a migration without having to implement all functions anew.

6.1   Variables in Planning

SAP BW-BPS and SAP NetWeaver BI Integrated Planning vary considerably with regard to variables because the variables and exits used in the Business Explorer (BEx) continued to be used due to the integration of the planning layout with the query. Therefore, the following sections mainly discuss the variables of SAP BW-BPS. For further information on SAP NetWeaver BI Integrated Planning refer to Section 5.1, Variable Exit RSR00001.

6.1.1   Variables in SAP BW-BPS

The variable concept in SAP BW-BPS is completely different from the variable concept in BEx and in SAP NetWeaver BI Integrated Planning. Hence, you're provided with a brief introduction to this concept, which is followed by the description of the actual implementation.

In the variable exit of reporting, you directly fill the attributes to be used in the report. In the variables in SAP BW-BPS, by contrast, the permitted attributes are filled by means of exits, and the user may select a value. This stands in contrast to the variables in BEx, which either can be filled completely without user input or the user can select any valid value. If the value isn't permitted in a specific context, a message is sent.

Another difference is that variables are saved across sessions. You can display the current variable values in Transaction BPS0 by clicking the SET VARIABLES button (see Figure 6.1).

However, this may result in some undesirable side effects. If an exit reads the value of another variable to determine the variable value, the developers can't establish whether this other variable is used at all.

> **Example**
>
> Let's assume that you're responsible for planning car sales, and your planning includes an InfoObject for brands and another InfoObject for models. If you select a brand, the exit is supposed to provide all possible models of the brand currently available. According to this, you first read the variable of the brand and determine the models accordingly.
>
> It may be possible, however, that you use the variables for the models at the planning level, which contains all brands. Then, your exit would still read the variable of the brand although it isn't used in the current context. Effects like these often result in a large number of variables and planning levels.

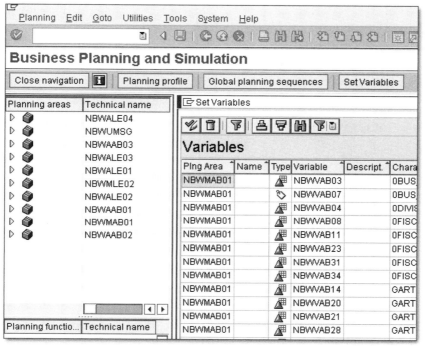

Figure 6.1 Setting Variables in SAP BW-BPS

If you take these cases into account for the implementation of variables, the actual exit can be implemented easily. It consists of a function module with a fixed interface. This function module can then be entered in one or more variables. You must note here that within the function module, the different variables are considered.

Similarly to the variables for reporting, a distinction is made for variables that return values dependent and independent of other variable values. In the following sections, you learn more about the difference between returning single values and returning value sets.

Returning a Single Value Without Dependency of Other Variables

The example shown in Listing 6.1 assumes that different kinds of planning are implemented in the course of a year (medium-term planning, annual planning, forecast) that all use the same layouts and planning levels. To not change all planning levels prior to every planning session, you want to enter the plan version in a central table. The version is read from this table and returned to it.

```
FUNCTION Z_VAR_VAL_PLANVERSION.
*"----------------------------------------------------------
*"*"Local interface:
*"  IMPORTING
*"     VALUE(I_AREA) TYPE  UPC_Y_AREA
*"     VALUE(I_VARIABLE) TYPE  UPC_Y_VARIABLE
*"     VALUE(I_CHANM) TYPE  UPC_Y_CHANM OPTIONAL
*"     VALUE(ITO_CHANM) TYPE  UPC_YTO_CHA
*"  EXPORTING
*"     REFERENCE(ETO_CHARSEL) TYPE  UPC_YTO_CHARSEL
*"  EXCEPTIONS
*"      FAILED
*"----------------------------------------------------------
* Input parameter:
* i_area     : Planning area, in which the variable
*              is defined.
* i_variable : Variable name.
* i_chanm    : As of Release 3.0B, the variables were
*              extended and can contain more than one
*              characteristic(in Release 3.0A, only one was
*              contained). To maintain the existing exits
*              Parameter i_chanm is filled if the variables
*              only contain one characteristic.
* ito_chanm  : The table of characteristics for which the
*              variable was defined. It is always filled
*              independent of the number of characteristics.

* Export parameter :
* eto_charsel : Selection table for the variable in
*               Structure upc_ys_charsel

* Exceptions:
* Exceptions in the Exit function module can be output
* using the  message ... raising <exception name> command.
* All exceptions can be used and the error is
* captured.
* ----------------------------------------------------------
* The structure
*           UPC_YS_CHARSEL
*   Fields: CHANM - Characteristic
```

```
*           SEQNO - Sequential number
*           SIGN  - I/E for Include/Exclude
*           OPT   - Selection condition  (EQ, BT, ...)
*           LOW   - Lower limit or single value
*           HIGH  - Upper limit
* -------------------------------------------------------


  DATA l_eto_charsel_wa TYPE upc_ys_charsel.
  DATA: l_t_plan_zentra TYPE STANDARD TABLE OF
                         z_plan_zentra,
       wa_plan_zentra TYPE z_plan_zentra,
       l_d_version TYPE /bi0/oiversion.

* CLEAR export table
  CLEAR eto_charsel.

*Transparent table read with key from column ZV
SELECT * FROM z_plan_zentra INTO TABLE l_t_plan_zentra.
READ TABLE l_t_plan_zentra INTO wa_plan_zentra
           WITH KEY ZZ_PLAN = ‚PLN'.
    IF sy-subrc NE 0.
    ENDIF.
    l_d_version = wa_nbw_zentra-ZZ_VERSion.

* Fill selection condition
  l_eto_charsel_wa-chanm = i_chanm.
  l_eto_charsel_wa-seqno = '0001'.
  l_eto_charsel_wa-sign  = 'I'.
  l_eto_charsel_wa-opt   = 'EQ'.
  l_eto_charsel_wa-low   = l_d_version.
  l_eto_charsel_wa-high  = ' '.
  INSERT l_eto_charsel_wa INTO TABLE eto_charsel.

* Check InfoObject
  IF i_chanm IS INITIAL OR i_chanm NE 'OVERSION'.
* Error occurred in user exit for variables
    Message e538(upc) raising FAILED.
  ENDIF.

ENDFUNCTION.
```

Listing 6.1 Example for BPS Variable Delivering a Single Value

Returning a Value Set Without Dependency of Other Variables

The example shown in Listing 6.2 indicates how you can use variables for implementing time-dependent validities. The example assumes that the planning is based on the characteristic of the product group PRODGRP, that the product groups change frequently, and that they aren't available for planning all of the time. For this reason, there are two attributes, VALIDFROM and VALIDTO, which indicate whether a product group is currently valid.

The basic idea is to read all values that are valid for the year to be planned, that is, for which "Valid from" is smaller or equal to the last day of the year, and "Valid to" is larger or equal to the first day of the year.

If you select the RESTRICTION OF VALUES REQUIRED BY USER option when you create the variable, you can select from these values. However, for planning functions, such as the pre-assignment of planning, it may be useful to restrict to the entire value set. This enables you to pre-assign only those product groups that are actually planned.

```
FUNCTION Z_GUELTIGE_PRODGRP.
*"----------------------------------------------------------
*"*"Local interface:
*"  IMPORTING
*"     REFERENCE(I_AREA) TYPE  UPC_Y_AREA
*"     REFERENCE(I_VARIABLE) TYPE  UPC_Y_VARIABLE
*"     REFERENCE(I_CHANM) TYPE  UPC_Y_CHANM
*"     REFERENCE(ITO_CHANM) TYPE  UPC_YTO_CHA
*"  EXPORTING
*"     REFERENCE(ETO_CHARSEL) TYPE  UPC_YTO_CHARSEL
*"----------------------------------------------------------
*
  DATA: lto_chasel TYPE upc_yto_chasel,
        lto_chasel_wa TYPE upc_ys_chasel,
        lto_attr_chasel TYPE upc_yt_charng,
        lto_attr_chasel_wa TYPE upc_ys_charng.
  FIELD-SYMBOLS: <f_chasel> TYPE upc_ys_charsel.
  DATA:
        r_var TYPE REF TO cl_sem_variable,
        rr_variable TYPE REF TO cl_sem_variable,
        lto_value TYPE upc_yto_charsel,
        ls_value  like line of lto_value,
        l_d_var   type upc_y_variable.
```

```
   DATA: ltr_prodgrp   TYPE HASHED TABLE
                       OF /bic/pprodgrp
                       WITH UNIQUE KEY /bic/prodgrp,
         l_s_prodgrp   TYPE  /bic/pprodgrp,
         l_d_jahr      TYPE /bi0/oifiscyear,
         l_d_last_datefrom  type d,
         l_d_first_dateto   type d.

   DATA: leto_chavl TYPE upc_yto_chavl.

   DATA: ltmp_s_chavl TYPE upc_ys_chavl,
         leto_charsel_wa TYPE upc_ys_charsel.
   SELECT SINGLE jahr FROM  z_plan_zentra into l_d_jahr
         WHERE  zz_plan_runde  = 'ZV'.
   l_d_last_datefrom(4)    = l_d_jahr.
   l_d_last_datefrom+4(4)  = '1231'.
   l_d_first_dateto(4)     = l_d_jahr.
   l_d_first_dateto+4(4)   = '0101'.

* Write characteristic values in selection table
   leto_charsel_wa-seqno = 0.
   SELECT        * FROM  /bic/pprodgrp INTO l_s_prodgrp.
         WHERE  /bic/validfrom   <= l_d_last_datefrom
         AND    /bic/validto     <= l_d_first_dateto.
     leto_charsel_wa-chanm  = 'PRODGRP'.
     leto_charsel_wa-sign   = 'I'.
     leto_charsel_wa-opt    = 'EQ'.
     leto_charsel_wa-low    = l_s_prodgrp-/bic/prodgrp.
     READ TABLE eto_charsel TRANSPORTING NO FIELDS
         WITH KEY low = l_s_prodgrp-/bic/prodgrp.
     IF sy-subrc <> 0.
       ADD 1 to leto_charsel_wa-seqno.
       INSERT leto_charsel_wa INTO TABLE eto_charsel.
     ENDIF.
   ENDSELECT.

ENDFUNCTION.
```

Listing 6.2 Example of a Variable Returning a Value Set

Returning a Value Set Depending on a User Variable

The example shown in Listing 6.2 is extended in Listing 6.3. You can use another variable in planning, such as 0DIVISION, if the number of product group is still too high to enable a reasonable search. The following example only reads the values to which the user restricted the DIVISION variable and provides those product groups that have the corresponding attribute. It can always be assumed that the user has not restricted to one unique value but to several or all values. The results of the variable are read in a RANGES table.

```
FUNCTION Z080N_NBW_TYPKL_AUS_AG_SPAR.
*"----------------------------------------------------------
*"*"Local interface:
*"  IMPORTING
*"     REFERENCE(I_AREA) TYPE  UPC_Y_AREA
*"     REFERENCE(I_VARIABLE) TYPE  UPC_Y_VARIABLE
*"     REFERENCE(I_CHANM) TYPE  UPC_Y_CHANM
*"     REFERENCE(ITO_CHANM) TYPE  UPC_YTO_CHA
*"  EXPORTING
*"     REFERENCE(ETO_CHARSEL) TYPE  UPC_YTO_CHARSEL
*"----------------------------------------------------------
  DATA: lto_chasel TYPE upc_yto_chasel,
        lto_chasel_wa TYPE upc_ys_chasel,
        lto_attr_chasel TYPE upc_yt_charng,
        lto_attr_chasel_wa TYPE upc_ys_charng.
  FIELD-SYMBOLS: <f_chasel>  TYPE upc_ys_charsel.
  DATA:
        r_var TYPE REF TO cl_sem_variable,
        rr_variable TYPE REF TO cl_sem_variable,
        lto_value TYPE upc_yto_charsel,
        ls_value  like line of lto_value,
        l_d_var   type upc_y_variable.
  DATA: ltr_division TYPE RANGE of /bi0/oidivision,
        l_s_division like line of ltr_division,
        ltr_prodgrp  TYPE HASHED TABLE
                 OF /bic/pprodgrp
                 WITH UNIQUE KEY /bic/prodgrp,
        l_s_prodgrp  TYPE  /bic/pprodgrp,
        l_d_jahr   TYPE /bi0/oifiscyear,
        l_d_last_datefrom  type d,
        l_d_first_dateto   type d.
```

```
  DATA: leto_chavl TYPE upc_yto_chavl.
* Read division from variable
  CALL METHOD cl_sem_variable=>get_instance
    EXPORTING
*    Specify area
      i_area      = i_area
*    Specify variable
      i_variable   = ,VSPARTE'
    RECEIVING
      rr_variable  = r_var
    EXCEPTIONS
      not_existing = 1
      OTHERS       = 2.

  CALL METHOD r_var->get_value
    RECEIVING
      rto_value = lto_value
    EXCEPTIONS
      error       = 1
      OTHERS      = 2.
*        **
  LOOP AT lto_value INTO ls_value.
    l_s_division-sign   = ls_value-sign.
    l_s_division-option = ls_value-opt.
    l_s_division-low    = ls_value-low.
    l_s_division-high   = ls_value-high.
     INSERT l_s_division INTO TABLE ltr_division.
  ENDLOOP.
  DATA: ltmp_s_chavl TYPE upc_ys_chavl,
        leto_charsel_wa TYPE upc_ys_charsel.
  SELECT SINGLE zz_jahr FROM
                     z080n_nbw_zentra into l_d_jahr
       WHERE  zz_plan_runde  = ,ZV'.
  l_d_last_datefrom(4)    = l_d_jahr.
  l_d_last_datefrom+4(4)  = ,1231'.
  l_d_first_dateto(4)     = l_d_jahr.
  l_d_first_dateto+4(4)   = ,0101'.

* Write characteristic values in selection table
  leto_charsel_wa-seqno = 0.
  SELECT        * FROM  /bic/pprodgrp INTO l_s_prodgrp.
       WHERE  /bic/validfrom  <= l_d_last_datefrom
       AND    /bic/validto    <= l_d_first_dateto
```

```
        AND     division          IN ltr_division.
    leto_charsel_wa-chanm  = ,PRODGRP'.
    leto_charsel_wa-sign   = ,I'.
    leto_charsel_wa-opt    = ,EQ'.
    leto_charsel_wa-low    = l_s_prodgrp-/bic/prodgrp.
    READ TABLE eto_charsel TRANSPORTING NO FIELDS
        WITH KEY low = l_s_prodgrp-/bic/prodgrp.
    IF sy-subrc <> 0.
      ADD 1 to leto_charsel_wa-seqno.
      INSERT leto_charsel_wa INTO TABLE eto_charsel.
    ENDIF.
  ENDSELECT.
ENDFUNCTION.
```

Listing 6.3 Example for Reading BPS Variables in Other Variables

6.1.2 Variables in SAP NetWeaver BI Integrated Planning

The variables in SAP NetWeaver BI Integrated Planning have basically been described in Chapter 5, User Exits and BAdIs in Reporting. These are the same variables that are also used in the query creation. However, it often happens that SAP NetWeaver BI Integrated Planning and old SAP BW-BPS planning functions need to be integrated and implemented. This section provides the information you need to read SAP BW-BPS variables for processing variables of SAP NetWeaver BI Integrated Planning and to set SAP BW-BPS variables. In this context, it's important to understand that only SAP BW-BPS variables can store values user-dependently. This isn't possible for the variables in SAP NetWeaver BI Integrated Planning.

Reading SAP BW-BPS Variables in the Query Variable Exit

As a general rule, you should map SAP BW-BPS variables on a 1:1 basis. Consequently, the naming conventions should be selected in such a way that the name of the SAP BW-BPS variable is identical to the name of the BEx variable. The code shown in Listing 6.4 provides the content of the SAP BW-BPS variable for all variables starting with "BPS."

```
INCLUDE zxrsru01.
...
IF i_vnam(3) = 'BPS'
  DATA: l_s_variable TYPE UPC_Y_VARIABLE,
    L_s_area  = upc_y_area.
```

```
DATA:
     r_var TYPE REF TO cl_sem_variable,
     lto_value TYPE upc_yto_charsel,
     l_s_value  LIKE LINE OF lto_value.
  L_s_area  = 'DEMOAREA'.
  L_s_variable = i_vnam.
  CALL METHOD cl_sem_variable=>get_instance
    EXPORTING
*    Specify area
     i_area        = l_s_area
*    Specify variable
     i_variable   = l_s_variable
    RECEIVING
     rr_variable  = r_var
    EXCEPTIONS
     not_existing = 1
     OTHERS       = 2.

  CALL METHOD r_var->get_user_restriction
*    EXPORTING
*      I_USER     = SY-UNAME
    RECEIVING
     rto_value = lto_value.

  IF lines( lto_value ) = 0.
    CALL METHOD r_var->get_value
*      EXPORTING
*        I_USER     = SY-UNAME
*        I_RESTRICT = 'X'
     receiving
       rto_value  = lto_value
       EXCEPTIONS
         ERROR     = 1
         others    = 2
           .
    IF sy-subrc <> 0.
*      MESSAGE ID SY-MSGID TYPE SY-MSGTY NUMBER SY-MSGNO
*                 WITH SY-MSGV1 SY-MSGV2 SY-MSGV3 SY-MSGV4.
    ENDIF.

  ENDIF.

***
```

```
LOOP AT lto_value INTO l_s_value.
  move-corresponding l_s_value TO l_s_range.
  APPEND l_s_range TO e_t_range.
ENDLOOP.
```

Listing 6.4 Transferring BPS Variables to IP Variables

This example assumes that all variables are defined as selection option variables. If you're sure that the variable is restricted to a single value, you can adapt the code accordingly. You must consider, however, that a default value is set in case of doubt because the SAP BW-BPS variable is usually filled when the user calls an SAP BW-BPS application. If a user carries out a BEx query without having implemented an SAP BW-BPS application, he receives an error message stating that the single value variable isn't clearly restricted.

Writing SAP BW-BPS Variables in the Query Variable Exit

You can use Step 3 of the exit (I_STEP = 3) to write back the SAP BW-BPS variable. During this step, all variable values—both the exit variables and the normal input variables—are transferred to the exit so that you can access all variables. You can use Listing 6.5 to search for all variables starting with "BPS" and to transfer the variable value to the relevant SAP BW-BPS variable using SAP BW-BPS-API.

```
IF i_step = 3.
   data: l_s_bps_var  TYPE UPC_YS_API_VARSEL,
         l_t_bps_var  TYPE STANDARD TABLE
                      OF UPC_YS_API_VARSEL.
   LOOP AT i_t_var_range INTO l_s_var_range.
     IF l_s_var_range-vnam(3) = 'NBW'.
       REFRESH l_t_bps_var.
       CLEAR l_s_bps_var.
       MOVE-CORRESPONDING l_s_var_range TO l_s_bps_var.
       l_s_bps_var-option = l_s_var_range-opt.
       l_s_bps_var-chanm  = l_s_var_range-iobjnm.
       l_s_bps_var-seqno  = 1.
       INSERT l_s_bps_var INTO TABLE l_t_bps_var.
       CALL FUNCTION 'API_SEMBPS_VARIABLE_SET'
         EXPORTING
           I_AREA            = 'DEMOAREA'
           I_VARIABLE        = l_s_var_range-vnam
*          I_NUMVALUE        =
*          IS_HIESEL         =
```

```
*       IMPORTING
*         E_SUBRC          =
*         ES_RETURN        =
          TABLES
            ITK_VARSEL       = l_t_bps_var
*         ITK_HIEDEP       =
                         .
      ENDIF.
    ENDLOOP.
  ENDIF.
```

Listing 6.5 Writing Back Query Variables to BPS Variables

6.2   Characteristic Value Derivations

Characteristic value derivations are used for three different functions in SAP NetWeaver BI Planning Integration.

▶ First, you can check whether a certain combination of characteristic values is valid.

▶ Second, you can generate a list of valid combinations, for example, for a planning layout in which all possible combinations are displayed. These two functions must correspond; that is, each combination declared as valid in the first function must be returned in the second function and vice versa.

▶ The third and probably most frequently used function serves to derive a value for another characteristic from a quantity of characteristic values. This is required in particular if these characteristics don't exist at the planning level but are still to be used in reporting later on.

6.2.1   Characteristic Value Derivations in SAP BW-BPS

Characteristic value derivations in SAP BW-BPS are always maintained for the basic planning area. In principle, you must differentiate characteristic value derivations per attribute, per hierarchy, or per exit. The following sections particularly describe the derivations per exit.

Characteristic value derivations in SAP BW-BPS are always maintained for the basic planning area but never for the multi-planning areas.

1. For this purpose, in the basic planning area, select CHANGE AREA and then go to the last tab, CHARACTERISTIC RELS (see Figure 6.2).

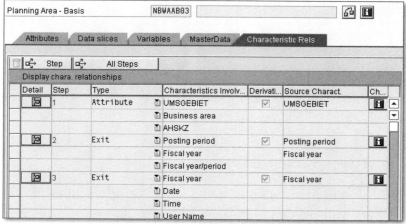

Figure 6.2 Maintaining Characteristic Relationships in SAP BW-BPS

2. Select the derivation type, EXIT.

3. Click on the left-most column, DETAIL, to go to the screen displayed in Figure 6.3.

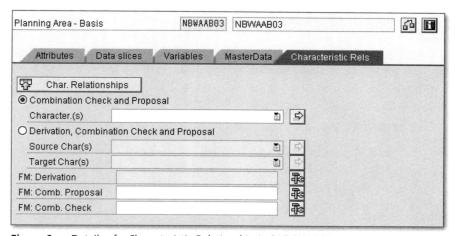

Figure 6.3 Details of a Characteristic Relationship in SAP BW-BPS

4. You have two options. You can either select a combination check and a combination proposal, or you can select a derivation with combination check and proposal. In the former case, you must select the characteristics for the combination check; in the latter, you must select the source and target characteristics.

5. In the lower part of the screen, you can set up two or three function modules depending on the variant. SAP BW-BPS provides three different modules for the characteristic value derivations per exit: UPF_TIME_EXIT_FISC_CHECK, UPF_TIME_EXIT_FISC_CREATE, and UPF_TIME_EXIT_FISC_DERIVE.

Checking Characteristic Value Combinations in SAP BW-BPS

Initially, the characteristic value combinations are checked: This exit is called once per data record after new planning records have been created. The characteristics to be checked are entered in the definition of the characteristic value derivation.

For the sake of simplicity, you should select a characteristic value derivation per hierarchy or attribute derivation whenever possible. However, this isn't possible for more complex combinations.

Listing 6.6 continues the example provided for the variables. There is a product group (PRODGRP) that includes the following attributes: division (0DIVISION), a "Valid from" date (VALIDFROM), and a "Valid to" date (VALIDTO). In the exit, you now want to check whether the month is within the validity period for a product group, a calendar year, and a calendar month. If this isn't the case, you must trigger exception INVALID.

```
FUNCTION Z_DERIVE_PRODGRP_CHECK.
*"----------------------------------------------------------
*"*"Local interface:
*"  IMPORTING
*"     REFERENCE(I_AREA) TYPE  UPC_Y_AREA
*"     REFERENCE(IS_CHAS) TYPE  ANY
*"     REFERENCE(ITO_CHA) TYPE  UPC_YTO_CHA
*"     REFERENCE(ITO_CHASEL) TYPE  UPC_YTO_CHASEL OPTIONAL
*"  EXCEPTIONS
*"      FAILED
*"      INVALID
*"----------------------------------------------------------

  FIELD-SYMBOLS: <f_prodgrp>  TYPE /bic/oiprodgrp,
                 <f_year>    TYPE /bi0/oifiscyear,
```

```
                  <f_per3>   TYPE /bi0/oifiscper3,
                  <f_chas>   TYPE ANY.
    DATA: l_s_prodgrp like line of g_t_prodgrp,
          l_d_valid     type c,
          l_d_min_to    type d,
          l_d_max_from  type d.

* First, the required fields of the structure
* are assigned to field symbols.
    ASSIGN COMPONENT 'PRODGRP' OF STRUCTURE is_chas
                                       TO <f_prodgrp>.
    ASSIGN COMPONENT '0FISCPER3' OF STRUCTURE is_chas
                                       TO <f_per3>.
    ASSIGN COMPONENT '0FISCYEAR' OF STRUCTURE is_chas
                                       TO <f_year>.

    IF lines( g_t_prodgrp ) = 0.
      SELECT * FROM /bic/pprodgrp INTO TABLE g_t_prodgrp
            WHERE OBJVERS = 'A'.
    ENDIF.

    l_d_valid = '-'.
    LOOP AT  g_t_prodgrp into l_s_prodgrp
        WHERE
            /bic/prodgrp    = <f_prodgrp> AND
            OBJVERS         = 'A'.
* Record valid?
      l_d_min_to(4) = l_d_max_from(4)  = <f_year>.

      IF <f_per3> > '012' OR <f_per3> = '000'.
*       Only check year
        l_d_min_to+4(4) = '1231'.
        l_d_max_from+4(4) = '0101'.
      ELSE.
*     Check period only from 1-12.
        l_d_max_from+4(2) = <f_per3>.
        l_d_max_from+6(2) = '01'.
        l_d_min_to        = l_d_max_from.
        l_d_min_to        = l_d_min_to + 31.
        l_d_min_to+6(2)   = '01'.
        l_d_min_to        = l_d_min_to  - 1.
      ENDIF.
      IF  l_s_typklasse-/bic/validfrom <= l_d_min_to AND
```

```
          l_s_typklasse-/bic/validto   >= l_d_max_from.
        l_d_valid  = '+'.
     ENDIF.
   ENDLOOP.
   IF l_d_valid = '-'.
     MESSAGE e101(z_bps) WITH <f_prodgrp>
                              <f_per3> <f_year>
*    Product group &1 is &2/&3 not valid.
         RAISING INVALID.
   ENDIF.
 ENDFUNCTION.
```

Listing 6.6 Sample Check of Characteristic Combinations

For the function module, you can use the sample function module, UPF_TIME_EXIT_FISC_CHECK.

Creating Characteristic Value Combinations in SAP BW-BPS

The corresponding function is the creation of a list that comprises valid combinations. As described previously, you must determine these combinations as valid combinations in the other exit. The simplest option is to determine all possible combinations and call the first function module. However, this process usually takes a long time; therefore, it's easier to determine the valid combinations directly. The corresponding function module then appears as shown in Listing 6.7.

```
FUNCTION z_derive_prodgrp_create.
*"----------------------------------------------------------
*"*"Local Interface:
*"  IMPORTING
*"     REFERENCE(I_AREA) TYPE  UPC_Y_AREA
*"     REFERENCE(ITO_CHA) TYPE  UPC_YTO_CHA
*"     REFERENCE(ITO_CHASEL) TYPE  UPC_YTO_CHASEL OPTIONAL
*"  EXPORTING
*"     REFERENCE(ETH_CHAS) TYPE  HASHED TABLE
*"  EXCEPTIONS
*"      FAILED
*"----------------------------------------------------------

* Determination of valid characteristics for product group,
* fiscal year, period
```

```
    DATA: l_s_chasel TYPE upc_ys_chasel,
          l_s_chas1  TYPE /1sem/_ys_chas_100demoarea,
          l_s_chas3  TYPE /1sem/_ys_chas_100demoar2,
          l_s_chas   TYPE REF TO DATA,
          l_s_charng TYPE upc_ys_charng.

    FIELD-SYMBOLS: <f_prodgrp>  TYPE /bic/oiprodgrp,
                   <f_year>     TYPE /bi0/oifiscyear,
                   <f_per3>     TYPE /bi0/oifiscper3,
                   <f_varnt>    TYPE /bi0/oifiscvarnt,
                   <f_chas>     TYPE ANY.

    DATA: l_tr_prodgrp  TYPE RANGE OF /bic/oiprodgrp,
          l_tr_year     TYPE RANGE OF /bi0/oifiscyear,
          l_tr_per3     TYPE RANGE OF /bi0/oifiscper3,
          l_sr_progrp   LIKE LINE OF l_tr_prodgrp,
          l_sr_year     LIKE LINE OF l_tr_year,
          l_sr_per3     LIKE LINE OF l_tr_per3.

    DATA: l_s_prodgrp   TYPE /bic/pprodgrp,
          l_d_datum     TYPE d,
          l_d_year      TYPE /bi0/oifiscyear,
          l_d_per3      TYPE /bi0/oifiscper3,
          l_s_zentra TYPE z_pln_zentra.

  CREATE DATA l_s_chas LIKE LINE OF eth_chas.
  ASSIGN      l_s_chas->* TO <f_chas>.
* Initialization of field symbols
  ASSIGN COMPONENT ,PRODGRP'   OF STRUCTURE <f_chas>
                                            TO <f_prodgrp>.
  ASSIGN COMPONENT ,0FISCYEAR'  OF STRUCTURE <f_chas>
                                            TO <f_year>.
  ASSIGN COMPONENT ,0FISCPER3'  OF STRUCTURE <f_chas>
                                            TO <f_per3>.
  ASSIGN COMPONENT ,0FISCVARNT' OF STRUCTURE <f_chas>
                                            TO <f_varnt>.

  LOOP AT ito_chasel INTO l_s_chasel.
    IF l_s_chasel-chanm = ,PRODGRP'.
      LOOP AT l_s_chasel-t_charng INTO l_s_charng.
        MOVE-CORRESPONDING l_s_charng TO l_sr_prodgrp.
        INSERT l_sr_prodgrp INTO TABLE l_tr_prodgrp.
      ENDLOOP.
```

```
    ENDIF.
  IF l_s_chasel-chanm = ‚0FISCYEAR‘.
    LOOP AT l_s_chasel-t_charng INTO l_s_charng.
      MOVE-CORRESPONDING l_s_charng TO l_sr_year.
      INSERT l_sr_year into table l_tr_year.
    ENDLOOP.
  ENDIF.
   IF l_s_chasel-chanm = ‚0FISCPER3‘.
     LOOP AT l_s_chasel-t_charng INTO l_s_charng.
       MOVE-CORRESPONDING l_s_charng TO l_sr_per3.
       INSERT l_sr_per3 INTO TABLE l_tr_per3.
     ENDLOOP.
   ENDIF.
  ENDLOOP.

* Create table for year
  SELECT SINGLE * FROM  z_plan_zentra
         INTO l_s_zentra
         WHERE  zz_plan_runde  = ‚ZV‘.

  l_d_per3 = ‚000‘.
  SELECT * FROM /bic/pprodgrp INTO l_s_prodgrp
         WHERE objvers        = ‚A‘
           AND /bic/prodgrp IN l_tr_prodgrp.
    l_d_datum = l_s_prodgrp-/bic/validfrom.
    IF l_d_datum(4)   < l_s_nbw_zentra-planjahr.
      l_d_datum(4)    = l_s_nbw_zentra-planjahr.
      l_d_datum+4(4)  = ‘0101’.
    ENDIF.
    IF l_s_prodgrp-/bic/validto(4)  >
               l_s_plan_zentra-planjahr.
      l_s_typkl-/bic/validto(4)  = l_s_plan_zentra-planjahr.
      l_s_typkl-/bic/validto+4(4) = ‚1231‘.
    ENDIF.
    WHILE l_d_datum <= l_s_prodgrp-/bic/validto.
*     Insert periods # and 16 , if at least one
*     combination is valid.
      l_d_per3+1(2) = l_d_datum+4(2).
      l_d_year      = l_d_datum(4).
      if l_d_year in l_tr_year.
        <f_varnt>    = ‚K4‘.
        <f_prodgrp>  = l_s_typkl-/bic/prodgrp.
        <f_year>     = l_d_year.
```

```
          IF ‚016' IN l_tr_per3.
            <f_per3>    = ‚016'.
            INSERT <f_chas> INTO TABLE eth_chas.
          ENDIF.
          IF ‚000' IN l_tr_per3.
            <f_per3>    = ‚000'.
            INSERT <f_chas> INTO TABLE eth_chas.
          ENDIF.
          IF l_d_per3 IN l_tr_per3.
*           valid combination
            <f_prodgrp>    = l_s_typkl-/bic/prodgrp.
            <f_year>       = l_d_year.
            <f_per3>       = l_d_per3.
            INSERT <f_chas> INTO TABLE eth_chas.
          ENDIF.
        ENDIF.
*     Increment date
        l_d_datum+6(2) = ‚01'.
        l_d_datum      = l_d_datum + 31.
      ENDWHILE.
    ENDSELECT.
ENDFUNCTION.
```

Listing 6.7 Example of the CREATE Function of the Characteristic Value Derivation

Derivation of Characteristics in SAP BW-BPS

The last function of the characteristic value derivation includes the enrichment of fields that don't exist at planning level. You can use this option in various ways. For instance, a project may require that plan line items must be written to trace who changed which plan value and when. At first glance, this seems impossible within SAP NetWeaver BI; but with the characteristic value derivation, it can be implemented easily.[1]

---

1 This example is based on the document, "How to … line items in SAP BW-BPS." It was selected because it fits in this context and is easy to implement. Most of the other examples are too complex to be described within the scope of in this book or could be better implemented by means of attribute or hierarchy derivations.

You simply include three InfoObjects for the user (0USERNAME), date (0DATE), and time (0TIME) and fill these via the exit for the characteristic value derivation. Note that you must always enter a source characteristic for the exit, for instance, the fiscal year, 0FISCYEAR. The exit then appears as shown in Listing 6.8.

```
FUNCTION Z_DERIVE_0USERNAME.
*"----------------------------------------------------------
*"*"Local interface:
*"  IMPORTING
*"     VALUE(I_AREA) TYPE  UPC_Y_AREA
*"     REFERENCE(ITO_CHA) TYPE  UPC_YTO_CHA
*"  CHANGING
*"     REFERENCE(XS_CHAS) TYPE  ANY
*"  EXCEPTIONS
*"      FAILED
*"----------------------------------------------------------
  FIELD-SYMBOLS: <l_chavl> TYPE ANY.

* fill user
  ASSIGN COMPONENT '0USERNAME' OF STRUCTURE xs_chas
                              TO <l_chavl>.
  IF sy-subrc = 0.
    <l_chavl> = sy-uname.
  ENDIF.
* fill date
  ASSIGN COMPONENT '0DATE' OF STRUCTURE xs_chas
                              TO <l_chavl>.
  IF sy-subrc = 0.
    <l_chavl> = sy-datum.
  ENDIF.
*** fill time
  ASSIGN component '0TIME' OF STRUCTURE xs_chas
                              TO <l_chavl>.
  IF sy-subrc = 0.

    <l_chavl> = sy-uzeit.
  ENDIF.
ENDFUNCTION.
```

Listing 6.8 Sample Implementation for Deriving Characteristic Values

6.2.2 Characteristic Value Derivations in SAP NetWeaver BI Integrated Planning

The characteristic value derivation in SAP NetWeaver BI Integrated Planning functions analogously; however, you must implement a class with corresponding interfaces instead of one or more function modules. Then, you must enter this class in the Modeler.

In many projects, you can select between SAP BW-BPS and SAP NetWeaver BI Integrated Planning or a combination of old SAP BW-BPS applications and new SAP NetWeaver BI Integrated Planning applications. For better comparability, in the following sections, the same exits as in SAP BW-BPS are implemented.

1. Create a new class in ABAP Workbench (Transaction SE80). Enter the name "ZCL_DERIVE_SAMPLE".

2. In this class, the `CL_RSPLS_CR_EXIT_BASE` superclass is entered in the properties screen.

3. Now, you can redefine the following methods from interface `IF_RSPLS_CR_METHODS`:

   ▶ The `IF_RSPLS_CR_METHODS~CHECK` method to implement checks of characteristic value combinations

   ▶ The `IF_RSPLS_CR_METHODS~CREATE` method to implement creations of characteristic combinations

   ▶ The `IF_RSPLS_CR_METHODS~DERIVE` method to derive characteristic values

IF_RSPLS_CR_METHODS~CHECK Method

The `IF_RSPLS_CR_METHODS~CHECK` method is used to check whether specific characteristic combinations are valid. It has the signature illustrated in Figure 6.4.

Ty.	Parameter	Type spec.	Description
▶□	I_S_CHAS	TYPE ANY	Characteristics Combination
□▶	E_T_MESG	TYPE IF_RSPLS_CR_TYPES=>TN_T_MESG	Messages
□▶	VALUE(E_IS_VALID)	TYPE RS_BOOL	Boolean

Figure 6.4 Signature of the CHECK Method in SAP NetWeaver BI Integrated Planning

The parameters are straightforward: `I_S_CHAS` contains the characteristics currently planned. Note that the key figure values aren't considered here. You can't carry out checks to determine whether specific combinations have positive or negative values.

The E_IS_VALID parameter returns the results whether a value is valid or not. This parameter is of the RS_BOOL type and is filled with X if the record is valid, and it is filled with SPACE if the record isn't valid. If a corresponding message is to be returned for invalid records, you can specify this in table E_T_MESG.

This method is called frequently for planning functions, so you should buffer the results, particularly if the check is complex and includes several steps. For this reason, the implementation of interface IF_RSPLS_CR_METHODS comprises a sample code for the buffer implementation. The example in Listing 6.9 shows how the SAP BW-BPS planning appears in SAP NetWeaver BI Integrated Planning.

```
METHOD if_rspls_cr_methods~check.
*-------------------------------------------------------*
*   --> i_s_chas     characteristics combination
*   <-- e_t_mesg     messages
*   <-- e_is_valid   flag, record is valid or not
*-------------------------------------------------------*

* begin example code:
* infrastructure needed by the buffer:
  DATA: l_s_mesg TYPE if_rspls_cr_types=>tn_s_mesg.

  FIELD-SYMBOLS: <l_th_buf> TYPE HASHED TABLE,
                 <l_s_buf>  TYPE ANY.
* end example code:


  CLEAR e_t_mesg.


* begin of example code:
* use the buffer?
* o_use_buffer is switched on by default in the
* constructor
  IF o_use_buffer = rs_c_true.
*    yes:
     ASSIGN o_r_th_buf->* TO <l_th_buf>.
     ASSIGN o_r_s_buf->*  TO <l_s_buf>.
     <l_s_buf> = i_s_chas.
```

```
      READ TABLE <l_th_buf> INTO <l_s_buf> FROM <l_s_buf>.
      IF sy-subrc = 0.
        e_is_valid = o_r_is_valid->*.
        IF e_is_valid = rs_c_false
           AND e_t_mesg IS SUPPLIED.
          APPEND o_r_s_mesg->* TO e_t_mesg.
        ENDIF.
        RETURN.
      ENDIF.
   ENDIF.
 * implement your algorithm to check the combination here
   Field-symbols: <f_prodgrp> TYPE /bic/oiprogrp,
                   <f_year>    TYPE /bi0/oifiscyear,
                   <f_per3>    TYPE /bi0/oifiscper3,
                   <f_chas>    TYPE ANY.
 * _t_progrp is an attribute of the implementing class
 * of a hashed table with structure /bic/pprodgrp
 DATA: l_s_prodgrp like line of g_t_prodgrp,
         l_d_valid     type c,
         l_d_min_to    type d,
         l_d_max_from  type d.

 * First, the required fields of the structure
 * are assigned to field symbols
   ASSIGN COMPONENT 'PRODGRP' OF STRUCTURE i_s_chas
                                         TO <f_prodgrp>.
   ASSIGN COMPONENT 'OFISCPER3' OF STRUCTURE i_s_chas
                                         TO <f_per3>.
   ASSIGN COMPONENT 'OFISCYEAR' OF STRUCTURE i_s_chas
                                         TO <f_year>.

   IF lines( g_t_prodgrp ) = 0.
     SELECT * FROM /bic/pprodgrp INTO TABLE g_t_prodgrp
           WHERE OBJVERS = 'A'.
   ENDIF.

   l_d_valid = '-'.
   LOOP AT  g_t_prodgrp into l_s_prodgrp
       WHERE
           /bic/prodgrp   = <f_prodgrp> AND
           OBJVERS        = 'A'.
 * Record valid?
     l_d_min_to(4) = l_d_max_from(4)  = <f_year>.
```

```
       IF <f_per3> > '012' OR <f_per3> = '000'.
*        Only check year
         l_d_min_to+4(4) = '1231'.
         l_d_max_from+4(4) = '0101'.
       ELSE.
*      Check period only for 1-12.
         l_d_max_from+4(2) = <f_per3>.
         l_d_max_from+6(2) = '01'.
         l_d_min_to        = l_d_max_from.
         l_d_min_to        = l_d_min_to + 31.
         l_d_min_to+6(2)   = '01'.
         l_d_min_to        = l_d_min_to  - 1.
       ENDIF.
       IF  l_s_typklasse-/bic/validfrom <= l_d_min_to AND
           l_s_typklasse-/bic/validto   >= l_d_max_from.
         l_d_valid  = '+'.
       ENDIF.
     ENDLOOP.
     IF l_d_valid = '-'.
       e_is_valid = rs_c_false.
       l_s_mesg-msgty = 'E'.
       l_s_mesg-msgid = 'z_bps'.
       l_s_mesg-msgno = '101'.
       l_s_mesg-msgv1 = <f_prodgrp>.
       l_s_mesg-msgv2 = <f_per3>.
       l_s_mesg-msgv3 = <f_year>.
*      Product group &1 is &2/&3 not valid.
       APPEND l_s_mesg TO e_t_mesg.
     ELSE.
       E_is_valid = rs_c_true.
     ENDIF.

* update the buffer with the result:
* l_s_mesg should contain a message in the 'invalid'
* case
     IF o_use_buffer = rs_c_true.
       o_r_is_valid->* = e_is_valid.
       IF o_r_is_valid->* = rs_c_false
         AND e_t_mesg IS SUPPLIED.
         o_r_s_mesg->* = l_s_mesg.
       ENDIF.
       INSERT <l_s_buf> INTO TABLE <l_th_buf>.
```

```
    ENDIF.
* end of example code

ENDMETHOD.
```

Listing 6.9 Sample Implementation of the CHECK Method

IF_RSPLS_CR_METHODS~CREATE Method

Like in SAP BW-BPS, SAP NetWeaver BI Integrated Planning also includes a method that provides all valid characteristic combinations (see Figure 6.5). The signature of this method is more complex than the signature of the CHECK method.

Ty.	Parameter	Type spec.	Description
▸▫	I_TSX_SELDR	TYPE RSDD_TSX_SELDR	Selection to the Data Manager
◻▸	E_T_MESG	TYPE IF_RSPLS_CR_TYPES=>TN_T_MESG	Message Table
◻▸	E_TH_CHAS	TYPE HASHED TABLE	Characteristics combinations
◫	CX_RSPLS_FAILED		Method Failed

Figure 6.5 Signature of the CREATE Method in SAP NetWeaver BI Integrated Planning

Table I_TSX_SELDR comprises the characteristic selections that are stored in the query, for example. You may only create combinations that are contained in the selection. Although the structure of table I_TSX_SELDR is complex, you only have to consider two fields: the CHANM field and the RANGE structure (or more precisely table RANGE-RANGE). It contains restrictions in the form of a RANGES table, which belongs to the characteristic included in CHANM.

In addition to table E_T_MESG known from the CHECK method, you're provided with table E_TH_CHAS to return combinations. This is a hashed table that contains the valid combinations. An empty table E_TH_CHAS means that all combinations are valid.

It makes sense to fill the buffer table of the CHECK method already in the CREATE method. This enables you to immediately check the validity of new records that are created during planning.

Listing 6.10 shows the current example.

```
METHOD if_rspls_cr_methods~create.
*------------------------------------------------------*
*   --> i_tsx_seldr       selection criteria
```

```
*  <-- e_t_mesg         messages
*  <-- e_th_chas        valid combinations
*  <<- cx_rspls_failed  exception
*-------------------------------------------------------*


* Infrastructure needed by the buffer:
  FIELD-SYMBOLS: <l_th_buf> TYPE HASHED TABLE,
                 <l_s_buf>  TYPE ANY,
                 <l_s_chas> TYPE ANY.

  CLEAR e_t_mesg.
  CLEAR e_th_chas.


* Implement your algorithm to create valid combinations
* make sure that only records contained in the selection
* table i_tsx_seldr will be generated here!
* Determine valid characteristics for the product group,
* fiscal year, period

  FIELD-SYMBOLS: <f_prodgrp>  TYPE /bic/oiprodgrp,
                 <f_year>     TYPE /bi0/oifiscyear,
                 <f_per3>     TYPE /bi0/oifiscper3,
                 <f_varnt>    TYPE /bi0/oifiscvarnt,
                 <f_chas>     TYPE ANY,
                 <f_seldr>    TYPE RSDD_SX_SELDR,
                 <f_range>    TYPE RRRANGESID.

  DATA: l_tr_prodgrp  TYPE RANGE OF /bic/oiprodgrp,
        l_tr_year     TYPE RANGE OF /bi0/oifiscyear,
        l_tr_per3     TYPE RANGE OF /bi0/oifiscper3,
        l_sr_progrp   LIKE LINE OF l_tr_prodgrp,
        l_sr_year     LIKE LINE OF l_tr_year,
        l_sr_per3     LIKE LINE OF l_tr_per3.

  DATA: l_s_prodgrp   TYPE /bic/pprodgrp,
        l_d_datum     TYPE d,
        l_d_year      TYPE /bi0/oifiscyear,
        l_d_per3      TYPE /bi0/oifiscper3,
        l_s_zentra TYPE z_pln_zentra.

  CREATE DATA l_s_chas LIKE LINE OF eth_chas.
  ASSIGN      l_s_chas->* TO <f_chas>.
* Initialization of field symbols
```

```
      ASSIGN COMPONENT ‚PRODGRP‘    OF STRUCTURE <f_chas>
                                                 TO <f_prodgrp>.
      ASSIGN COMPONENT ‚0FISCYEAR‘  OF STRUCTURE <f_chas>
                                                 TO <f_year>.
      ASSIGN COMPONENT ‚0FISCPER3‘  OF STRUCTURE <f_chas>
                                                 TO <f_per3>.
      ASSIGN COMPONENT ‚0FISCVARNT‘ OF STRUCTURE <f_chas>
                                                 TO <f_varnt>.

    LOOP AT i_tsx_seldr ASSIGNING <f_seldr>.
      IF <f_seldr>-chanm = ‚PRODGRP‘.
        LOOP AT <f_seldr>-range-range ASSIGNING <f_range>.
          MOVE-CORRESPONDING <f_range> TO l_sr_prodgrp.
          INSERT l_sr_prodgrp INTO TABLE l_tr_prodgrp.
        ENDLOOP.
      ENDIF.
      IF <f_seldr>-chanm = ‚0FISCYEAR‘.
        LOOP AT <f_seldr>-range-range ASSIGNING <f_range>.
          MOVE-CORRESPONDING <f_range> TO l_sr_year.
          INSERT l_sr_year into table l_tr_year.
        ENDLOOP.
      ENDIF.
      IF <f_seldr>-chanm = ‚0FISCPER3‘.
        LOOP AT <f_seldr>-range-range ASSIGNING <f_range>.
          MOVE-CORRESPONDING <f_range> TO l_sr_per3.
          INSERT l_sr_per3 INTO TABLE l_tr_per3.
        ENDLOOP.
      ENDIF.
    ENDLOOP.

* Create table for year
    SELECT SINGLE * FROM  z_plan_zentra
           INTO l_s_zentra
           WHERE  zz_plan_runde  = ‚ZV‘.

    l_d_per3 = ‚000‘.
    SELECT * FROM /bic/pprodgrp INTO l_s_prodgrp
           WHERE objvers        = ‚A‘
             AND /bic/prodgrp IN l_tr_prodgrp.
      l_d_datum = l_s_prodgrp-/bic/validfrom.
      IF l_d_datum(4)   < l_s_nbw_zentra-planjahr.
        l_d_datum(4)    = l_s_nbw_zentra-planjahr.
        l_d_datum+4(4)  = ‘0101’.
```

```
    ENDIF.
    IF l_s_prodgrp-/bic/validto(4)  >
               l_s_plan_zentra-planjahr.
      l_s_typkl-/bic/validto(4)  = l_s_plan_zentra-planjahr.
      l_s_typkl-/bic/validto+4(4) = ‚1231‘.
    ENDIF.
    WHILE l_d_datum <= l_s_prodgrp-/bic/validto.
*     Insert periods # and 16 , if at least one
*     combination is valid
      l_d_per3+1(2) = l_d_datum+4(2).
      l_d_year      = l_d_datum(4).
      if l_d_year in l_tr_year.
        <f_varnt>    = ‚K4‘.
        <f_prodgrp>  = l_s_typkl-/bic/prodgrp.
        <f_year>     = l_d_year.

        IF ‚016‘ IN l_tr_per3.
          <f_per3>    = ‚016‘.
          INSERT <f_chas> INTO TABLE eth_chas.
        ENDIF.
        IF ‚000‘ IN l_tr_per3.
          <f_per3>    = ‚000‘.
          INSERT <f_chas> INTO TABLE eth_chas.
        ENDIF.
        IF l_d_per3 IN l_tr_per3.
*         valid combination
          <f_prodgrp>  = l_s_typkl-/bic/prodgrp.
          <f_year>     = l_d_year.
          <f_per3>     = l_d_per3.
          INSERT <f_chas> INTO TABLE eth_chas.
        ENDIF.
      ENDIF.
*   Increment date
      l_d_datum+6(2) = ‚01‘.
      l_d_datum      = l_d_datum + 31.
    ENDWHILE.
  ENDSELECT.
* Use the buffer?
* o_use_buffer is switched on by default in the
* constructor
  IF o_use_buffer = rs_c_true.
*   update the buffer with the created records
    ASSIGN o_r_th_buf->* TO <l_th_buf>.
```

```
      ASSIGN o_r_s_buf->*  TO <l_s_buf>.
      LOOP AT e_th_chas ASSIGNING <l_s_chas>.
        <l_s_buf>       = <l_s_chas>.
        o_r_is_valid->* = rs_c_true.
        INSERT <l_s_buf> INTO TABLE <l_th_buf>.
      ENDLOOP.
    ENDIF.


ENDMETHOD.
```

Listing 6.10 Sample Implementation of the CREATE Method

IF_RSPLS_CR_METHODS~DERIVE Method

The IF_RSPLS_CR_METHODS~DERIVE method is different from the CREATE and CHECK methods because the DERIVE method addresses characteristics that aren't at aggregation level. These characteristics are filled using the DERIVE method. Just like in the CHECK method, it's implemented at the level of individual records. Hence, the signature of this method is practically identical (see Figure 6.6).

Ty.	Parameter	Type spec.	Description
▢▸	E_T_MESG	TYPE IF_RSPLS_CR_TYPES=>TN_T_MESG	Message Table
▸▢▸	C_S_CHAS	TYPE ANY	Characteristics combination
▨	CX_RSPLS_FAILED		Method Failed

Figure 6.6 Signature of the DERIVE Method in SAP NetWeaver BI Integrated Planning

Because you change characteristic values, you need to use the C_S_CHAS changing parameter instead of the I_S_CHAS importing parameter that has the same structure. Table E_T_MESG is identical to the table parameters in the CHECK and CREATE methods. Instead of the E_IS_VALID parameter of the CHECK method, you're provided with the CX_RSPLS_FAILED exception. This exception should only be triggered if serious errors or illogical selection conditions (e.g., "Valid from" is larger than "Valid to") occur in the database because it aborts the entire planning function.

For SAP NetWeaver BI Integrated Planning, Listing 6.11 shows a derivation of user and time information taken from the SAP BW-BPS example.

```
METHOD if_rspls_cr_methods~derive.
*------------------------------------------------------------*
*   <-- e_t_mesg          messages
*   <-> c_s_chas     *       characteristic combination:
```

```
*                           source and target
*       fields included; do not change the source fields
*       <<- cx_rspls_failed  exception
*------------------------------------------------------------*

  CLEAR e_t_mesg.
  FIELD-SYMBOLS: <l_chavl> TYPE ANY.
* fill user
  ASSIGN COMPONENT 'OUSERNAME' OF STRUCTURE c_s_chas
                              TO <l_chavl>.
  IF sy-subrc = 0.
    <l_chavl> = sy-uname.
  ENDIF.
* fill date
  ASSIGN COMPONENT 'ODATE' OF STRUCTURE c_s_chas
                          TO <l_chavl>.
  IF sy-subrc = 0.
    <l_chavl> = sy-datum.
  ENDIF.
*** fill time
  ASSIGN COMPONENT 'OTIME' OF STRUCTURE c_s_chas
                          TO <l_chavl>.
  IF sy-subrc = 0.
    <l_chavl> = sy-uzeit.
  ENDIF.

ENDMETHOD.
```

Listing 6.11 Sample Implementation of the DERIVE Method

The different methods indicate that they can be changed easily. You can even call the original function module if you want to transform a project from SAP BW-BPS to SAP NetWeaver BI Integrated Planning.

6.3   Exit Functions in Planning

Finally, you're presented with the most powerful tool of planning—the exit function. Both in SAP BW-BPS and in SAP NetWeaver BI Integrated Planning, you can manipulate the entire dataset via an exit.

6.3.1 Exit Functions in SAP BW-BPS

Exit functions in SAP BW-BPS are an essential part of many BPS implementations. The option to manipulate entire sets of data offers many opportunities that should not be left unexploited.

> **Example**
>
> My first project in the BPS environment included the challenge that several dozens of subsidiaries were supposed to upload their data from a file in a decentralized manner and have immediate information about whether their master data was valid, whether all records were transferred, and so on. The solution included a BPS exit function, in which we loaded the file using the then available WS_UPLOAD function, checked the data, and posted it subsequently. This way, we were able to send all error messages already during data loading—a function that wasn't possible in SAP BW due to asynchronous processing of requests.

The exit function itself consists of one or two function modules.

► The first module is mandatory because it implements the actual logic.

► The second module is optional and is required if you want to create new records for characteristic combinations that do not yet exist.

This is described in detail in the following sections. For this purpose, you create an exit function that reads all cost center master data containing an 'X' in the IST_HKST field and writes these entries and their plan values into a transparent table.

Creating the Planning Function

To create an exit function, proceed as follows:

1. First select the planning level to be used, and then right-click CREATE PLANNING FUNCTION in the lower part of the PLANNING FUNCTION subscreen. The screen shown in Figure 6.7 appears.

2. Assign a technical name and function name, select the exit function from the ALL FUNCTIONS subtree, and press the Enter key to confirm your selection.

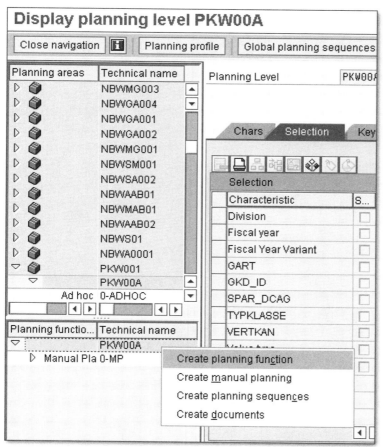

Figure 6.7 Creating a Planning Function

3. The maintenance of the exit function is displayed. The upper part includes two fields for the exit function module (`Function Module`) and the `init` function module (`FM Initialization`) where you can define your own parameters to use in the exit function.

   The two fields on the right-hand side, FIELDS TO BE CHANGED and FIELD SELECTION, are important. You can use these fields to determine the level of detail of the data with which the actual exit function module is called. These characteristics must be added to the fields to be changed, particularly if you require data from different characteristic attributes.

Example: Effects of Fields to Be Changed

At a planning level, you consider the total amount (0AMOUNT) per cost center (0COST-CENTER), the version (0VERSION), and the fiscal year (0FISCYEAR). The corresponding InfoCube comprises the values for the fiscal year 2008 (see Table 6.1).

0FISCYEAR	0VERSION	0COSTCENTER	0AMOUNT
2008	ACTUAL	1000	100
2008	ACTUAL	2000	200
2008	ACTUAL	3000	300
2008	PLAN	1000	400
2008	PLAN	2000	500
2008	PLAN	4000	600

Table 6.1 Data for the Field Selection Example in Planning Functions

The following cases are possible.

▶ **Case 1: All characteristics are in the field selection**
In this case, the exit function module is called six times, once for each data record of the previous table. You can't create new records because they must have identical cost centers and versions. In a hashed table, only one record per key may exist.

▶ **Case 2: 0COSTCENTER is in the fields to be changed; 0VERSION is in the field selection**
The exit function module is called twice, once for the three records of the ACTUAL version and once for the three records of the PLAN version. Newly created records and their versions must be identical to the other records.

▶ **Case 3: 0VERSION is in the fields to be changed; 0COSTCENTER is in the field selection**
Here, the exit function module is called four times, once for each cost center (1000, 2000, 3000, and 4000). Two records are transferred to the function module for the cost centers 1000 and 2000, and one record for the cost centers 3000 and 4000. Newly created records and their cost centers must be identical to the other records.

▶ **Case 4: All characteristics are in the fields to be changed**
The exit function module is called once, including all six records. You can create as many new records as required if corresponding master data exists.

Init Function Module

Let's take a look at Case 3, in which the exit function module is called once per cost center. It may be possible that you need to create data records for cost center 5000 due to business reasons. This wouldn't be possible in the exit function module because the module is only called for the cost centers 1000 to 4000. This problem can be solved with the `init` function module.

The `init` function module is used to create additional characteristic combinations with which the exit function module is called. To do that, an `ETO_CHAS` table is transferred to the function module. This table is usually typed as `ANY TABLE` so that you must access it using field symbols. If the function module is used for one single planning area, you can type it. The corresponding table type is called `/1SEM/_YTO_CHAS_<client><planning area>`, and the corresponding structure `/1SEM/_YS_CHAS_<client><planning area>`.

Although the interface of the function module appears very large, it's straightforward.

▶ The parameters, `I_AREA` (planning area), `I_PLEVEL` (planning level), `I_PACK-AGE` (planning package), `I_METHOD` (planning function), and `I_PARAM` (parameter group), specify which planning function is carried out in which parameter group.

▶ Table `IT_EXITP` comprises the exit parameters defined in the planning_function and the corresponding attributes determined in the parameter group.

▶ Tables `ITO_CHA` (characteristics) and `ITO_KYF` (key figures) comprise the characteristics and key figures defined at the planning level. Characteristics that aren't contained in the planning level may not be filled in the `ETO_CHAS` return table; otherwise, you receive an error message.

▶ Table `ITO_CHASEL` comprises the characteristic restrictions defined in the planning level and in the planning package. It may be possible that the cost center is restricted to the interval ranging from 1000 to 4000 at the planning level. In this case, you may not insert a record in table `ETO_CHAS` that includes cost center 5000.

▶ Table `ETO_CHAS` is the table of the characteristic combinations with which the exit function module is supposed to be called. All characteristic combinations that contain data are definitely transferred even if they don't exist in table `ETO_CHAS`. Deleting records from table `ETO_CHAS` has no effect at all.

▶ Table `ET_MESG` is a normal table for returning messages.

Listing 6.12 shows how the `init` function module must look to write cost center data in a transparent table. The aim of the function module is to include all cost centers that are to be written in the table in the characteristic combinations. This is necessary because the table can contain values that have been deleted in a previous planning function.

```
FUNCTION Z_KST_IN_TABELLE_INIT.
*"----------------------------------------------------------
*"*"Local interface:
*"  IMPORTING
*"     REFERENCE(I_AREA) TYPE  UPC_Y_AREA
*"     REFERENCE(I_PLEVEL) TYPE  UPC_Y_PLEVEL
*"     REFERENCE(I_PACKAGE) TYPE  UPC_Y_PACKAGE
*"     REFERENCE(I_METHOD) TYPE  UPC_Y_METHOD
*"     REFERENCE(I_PARAM) TYPE  UPC_Y_PARAM
*"     REFERENCE(IT_EXITP) TYPE  UPF_YT_EXITP
*"     REFERENCE(ITO_CHASEL) TYPE  UPC_YTO_CHASEL
*"     REFERENCE(ITO_CHA) TYPE  UPC_YTO_CHA
*"     REFERENCE(ITO_KYF) TYPE  UPC_YTO_KYF
*"  EXPORTING
*"     REFERENCE(ETO_CHAS) TYPE  ANY TABLE
*"     REFERENCE(ET_MESG) TYPE  UPC_YT_MESG
*"----------------------------------------------------------


data: l_s_chasel  type upc_ys_chasel,
      l_s_charng  type upc_ys_charng.

data: l_r_co_area type range of /bi0/oico_area,
      l_s_co_area like line of l_r_co_area,
      l_s_costcenter type /bi0/pcostcenter.

* Characteristic structure for Planning Area DEMOAREA
* in Client 100
data: l_s_chas type /1SEM/_YS_CHAS_100DEMOAREA.
field-symbols: <f_coar>  type /bi0/oico_area,
               <f_year>  type /bi0/oifiscyear,
               <f_varnt> type /bi0/oifiscvarnt,
               <f_cctr>  type /bi0/oicostcenter.

  assign component: 'OFISCVARNT' of structure l_s_chas
                    TO <f_varnt>,
                    'OFISCYEAR'  of structure l_s_chas
                    TO <f_year>,
                    'OCO_AREA'   of structure l_s_chas
                    TO <f_hndl>,
```

```
                          'OCOSTCENTER'  of structure l_s_chas
                          TO <f_umsg>.

* Determine controlling area
    READ TABLE ito_chasel INTO l_s_chasel
        WITH KEY chanm = 'OCO_AREA'.
    IF sy-subrc <> 0.
      RAISE co_area_missing.
    ENDIF.
    LOOP AT l_s_chasel-t_charng INTO l_s_charng.
      MOVE-CORRESPONDING l_s_charng TO l_s_co_area.
      INSERT l_s_co_area INTO TABLE l_r_co_area.
    ENDLOOP.

* Determine fiscal year
    <f_varnt> = 'K4'.
    READ TABLE ito_chasel INTO l_s_chasel
        WITH KEY chanm = 'OFISCYEAR'.
    IF sy-subrc <> 0.
      RAISE fiscyear_missing.
    ENDIF.
    READ TABLE l_s_chasel-t_charng INTO l_s_charng index 1.
    IF sy-subrc <> 0.
      RAISE program_error.
    ENDIF.
    <f_year> = l_s_charng-low(4).

    SELECT * FROM /bi0/pcostcenter INTO l_s_costcenter
        WHERE co_area IN l_r_co_area
        AND   /bic/ist_hkst = 'X'
        AND   objvers       =  'A'.
      <f_coar>  = l_s_costcenter-co_area.
      <f_cctr>  = l_s_costcenter-costcenter.
      INSERT l_s_chas INTO TABLE eto_chas.
    ENDSELECT.
ENDFUNCTION.
```

Listing 6.12 Sample Implementation of the Init Function Module

Exit Function Module

The interface of the exit function module and the `init` function module is almost identical. These are the only differences:

6 | User Exits in Planning

▶ Table `ITO_CHASEL` contains a unique value for the characteristic values in the field selection, that is, the value of the characteristic in the current characteristic combination.

▶ Table `XTH_DATA` contains the data of the current characteristic combination. This is a hashed table that contains all characteristics as a key.

The row structure is as follows. Each row of the table contains two structures: `S_CHAS` and `S_KYFS`. `S_CHAS` is the key of the table and comprises all characteristics of the planning area, including the units for the key figures. `S_KYFS` comprises all key figures of the planning area. If new records are created or if existing records are changed, you may fill only those characteristics and key figures that are included in table `ITO_CHA` or table `ITO_KYF`; otherwise, you may receive error messages.

▶ In the sample function module, table `XTH_DATA` is typed generically as a hashed table. Then, you must access it using field symbols. If the function module is used in only one planning area, you can also use the generated table type `/1SEM/_YTH_DATA_<client><planning area>` with row structure `/1SEM/_YS_DATA_<client><planning area>`. As a result, the function module must contain the records that will be included in the InfoCube for subsequent characteristic combination. SAP BW-BPS then automatically determines the difference from the already existing records.

▶ To delete the records, you can either delete the record from table `XTH_DATA` or set all key figures of the `S_KYFS` structure to zero. SAP BW-BPS interprets records whose key figures are set to zero as not existent.

▶ New records can be added to the table if the characteristic values correspond to the selections in table `ITO_CHASEL`.

To get some practice, you should not write the first planning functions generically but specifically to get a general understanding of how SAP BW-BPS uses this data. The function module shown in Listing 6.13 describes how a transparent table is written.

```
FUNCTION Z_KST_IN_TABELLE.
*"----------------------------------------------------------
*"*"Local interface:
*"  IMPORTING
*"     REFERENCE(I_AREA) TYPE  UPC_Y_AREA
*"     REFERENCE(I_PLEVEL) TYPE  UPC_Y_PLEVEL
*"     REFERENCE(I_METHOD) TYPE  UPC_Y_METHOD
```

```
*"      REFERENCE(I_PARAM) TYPE   UPC_Y_PARAM
*"      REFERENCE(I_PACKAGE) TYPE   UPC_Y_PACKAGE
*"      REFERENCE(IT_EXITP) TYPE   UPF_YT_EXITP
*"      REFERENCE(ITO_CHASEL) TYPE   UPC_YTO_CHASEL
*"      REFERENCE(ITO_CHA) TYPE   UPC_YTO_CHA
*"      REFERENCE(ITO_KYF) TYPE   UPC_YTO_KYF
*"  EXPORTING
*"      REFERENCE(ET_MESG) TYPE   UPC_YT_MESG
*"  CHANGING
** For simplicity reasons, the table is typed because
** it is to be used in planning area DEMOAREA only
*"      REFERENCE(XTH_DATA) TYPE
*"                          /1SEM/_YTH_DATA_100DEMOAREA
*"----------------------------------------------------------
* Field symbol for the row of Table XTH_DATA
field-symbols: <s_data> TYPE /1SEM/_YS_DATA_100DEMOAREA.
data: l_s_cctr_tab type Z_KST_DATEN,
      l_s_chasel  type upc_ys_chasel,
      l_s_charng  type upc_ys_charng.

  clear l_s_cctr_tab.
* The following assumes that the cost center, the
* fiscal year, and the controlling area are
* in the field selection. Therefore, they are unique
* in the selections.

* Determine business year
 READ TABLE ito_chasel INTO l_s_chasel
      WITH TABLE KEY chanm  = '0FISCYEAR'.
  IF sy-subrc <> 0.
    RAISE fiscyear_missing.
  ENDIF.
  READ TABLE l_s_chasel-t_charng INTO l_s_charng index 1.
  IF sy-subrc <> 0.
    RAISE fiscyear_missing.
  ENDIF.
  l_s_cctr_tab-FISCYEAR = l_s_charng-low(4).
* Determine cost center
  READ TABLE ito_chasel INTO l_s_chasel
      WITH TABLE KEY chanm  = '0COSTCENTER'.
  IF sy-subrc <> 0.
    RAISE kostenstelle_missing.
  ENDIF.
```

```
    READ TABLE l_s_chasel-t_charng INTO l_s_charng index 1.
    IF sy-subrc <> 0.
      RAISE kostenstelle_missing.
    ENDIF.
    l_s_cctr_tab-costcenter = l_s_charng-low(10).
*   Determine controlling area
    READ TABLE ito_chasel INTO l_s_chasel
         WITH TABLE KEY chanm  = '0CO_AREA'.
    IF sy-subrc <> 0.
      RAISE kostenrechnungskreis_missing.
    ENDIF.
    READ TABLE l_s_chasel-t_charng INTO l_s_charng index 1.
    IF sy-subrc <> 0.
      RAISE kostenrechnungskreis_missing.
    ENDIF.
    l_s_cctr_tab-co_area = l_s_charng-low(4).
    l_s_cctr_tab-mandt  = sy-mandt.
*   Now, value AMOUNT is determined as the total
*   of all rows.
    CLEAR l_s_cctr_tab-amount
    LOOP AT xth_data assigning <s_data>.
      CHECK <s_data>-s_kyfs-amount <> 0.
      ADD <s_data>-s_kyfs-0amount TO l_s_cctr_tab-amount.
    ENDLOOP.
    UPDATE Z_KST_DATEN FROM l_s_cctr_tab.
*   New record?
    IF sy-subrc <> 0.
      INSERT Z_KST_DATEN FROM l_s_cctr_tab.
    ENDIF.

ENDFUNCTION.
```

Listing 6.13 Sample Implementation of the Exit Function Module

6.3.2 Exit Functions in SAP NetWeaver BI Integrated Planning

You can create exit functions in SAP NetWeaver BI Integrated Planning by generating a class that implements one of the interfaces, IF_RSPLFA_SRVTYPE_IMP_EXEC or IF_RSPLFA_SRVTYPE_IMP_EXEC_REF. The first interface is used for functions that don't require any reference data, and the second interface is used for functions with reference data.

Reference data is data that is required in the planning function but isn't changed. Originally, SAP BW-BPS only included a planning function without reference data; that's why all used data was locked and could be changed accidentally in case of program errors. So if you wrote a planning function that should change the plan data depending on actual data values, a programming error could lead to a change of the actual data. As of Release 7.0, reference data is no longer locked and protected from being overwritten. Because many functions require reference data, the following sections present an implementation of a function with reference data. The function without reference data can be carried out in the same way.

Interface `IF_RSPLFA_SRVTYPE_IMP_EXEC_REF` contains the following methods (see Table 6.2).

Method	Description
`INIT_EXECUTION`	Initialization of the execution
`GET_REF_DATA_SEL`	Determine selection for reference data
`ADD_NEW_BLOCKS`	Add new blocks
`EXECUTE`	Execution
`FINISH_EXECUTION`	Actions at the end of execution

Table 6.2 Methods in Interface IF_RSPLFA_SRVTYPE_IMP_EXEC_REF

INIT_EXECUTION Method

The `INIT_EXECUTION` method (see Figure 6.8) is used to implement the required initializations before the actual data is read. The method comprises the following parameters:

▶ The `I_R_SRVTYPE_DEF` parameter contains information about the definition of the service type, for instance, the implementing class or whether reference data is necessary.

▶ The `I_R_SRV` parameter contains information about the planning function, for instance, the InfoProvider or the function types.

▶ The `I_R_INFOPROV_DESC` parameter contains information about the InfoProvider, for instance, the used characteristics and key figures.

▶ The `I_R_MSG` parameter is used to return messages. For this purpose, you must call the `ADD_MSG` method of the parameter. This method retrieves its information from the system fields SY-MSGNO, and so on; you don't have to transfer any parameters.

▶ The I_T_DATA_CHARSEL parameter contains the current filters, usually the navigation condition of the query, for which the planning function is called.

Ty.	Parameter	Type spec.	Description
▶◻	VALUE(I_R_SRVTYPE_DEF)	TYPE REF TO IF_RSPLFA_SRVTYPE_DEF	Service Type (Definition)
▶◻	VALUE(I_R_SRV)	TYPE REF TO IF_RSPLFA_SRV	Planning Service
▶◻	VALUE(I_R_INFOPROV_DESC)	TYPE REF TO IF_RSPLFA_INFOPROV_DESC	InfoProvider (Metadata)
▶◻	VALUE(I_R_MSG)	TYPE REF TO IF_RSPLFA_MSG	Messages
▶◻	VALUE(I_T_DATA_CHARSEL)	TYPE RSPLF_T_CHARSEL	Current filter

Figure 6.8 Signature of the INIT_EXECUTION Method

In most cases, the method remains empty or contains general selections only. A completely generic implementation is very time-consuming.

GET_REF_DATA_SEL Method

The GET_REF_DATA_SEL method is used to determine which data is transferred to the EXECUTE method as reference data. Reference data is data from the InfoProvider that can't be changed and hence isn't locked. The signature of the GET_REF_DATA_SEL method is illustrated in Figure 6.9.

Ty.	Parameter	Type spec.	Description
▶◻	VALUE(I_T_DATA_CHARSEL)	TYPE RSPLF_T_CHARSEL	Current Selection
▶◻	VALUE(I_R_PARAM_SET)	TYPE REF TO IF_RSPLFA_PARAM_SET	Current Parameter Record
▶◻	VALUE(I_R_MSG)	TYPE REF TO IF_RSPLFA_MSG	Messages
◻▶	E_TH_NO_REF_BLOCK_CHA	TYPE RSPLF_TH_IOBJ	InfoObjects Without Block Building
◻▶	E_T_REF_CHARSEL	TYPE RSPLF_T_CHARSEL	Reference Data Selection

Figure 6.9 Signature of the GET_REF_DATA_SEL Method

The I_T_DATA_CHARSEL and I_R_MSG parameters are identical to the INIT_EXECUTION method. The I_R_PARAM_SET parameter contains the parameters stored in the planning function.

The E_T_REF_CHARSEL and E_TH_NO_REF_BLOCK_DATA return parameters are important:

▶ E_T_REF_CHARSEL must be filled with selections that are supposed to be valid for the reference data. It usually makes sense to transfer those selections that have been delivered in `I_T_DATA_CHARSEL` to keep the amount of data to be read low.

▶ `E_TH_NO_REF_BLOCK_DATA` contains characteristics that are supposed to be excluded from the block creation of reference data.

Let's examine the example of Case 3 in Section 6.3.1, Exit Function in SAP BW-BPS: If you define the ACTUAL version as reference data and PLAN version as data to be processed, the `EXECUTE` method is called four times, once for each cost center. The data table and the reference table each contain one record for the cost centers 1000 and 2000, cost center 3000 comprises one record in the reference data but none in the plan data, and cost center 4000 has one record in the plan data but none in the reference data.[2]

Let's assume that no reference data is available, and the average of all cost center actual data is used as the reference date — this constitutes a problem because you receive the records per cost center. Therefore, you have the option to add InfoObject `0COSTCENTER` to `E_TH_NO_REF_BLOCK_DATA`. In this case, the data of all cost centers are transferred to the reference data table.

This method then appears as shown in Listing 6.14.

```
METHOD IF_RSPLFA_SRVTYPE_IMP_EXEC_REF~GET_REF_DATA_SEL.
  DATA: s_charsel TYPE RSPLF_S_CHARSEL,
        s_iobjnm  TYPE RSPLF_S_IOBJNM.
* Transfer all selections to reference data
* except for version
  LOOP AT i_t_data_charsel INTO s_charsel.
    IF s_charsel-iobjnm <> 'OVERSION'.
      APPEND s_charsel TO e_t_ref_charsel.
    ENDIF.
  ENDLOOP.
* Add ACTUAL version
  s_charsel-iobjnm  = 'OVERSION'.
  s_charsel-sign    = 'I'.
  s_charsel-opt     = 'EQ'.
  s_charsel-low     = 'IST'.
  INSERT s_charsel INTO TABLE e_t_ref_charsel.
```

---

2 Usually, this method isn't called for cost center 4000 because there is no plan data for this cost center. In this example, however, it's assumed that cost center 4000 is added in method `ADD_NEW_BLOCKS`, which is described in the following sections.

```
* Take cost center from block creation
  s_iobjnm           = 'OCOSTCENTER'.
  INSERT s_iobjnm INTO TABLE e_th_no_ref_block_cha.
ENDMETHOD.
```

Listing 6.14 Sample Implementation of the GET_REF_DATA_SEL Method

ADD_NEW_BLOCKS Method

The ADD_NEW_BLOCKS method (see Figure 6.10) works similar to the init function module of the BW-BPS exit function. It's used to generate characteristic combinations that don't appear in the data to be processed; for example, characteristic combinations that can only be found in the reference data. This example is frequently used in SAP development for the default copy function of SAP NetWeaver BI Integrated Planning that is implemented in class CL_RSPLFC_COPY.

Ty.	Parameter	Type spec.	Description
▶□	VALUE(I_R_PARAM_SET)	TYPE REF TO IF_RSPLFA_PARAM_SET	Record of Parameter Values
▶□	VALUE(I_TH_REF_DATA)	TYPE HASHED TABLE	Reference Data
▶□	VALUE(I_TS_EXISTING_BLOCKS)	TYPE SORTED TABLE	Existing Data Blocks
▶□	VALUE(I_R_MSG)	TYPE REF TO IF_RSPLFA_MSG	Messages
◁▶	E_TS_NEW_BLOCKS	TYPE SORTED TABLE	New Data Blocks

Figure 6.10 Signature of ADD_NEW_BLOCKS Method

The ADD_NEW_BLOCKS method contains the known parameters, I_R_PARAM_SET and I_R_MESG, as well as the following parameters:

▶ I_TH_REF_DATA comprises the reference data with the selections that were determined in the GET_REF_DATA_SEL method.

▶ I_TS_EXISTING_BLOCKS contains the combinations that are already included in the plan data. Similar to the SAP BW-BPS function, no combinations can be deleted here.

▶ E_TS_NEW_BLOCKS must be filled with additional combinations. If it includes combinations from I_TS_EXISTING_BLOCKS, this is neither a disadvantage nor an advantage.

Listing 6.15 shows the code of the method in class CL_RSPLFC_COPY.

```
METHOD IF_RSPLFA_SRVTYPE_IMP_EXEC_REF~ADD_NEW_BLOCKS.
  DATA: l_r_new_block TYPE REF TO data.
```

```
FIELD-SYMBOLS: <s_ref_data> TYPE ANY,
               <s_new_block> TYPE ANY.

* Generate a new (empty) record
  CREATE DATA l_r_new_block LIKE LINE OF e_ts_new_blocks.
  ASSIGN l_r_new_block->* TO <s_new_block>.

* Check reference data
  LOOP AT i_th_ref_data ASSIGNING <s_ref_data>.
*   Does plan data exist for reference data?
    MOVE-CORRESPONDING <s_ref_data> TO <s_new_block>.
    READ TABLE i_ts_existing_blocks
        TRANSPORTING NO FIELDS FROM <s_new_block>.
    IF sy-subrc <> 0.
*     No, insert new combination
      COLLECT <s_new_block> INTO e_ts_new_blocks.
    ENDIF.
  ENDLOOP.
ENDMETHOD.
```

Listing 6.15 Sample Implementation of the ADD_NEW_BLOCKS Method

EXECUTE Method

The EXECUTE method is the central method of the exit function in SAP NetWeaver BI Integrated Planning and must always be implemented. Just as in the SAP BW-BPS exit function, a C_TH_DATA table with the existing plan data is transferred that must then be changed. Figure 6.11 shows the signature of the method.

Ty.	Parameter	Type spec.	Description
▸☐	VALUE(I_R_PARAM_SET)	TYPE REF TO IF_RSPLFA_PARAM_SET	Parameter Record (Values)
▸☐	VALUE(I_TH_REF_DATA)	TYPE HASHED TABLE	Reference Data
▸☐	VALUE(I_S_BLOCK_LINE)	TYPE ANY	Current Data Block
▸☐	VALUE(I_R_MSG)	TYPE REF TO IF_RSPLFA_MSG	Messages
▸☐▸	C_TH_DATA	TYPE HASHED TABLE	Transaction Data

Figure 6.11 Signature of the EXECUTE Method

The I_R_PARAM_SET, I_TH_REF_DATA, and I_R_MSG parameters are already known; only the I_S_BLOCK_LINE parameter is new. This parameter contains the characteristics that are constant in the current data block.

The example shown in Listing 6.16 copies all values from the reference data of the corresponding cost center to the plan data. If no reference data exists in the cost center, the values of all cost centers are determined.

```
METHOD IF_RSPLFA_SRVTYPE_IMP_EXEC_REF~EXECUTE.
  FIELD-SYMBOLS: <f_cctr>       TYPE /bi0/oicostcenter,
                 <f_cctr_ref>   TYPE /bi0/oicostcenter,
                 <f_amount>     TYPE /bi0/oiamount,
                 <f_ref_data>   TYPE any,
                 <f_new_data>   TYPE ANY.

  DATA: l_r_data   TYPE REF TO DATA,
        l_d_amount TYPE /bi0/oiamount,
        l_d_count  TYPE i.

* Generate new (empty) record
  CREATE DATA l_r_data LIKE LINE OF c_th_data.
  ASSIGN l_r_data->*   TO <f_new_data>.

* Determine cost center
  ASSIGN COMPONENT 'OCOSTCENTER'
         OF STRUCTURE i_s_block_line
         TO <f_cctr>.
  IF sy-subrc <> 0.
*   Cost center not in block characteristics
    "Trigger error, wrong configuration
  ENDIF.

* Read reference data for cost center
  CLEAR l_d_count.
  LOOP AT i_th_ref_data ASSIGNING <f_ref_data>.
    ASSIGN COMPONENT 'OCOSTCENTER'
           OF STRUCTURE <f_ref_data>
           TO <f_cctr_ref>.
    IF <F_CCTR>  = <f_cctr_ref>.
      ADD 1 TO l_d_count.
      <f_new_data>  = <f_ref_data>.
      REFRESH c_th_data.
      INSERT <f_new_data> INTO TABLE c_th_data.
    ENDIF.
  ENDLOOP.
  IF l_d_count = 0.
```

```
*    No data found for the corresponding cost center
     CLEAR l_d_amount.
     LOOP AT i_th_ref_data ASSIGNING <f_ref_data> .
       ASSIGN COMPONENT 'OAMOUNT'
              OF STRUCTURE <f_ref_data>
              TO <f_amount>.
       IF sy-subrc <> 0.
         "Trigger error, wrong configuration
       ENDIF.
       <f_new_data>  = <f_ref_data>.
       ADD 1 TO l_d_count.
       ADD <f_amount> TO l_d_amount.
     ENDLOOP.
     ASSIGN COMPONENT 'OAMOUNT'
            OF STRUCTURE <f_new_data>
            TO <f_amount>.
     IF l_d_count <> 0.
       <f_amount> = l_d_amount / l_d_count.
     ELSE.
       <f_amount> = 0.
     ENDIF.
     REFRESH c_th_data.
     INSERT <f_new_data> INTO TABLE c_th_data.
   ENDIF.
ENDMETHOD.
```

Listing 6.16 Sample Implementation of the EXECUTE Method

FINISH_EXECUTION Method

The FINISH_EXECUTION method is used to release large internal tables and to carry out similar cleanup tasks. It has one parameter only: I_R_MSG. This parameter is used to return messages (see Figure 6.12). Usually, it should not be implemented.

Ty.	Parameter	Type spec.	Description
▶□	VALUE(I_R_MSG)	TYPE REF TO IF_RSPLFA_MSG	Messages

Figure 6.12 Signature of the FINISH_EXECUTION Method

6.4   Conclusion

In general, the option to use reference data makes the exit function in SAP NetWeaver BI Integrated Planning considerably more flexible. Those of you who become more engaged with this topic will have the option to write planning functions that would otherwise have resulted in locks within SAP BW-BPS. However, this implementation sets considerably higher demands on the developers because the options of object-oriented programming are used more intensively. You can recognize this by the object references in the interfaces.

But if you engage in this topic, you can obtain both better ABAP Object know-how and more powerful extension options in SAP NetWeaver BI Integrated Planning. If you can't get used to it at all, use class CL_RSPLFC_BPS_EXITS, which enables you to create a planning function in SAP NetWeaver BI Integrated Planning that calls function modules of the SAP BW-BPS exit function.

7   Summary

After a brief introduction to the issues surrounding system performance, this book from the SAP PRESS Essentials series introduced you to all user exits and BAdIs that are important in the data flow, from the source system to the report.

We started off with the extension of extractors. We described the option of using generic extractors as well as the extension of those extractors provided by SAP. The chapter on data staging first provided a detailed description of the transformation process that was introduced with SAP NetWeaver 7.0. We then took a detailed look at the transfer and update rules exclusively used in SAP Business Warehouse 3.x (SAP BW). Then, we treated the variable exit `RSR00001` in the chapter on reporting before taking a detailed look at the topics of virtual key figures and characteristics, the VirtualProvider, and the report-report interface. Then, you had the opportunity to learn more about the user exits in planning applications by means of SAP BW-BPS and SAP NetWeaver BI Integrated Planning and compare them.

You will have many opportunities to improve your knowledge of ABAP in SAP NetWeaver BI. While reading this book, you probably came up with ideas for creating your own applications. This book will also serve as a reference guide for many of you in your daily work.

I hope I was able to show you how important it is to always be creative when using SAP NetWeaver BI, in addition to mastering the many exits. You should use the exits to provide optimal solutions to the user, even though you sometimes may think at first glance that the requirements cannot be implemented. This process of finding a solution is what fascinates me every day about my work. I hope you will experience this fascination as well when you implement complex requirements with just a few lines of ABAP code.

Appendices

A   Additional Extension Options

A.1   Other BAdIs and User Exits in SAP NetWeaver BI

The majority of the most important BAdIs and user exits that are needed for standard reporting have been described in great detail during the course of this book. However, numerous other BAdIs are available that can be used for specific purposes. Here is a brief overview of those BAdIs, so that you know where to look in case of problems. If you have further questions, refer to the SAP Developer Network (*http://sdn.sap.com*).

A.1.1   BAdIs

▶ RSDBC_SQL_STATEMENT
This BAdI enables you to customize the SQL statement in DB connect.

▶ RSR_OLAP_AUTH_GEN
This BAdI enables you to customize user rights for reporting calls, which is helpful if users should have more rights for reporting than they have, for instance, for master data maintenance in the Administrator Workbench.

▶ OPENHUB_TRANSFORM
This BAdI adjusts the output of the open hub export so you can generate additional headers and footers or perform a different field conversion, among other tasks.

▶ RSRA_ALERT
This BAdI is used for alert handling in the reporting agent.

▶ RSAR_CONNECTOR
This BAdI enables you to edit customized functions in the formula editor. Here you can define your own functions and assign methods to those functions.

▶ BW_SCHEDULER
This BAdI is used for controlling follow-up jobs for InfoPackages.

▶ RSOD_DOC_BADI
This BAdI allows you to manage documents in the report view.

▶ RSOD_ITEM_DOC
This BAdI is used for the Web item "Single Document." It enables you to completely modify the generated HTML document.

▶ RSOD_ITEM_DOC_LIST
This is a BAdI for the Web item "Document List." The BAdI provides several functions for customizing selections, the ADDITIONAL FUNCTIONS button, the document list, and the entire HTML document.

▶ RSOD_WWW_DOC_MAINT
This BAdI is used to maintain text documents in the Web interface of SAP Business Explorer.

A.1.2 Exits

SAP BW-BPS provides additional options to manipulate the program flow in SAP NetWeaver BI. In addition to the CMOD exits, SEMBPS01 and SEMBPS02, the exit function deserves mention here because it enables you to manipulate any field content in a transactional InfoCube. Moreover, the *FOX formulas* play an important role in SAP BW-BPS because they enable you to carry out extensive calculations in the InfoCube without ABAP knowledge.

Process chains represent another important topic because they enable you to include normal ABAP programs into the process chain and to implement your own process types. You can do that by implementing the documented interfaces, IF_RSPC_*. The document "How to … Implement custom-defined process type" contains useful information to get started. You can download it from SAP Service Marketplace (*http://service.sap.com/bi*) at the following location: SERVICES & IMPLEMENTATION • HOW TO… GUIDES • GUIDE LIST SAP BW 3.0B/BW 3.1 CONTENT.

The *Analytics Process Designer* (APD) also enables you to integrate your own functions.

A.2 Generated Tables and Objects in SAP NetWeaver BI

To access data stored in SAP NetWeaver BI and to perform a results check, it's often very useful to know the data structures contained in the objects. For this reason, the remainder of this appendix lists the most important tables required for the programming process. Although having direct access to the objects is not recommended in all cases, this solution is always available as a last resort.

Note that for all of the following structures, the prefix does not necessarily have to be /BIC/. The prefix of objects from the business content, for instance, is /BIO/, whereas other SAP applications use different namespaces, depending on the application.

A.2.1 Tables in InfoCubes

Table Name	Description
/BIC/F<CUBENAME>	Fact table of the InfoCube for noncompressed data records.
/BIC/E<CUBENAME>	Fact table of the InfoCube for compressed data records.
/BIC/D<CUBENAME>X	Dimension table of the InfoCube. X is the hexadecimal number of the D(imension), P(ackage), U(nit), or T(ime).
/BIC/L<CUBENAME>	Data table for inventory values.
/BIC/V<CUBENAME>T	Structure containing all InfoObjects and navigation attributes.
/BIC/V<CUBENAME>F	FACTVIEW, a view of the E and F tables. The view can be used for a data mart selection, for example.
/BIC/V<CUBENAME>I	Structure containing the InfoObjects of the InfoCube.
/BIC/V<CUBENAME>N	Structure containing the navigation attributes of the InfoCube.
/BIC/V<CUBENAME>J	Structure containing the InfoObjects of the InfoCube.
/BIC/V<CUBENAME>M	Structure containing all InfoObjects and navigation attributes.
/BIC/V<CUBENAME>2	Structure containing InfoObjects and navigation attributes, as well as 0INFOPROV and 1ROWCOUNT.
/BIC/V<CUBENAME>H	Structure containing additional hierarchy surrogate IDs (SIDs).

Table A.1 Tables in InfoCubes

A.2.2 Tables in DataStore Objects

Table Name	Description
/BIC/A<DSNAME>00	Table containing activated data records of the DataStore object
/BIC/A<DSNAME>40	Table containing data records for updating the DataStore object
/BIC/A<DSNAME>50	Table for rolling back the DataStore object
/BIC/0012345678	Table of the change log (corresponds to a PSA table)

Table A.2 Generated Objects of a DataStore Object

A.2.3 Tables in InfoObjects

Table Name	Description
/BIC/P<IOBJNAME>	Table containing time-independent master data attributes
/BIC/Q<IOBJNAME>	Table containing time-dependent master data attributes
/BIC/S<IOBJNAME>	Table containing master data SIDs
/BIC/X<IOBJNAME>	Table containing SIDs for time-independent navigation attributes
/BIC/Y<IOBJNAME>	Table containing SIDs for time-dependent navigation attributes
/BIC/T<IOBJNAME>	Table containing master data texts
/BIC/H<IOBJNAME>	Table containing hierarchy nodes and leaves
/BIC/K<IOBJNAME>	Table containing SIDs for the hierarchy nodes
/BIC/I<IOBJNAME>	Table containing the SID structure
/BIC/J<IOBJNAME>	Table of hierarchy intervals
/BIC/OI<IOBJNAME>	Data element generated for the InfoObject
/BIC/O<IOBJNAME>	Domain generated for the InfoObject

Table A.3 Tables in InfoObjects

A.2.4   Data Structures in the Dataflow

Structure Name	Description
/BIC/0012345678	PSA table
/BIC/CC<XX><DATASRC>	Transfer structure
/BIC/CS<INFOSOURCE>	Communication structure

Table A.4   Structures in the Dataflow

A.2.5   Generated Objects in SAP NetWeaver BI

The following objects are database tables generated by SAP NetWeaver BI. They are listed here only for the sake of completeness; you shouldn't use them in your user exits or BAdIs. However, because basic customer support sometimes seems to have problems with these tables, they are listed here. You can also find information on them in SAP Note 449891.

Table Name	Description
/BI0/01...	Intermediate results for query processing
/BI0/02...	Intermediate results for external hierarchies that can be reused
/BI0/03...	Generated views for query processing
/BI0/04...	Stored procedures for compressing InfoCubes
/BI0/05...	Trigger for compressing InfoCubes
/BI0/06...	Similar to the /BI0/01... tables, but reusable
/BI0/0D...	Temporary tables for the open hub

Table A.5   Temporary Tables in SAP NetWeaver BI

B   The Author

After graduating with a degree in business mathematics from Technische Universität Berlin, Germany, **Dirk Herzog** started his career in 1996 in the CO-OM development department at SAP in Walldorf, Germany. His work focused on cost-center planning and the CO planning processor.

Four years later, he moved back to Berlin to join the BI consulting team at SAP Deutschland. Since then, he has led numerous national and international implementations of SAP NetWeaver Business Intelligence (SAP NetWeaver BI) and SAP Strategic Enterprise Management (SAP SEM). These included the world's first SAP BW 3.0 project, one of the first cube-based SEM-BCS implementations, and a large business planning for the German Sales of a large automotive manufacturer.

Dirk also has developed solutions and solution concepts for complex modeling and implementation. He is co-author of the PDEBWB course on "User Exits in SAP BW" and has taught the course several times. When he's not spending time with his two children, Dirk writes web logs in the SAP Developer Network (SDN) and answers questions.

Index

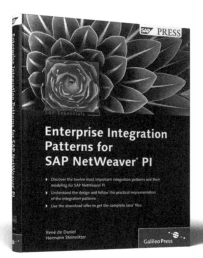

Discover the twelve most important integration patterns and their modeling for SAP NetWeaver XI

Understand the integration patterns' design and follow their practical implementation

Includes download offer for the complete Java files

René de Daniel, Hermann Steinrötter

Enterprise Integration Patterns for SAP NetWeaver PI

SAP PRESS Essentials 35

Enterprise Integration Patterns (EIP) are design patterns that enable the integration of enterprise applications. This practical workshop provides SAP NetWeaver XI developers with the most important patterns, from Aggregator, to Content Filter and Guaranteed Delivery, to Request – Reply and Splitter. The book describes the function and structure of individual EIPs, applies them to specific real-life problems, and ultimately implements them in Java for SAP NetWeaver XI. It also includes download offerings for the individual patterns.

223 pp., 2009, 68,– Euro / US$ 85
ISBN 978-1-59229-175-5

>> www.sap-press.de/1644

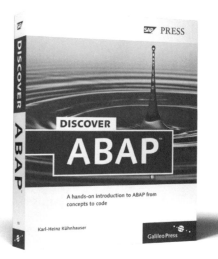

A hands-on introduction to ABAP from concepts to code

Task-focused education with coverage of all the most important commands

Short exercise units featuring a wealth of code examples and screenshots

Karl-Heinz Kühnhauser

Discover ABAP

This book, specifically designed for beginners, introduces you to all relevant ABAP language elements in a series of clearly structured lessons. Adhering to the motto, "As much theory as necessary and as little as possible," you'll methodically familiarize yourself with one ABAP programming aspect at a time — each directly relevant to solving the tasks described in the corresponding lesson. Based on an extended, real-life example that's referred to throughout the book, you'll quickly develop your own programming solutions, starting right from the first page. Then, take your new skills to the next level as you successfully use your custom source code in practice. By reading this book, you can develop the knowledge and skills needed to leverage ABAP tools and methods in your everyday work.

503 pp., 2008, 39,95 Euro / US$ 39.95
ISBN 978-1-59229-152-6

>> www.sap-press.de/1531

Second edition, updated and expanded to cover SAP NetWeaver Application Server Java (release 7.1)

Covers new topics, such as Java EE 5, EJB 3.0, SAP NetWeaver CE, and more

Includes sample applications on Web Dynpro, Visual Composer, CAF, and Developer Studio

Includes the SAP NetWeaver CE 7.1 Trial Version on DVD

Karl Kessler et al.

Java Programming with SAP NetWeaver

Explore all the innovations in SAP NetWeaver AS Java (release 7.1) with this completely updated and extended second edition of our standard work. You'll get profound insights into all topic areas linked to Java programming for SAP applications: business logic, persistence, scalability, maintainability, development in teams, and UI design. Three completely new chapters show you the development of composite applications with the Composition Environment. All other chapters have been revised and updated to Java EE 5.

696 pp., 2. edition 2008, with DVD 5, 69,95 Euro / US$ 69.95
ISBN 978-1-59229-181-6

>> www.sap-press.de/1657

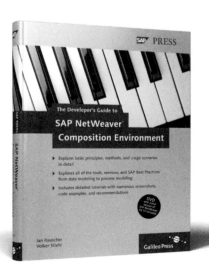

Explains basic principles, methods, and usage scenarios in detail

Explains all of the tools, services, and SAP Best Practices from data modeling to process modeling

Includes detailed tutorials with numerous screenshots, code examples, and recommendations

Jan Rauscher, Volker Stiehl

The Developer's Guide to the SAP NetWeaver Composition Environment

The SAP NetWeaver Composition Environment provides everything you need to develop composite applications quickly and efficiently using SAP NetWeaver CE 7.1, and this Developer's Guide shows you how to do exactly that. Based on numerous examples, you will learn how to use the development tools and methods to build composite applications using SAP NetWeaver CE in your daily work. The book helps you decide at any time which of the following tools is the best choice in your specific situation: Composite Application Framework (CAF), Web Dynpro, SAP NetWeaver Visual Composer, SAP Interactive Forms, or Guided Procedures.

365 pp., 2008, with DVD 5, 69,95 Euro / US$ 69.95
ISBN 978-1-59229-171-7

>> www.sap-press.de/1671